INVESTING IN
LIQUID
ASSETS

Uncorking Profits in Today's Global Wine Market

DAVID SOKOLIN

AND

ALEXANDRA BRUCE

Simon & Schuster

NEW YORK LONDON TORONTO SYDNEY

SIMON & SCHUSTER
Rockefeller Center
1230 Avenue of the Americas
New York, NY 10020

First Simon & Schuster hardcover edition May 2008

SIMON & SCHUSTER and colophon are registered trademarks of
Simon & Schuster, Inc.

For information about special discounts for bulk purchases,
please contact Simon & Schuster Special Sales at
1-800-456-6798 or business@simonandschuster.com

Designed by Paul Dippolito

Manufactured in the United States of America

1   3   5   7   9   10   8   6   4   2

Library of Congress Cataloging-in-Publication Data

Sokolin, David.
Investing in liquid assets : uncorking profits in today's
global wine market / David Sokolin.
p.   cm.
Includes bibliographical references and index.
1. Wine as an investment. I. Title.
HD9370.5.S646 2008
332.63—dc22   2007045248

ISBN-13: 978-1-4165-5018-1

ACKNOWLEDGMENTS

Alexandra "Chica" Bruce (Thank you so much for sticking with me), Al Zuckerman, Amanda Murray, Andrew Cader, Andy Lench, Bayo Ogunlesi, Beaver Truax, Benjamin James, Bill Dobrow, Bill Strang, BJ Calloway, Bob Dickenson, Bobby Gianos, Brendon Blake, Charlie Banta, Christina Pai, Christine Hawkins, Dan Loeb, David Cox, David Dorman, David James, David Smydo (YTM), Dede Goldstein, Denton Knezovich, Don Engel, Don Textor, Ed Pantzer, Eric Celt, Eric Freeman, Gerald Decock, Glenn Goldstein, Harry Hackett, Ian Gittler, Imre Pakh, Irving Geszel, Jack Meyer, James Suckling, Jean-Michel Cazes, Jeff Opedyke (A brilliant writer), Jeff Resnick, Jesse Harris, Jim Rosenthal, Joel Fitzpatrick, John Childs, John McWhinnie, Jonathan Lynne, Kate Ankofski, Kengo Watanabe, Kevin Kennedy, Kevin Parker, Kim Vernon, Koichi Okada, Larry Fink, Larry Lavine, Laurie Densen, Lexi Densen, Margaret Loeb, Maria Beaulieu, Marina Cazes, Marvin Shanken, Mel Vogel, Michael Lynch, Michael Lynne, Mike Densen (YTM), Mike Tiedemann, Morris Shirazi, Nick Weber, Ninah Lynne, Pat Mcmullan, Patty Scire, Peter Minikes, Peter Sabbeth, Rachel Schatz, Richard Gadbois, Rob Altman, Robert Parker, Rose Norton, Sandy Densen, Sandy Weill, Serena Altschul, Seth Berger, Steve Burickson, Stephen Tanzer, Steve Fink, Steve Hokanson, Sydney Stutterheim, the late Scott Chinery, Tod Perkins, Tom Black, Tom Tuft, Tony James, Tony Wilson, Trent Preszler, and Wingnut.

To my entire family: grandfather, grandmother, father, and mother, for giving me the opportunity to participate in one of the most pleasurable businesses on earth.

CONTENTS

INVESTING IN
LIQUID
ASSETS

INTRODUCTION

If you have never traded wine before, the idea of wine as an invest-ment might seem mystifying or impractical, given the physical heft of a dozen wine bottles cordoned off in a wooden case. Despite per-ceptions that wine is simply a beverage, or at best a collectible, the fact is that a particular category of Investment-Grade Wines (IGWs) has emerged in recent years as its own alternative investment class, with characteristics similar to high-yield bonds, gold, and fine art. These assets are largely uncorrelated with stocks, so they provide a greater level of portfolio diversification and risk reduction. You may be surprised to know that returns on IGW have dependably outper-formed blue-chip stocks over the past fifty years. Fine wines have become very easy to trade online and you don't even need your own cellar to store them. Despite rising prices, IGWs are still among the least expensive, easily tradable, and most profitable investment op-portunities around.

Blame it on the exploding popularity of fine wine as a consum-able. Though long associated with highbrow affairs like a gala, a black-tie event at a local museum, or maybe a dinner among invest-ment bankers celebrating the closing of a billion-dollar deal on Wall Street, wine is increasingly finding a fan base in more mainstream markets. It's now found for sale at Nascar races, and some tracks even offer wine-tasting programs for race patrons. One of Nascar's most famous sons, Jeff Gordon, makes wine under his own label and owns a collection of rare wines that has been featured in the pages of *Wine Spectator* magazine.

But it's outside America where the economic trends are really driving the growth in the finest wines. The rise of global wealth, particularly in Asia, Russia, and other emerging parts of the world, combined with increasing awareness about wine, has spawned an unprecedented demand for what I call investment-grade wines. Not among investors, mind you, but among consumers who suddenly have the discretionary dollars to splurge on some of the best wines money can buy. Due to the unique properties of these investment-worthy wines, the world has entered an era where continually decreasing supply meets continually increasing demand for the relatively limited supply of the world's greatest wines. Where this sort of supply-demand dynamic emerges, you suddenly have . . . an investment opportunity.

Little wonder, then, that Wall Street has latched onto the idea that fine wine now has investment-grade characteristics. Fine-wine investment funds have launched in the United Kingdom, the United States, and Australia in the last few years, and all are solely in the business of profiting off the price appreciation that is basically unavoidable in certain wines. Why is this price appreciation unavoidable? In a word, *consumption*. Unlike other assets, wine is drunk by buyers. Over time, fewer and fewer bottles exist of the comparatively small lot of the world's best wines that, themselves, are improving with age. The result: Every time someone pulls the cork on a bottle of 1982 Château Pétrus—one of the truly great wines—the remaining supply of that vintage rises in value. No one will ever own the last tradable share of IBM. But one day, someone will own the last known bottle of '82 Pétrus, and that bottle might just be worth enough to buy a winery.

Like stocks and bonds, fine wine even has its own index of prices now. The London International Vintners Exchange (Liv-ex) is an electronic exchange of about 150 merchants and professional traders in the global fine-wine market. Liv-ex produces the Liv-ex 100 Index, which is to wine what the Dow Jones Industrial Average is to U.S. stocks—the leading blue-chip index. In Liv-ex's case, the blue chips are 100 of some of the most widely traded fine wines from the French regions of Bordeaux, Burgundy, Champagne, and the

Rhône, as well as some of the Super Tuscans from Italy. The Liv-ex 100 is used by wine merchants, wine funds, and investors around the globe to price the wine they own or want to invest in.

In another sign that fine wine is a recognized investment class, in 2006 Bloomberg, the New York purveyor of global financial data, began listing the Liv-ex 100 alongside such storied investment indices as the Dow Jones Industrial Average and the Standard & Poor's 500.

Fact is, wine investing has become so easy that many wine enthusiasts have become accidental—and successful—investors almost overnight, simply by dint of what's tucked away in their cellar. Indeed, if you find yourself sitting on a small wine collection, you might already be a de facto wine investor. It is easier than ever to buy and sell investment-grade wine. Over the past decade, the market has radically shifted from a brick-and-mortar, merchant-centric business into one that is reviewer driven and Internet based, making it just as easy these days to research and trade wine as it is to trade stocks and mutual funds through an online brokerage firm. The online merchants provide the exchange through which to buy and sell; the reviewers and their universally recognized scores provide a standard of measure that crosses currencies, language, and tastes, and allows buyers in Hong Kong to effectively deal with sellers in New York on equal terms. In addition, the many professional wine-storage businesses that have popped up across the country in recent years have greatly helped to facilitate wine trading.

So, whether you're a wine lover who wants to become an investor or an investor who wants to know more about wine, this book is for you. I've written it to help collectors and investors alike make sense of the investment side of wine—all that you need to know to make appropriate decisions, everything from selecting the proper wines to storing them properly. In these pages you'll learn about the criteria I've used to identify successful wine investments over the years. My intent is to share the information that has helped me acquire one of the world's largest, most profitable rare wine portfolios.

And who am I to write authoritatively on wine?

Wine is my profession. As a third-generation wine merchant, I've had a front-row view of this business my entire life. I have experienced from an insider's perspective all of the dramatic market changes in an industry that, because of the global reach of the Internet, is transforming on a fundamental level. I know fine wine because I drink it, because I live it, and because I love it. I was fortunate enough to literally age alongside some of the world's finest of wines. While most of my friends were taking their first sips of beer from Dad's mug, I was sampling my father's 1961 Pétrus.

The business I now run—Sokolin LLC—was founded by my grandfather immediately after Prohibition was repealed in December 1933. For decades, the store then known as Dave's Liquors was among New York City's best-established purveyors of spirits. But when my father, William Sokolin, took over in the 1950s, he made the radical decision to focus solely on the sale of top-flight wines. During this time in America there was virtually no market awareness nor any notable appreciation of fine wines, let alone consumers. Bill's own fascination with wine was spurred by an Alfred Hitchcock movie he'd chanced to see, *Dial M for Murder,* starring Grace Kelly as the wife of the debonair Ray Milland, with glass in hand. The sophistication and glamour of that scene resonated in him, instilling a vision of what he wanted the family business to become. Ironically, the wine in that film was Mateus, a markedly unsophisticated rosé. At a time when cocktails were the beverages of choice among America's imbibers, Bill began his oenological education and that of his customers with the sale of this humble brand. To everyone's benefit, he later graduated from Mateus to Pétrus.

Bill changed the name of the business to D. Sokolin and began to emulate the business model established centuries ago by the wine traders of Great Britain. In 1959, he pioneered the sale of wine futures in America, allowing his customers to lock in a supply of fine French wines that the châteaux would not bottle and release to the public for another eighteen months or so. With unflagging enthusiasm, he played a role in educating New Yorkers about wines and the idea of holding fine wines for investment. He would tell customers to buy an extra case for each case they purchased, advising them that they could drink one case and later sell off a second case to finance their collection. His advice worked.

Under my management starting in 1996, D. Sokolin has evolved into a high-tech wine-sales and -storage facility located in Bridgehampton, New York. When I began my career in 1992, our most successful salespeople knew the vintage of Napoleon's favorite Pichon-Lalande. They were great storytellers with a passion for the history and the lore of wine. Today, our best brokers not only know the stories behind the wine, they also have a sense of the market and a keen knowledge of scores and prices. They see wine as not just a liquid but a liquid asset.

What you'll find in the coming pages is my personal experience distilled. This is the modern guide to wine from an investor's perspective. A lot has changed in the twenty years since my father coined the term investment-grade wines (IGW). My efforts not only cover the basics of wine investing, but they also explain how the wine market has dramatically changed because of the rise of the Internet, the emergence of cult boutique wines that work wine lovers into a frenzy, and the economic shifts that these days allow French châteaux to regularly ratchet the prices of their best Bordeaux higher.

Here's what you won't find: a wine education. Plenty of books have been written to help consumers become better wine drinkers. While you will certainly become intimately familiar with the names of the world's greatest wines, this book isn't designed to teach you how to become a wine connoisseur—though you probably will do a better job when ordering off restaurant wine lists.

Moreover, you won't find a lot about the competition that exists all over the Internet. While scores of merchants and online auction sites populate the Web, where you can buy and sell wines of various pedigree, truth is I don't know the criteria others use to make their wine-investment decisions, nor am I convinced that all of these sites operate in a manner conducive to a successful investor's needs.

One small example: You will find a number of do-it-yourself auction sites online, the eBays of wine, but you often have no way of proving a wine's authenticity or its provenance. Instead of owning an investment-grade wine, you could end up owning a fake or a poorly stored original that isn't worth what you paid.

There are those who miss the old days of wine, when investors weren't part of the market. They insist that the new generation of wine enthusiasts—particularly the investors—has lost touch with the essential, mysterious beauty that is fine wine. Some feel that the wealth generated in the late 1990s and the 2000s has turned wine buyers into lemmings, all chasing after the latest high-scoring bottles, in the process driving the price of great wines well beyond the pocketbook of all but the richest patrons, alienating lovers of wine the beverage, not wine the investment.

I don't see that from my perch. To the contrary, I see that the availability of information about fine wine has democratized the market, encouraging ever more people to refine their taste buds, empowering them to delve deeper into a field that was once clouded by a lack of information and to access a world that for centuries excluded all but the cognoscenti. The advent of Internet-based reviews, combined with the rise of wealth, has, during my tenure, enabled more people than ever to participate in what was formerly the domain of a much smaller, much more privileged class.

True, this increased focus on wine as an investment has priced some people out of the market, but that's a trait of every desirable asset. The more people educate themselves on the potential of some stock or some parcel of land, the greater the demand and the higher the price. That's the nature of free-market capitalism, and there's no reason it should be any different for wine just because you can drink it.

If you peer out over next two decades and visualize a larger client base for fine wines emerging in Asia, Eastern Europe, and South America, then you should easily see how demand is the crucial component behind rising prices. And if you're an investor in any other assets—such as stocks or real estate—you should immediately recognize the opportunity that lies before you. Individual investors who buy and properly store investment-grade wines are uniquely positioned to participate in the global expansion of wealth that is now under way.

The key difference between wine and any other asset is that "winning" in the wine market has one unique advantage. In the stock market, losing stocks are simply written off at tax time and, hopefully, forgotten. With wine, there's no such thing as a losing investment. Whenever you wish, you can "liquidate pleasurably," as my father likes to say, by drinking your "losers" with dinner. Of course, if you are investing in the right wines, it's going to be hard to lose even if some bottles don't appreciate as much as you'd like. They are fine wines, after all, and if history is any guide, the growing demand for the limited supply of the world's rarest beverages will continue to push prices higher for investment-grade wines.

So let's take a look at how fine wine has become more than a drink and has emerged as a great way to grow money.

PART I

Wine-Investing Basics

1

THE GRAPES OF MATH

The Finances of Fine Wine

Unless you're day-trading stocks or currencies for the thrill of the kill, investing generally isn't considered a game of fun. It's a much more sober affair for the most part, all cash flow analyses and financial ratios of one sort or another. The only time investment and wine generally mix is at cocktail parties, where there's always someone who has downed a bit too much Chardonnay and prattles on incessantly about the long-term potential of some nano-technology stock he's suddenly an expert on because of inside information he picked up at the barbershop from a friend of a friend who knows someone.

Wine, as you might imagine, is different. How can you invest in wine and not have fun? You can't drink a share of Microsoft, but you can certainly sample one of your bottles of '82 Château Latour and physically experience the character of the wine. You can't invite your friends over for a blind tasting of bonds, but nobody's missing the date if you arrange a vertical tasting of a half dozen of your back-vintage Latours in your private cellar.

Wine is just, well, fun.

Mix in a little profit potential, and suddenly it's a blast.

For many of my clients, collecting, sampling, and enjoying all that wine offers hedonistically overlaps seamlessly with wine as an investment—so much so that many never realize they've become investors until, by happenstance, they see somewhere that those bottles of '90 Château Le Pin they bought years ago for a few hundred dollars apiece are now worth nearly $5,000 each. That's when they realize they've become accidental wine investors. They're people not unlike Hans Denbaas, the subject of a 2007 *Wall Street Journal* story on the emergence of wine as a viable investment class. Years ago Mr. Denbaas bought for his own consumption cases of 1989 Château Haut-Brion, one of the premier wine producers in the Bordeaux region of France. His cost: less than $200 per bottle. By early 2007 those cases were selling for more than $12,000 each, leading the accidental wine investor to comment: "You start to ask yourself, 'Gee whiz, am I really going to pop the cork on a $1,000 bottle?' "

That's a good question. Most people don't start off buying wine with an investor's mind-set. Many of my clients are essentially Mr. Denbaas; they come to me with a passion for wine the liquid but at some point start seeing their wine as a liquid asset. Wine becomes a vehicle for profit, as well as pleasure.

Ironically, the largest sellers of wine on Earth—the wine merchants—are seldom holders of large stocks of investment-grade wine. The wine auction business is purely focused on brokerage, and very few wine merchants have the capital to hold on to stock over the long term. The role of the wine investor, therefore, is to step in and hold inventory of IGW for wealthy end consumers in a marketplace that has few holders of wine stock. In that role exists great opportunity for the individual investor.

But as with any investment, you need to understand the exogenous factors that move the asset you own.

Macroeconomic Factors Moving Wine Prices

Traditional, fairly obvious macroeconomic forces tug at wine prices just as they do with every other market from stocks to currencies.

When economies are rocking, stock markets are climbing higher, and a sense of economic well-being pervades the populace, wine prices do well. The increased wealth provides the necessary discretionary spending to fuel price spikes as consumers spend up to afford the best that they can, be that fancy cars or fine wine. When economies roll over and stock markets tank, wine prices soften as consumers rein in their spending. But prices don't tumble as you might expect with stock prices. That's because unique factors are at play in the wine market, and it's those idiosyncratic rhythms that wine investors need to understand.

Wine, for instance, is truly an agricultural commodity affected by climatic conditions that can have a defining impact on the available supplies from one vintage to the next. The best wines are in short supply in bad years—especially after a run of bad vintages—and are the ones most in demand during stellar vintages, which limits their supply as well.

At the same time, wine is a true collectible with demand that, while it can run slack during bad economies, never fades completely. No matter the state of the economy, people are forever consuming wine, so the float of available fine wines is continually shrinking, day by day. Imagine how much more Picassos or Dutch Masters would be worth if they started disappearing on a routine basis!

Bull markets in other assets tend to reflect in the wine market as well. In the heyday of the 1980s real estate boom, wine prices had a major run higher. During the tech bubble on Wall Street in the 1990s, wine prices surged. Even in the dark days following the 9/11 terrorist attack and the resulting stock market downturn, my company continued to grow at a rapid pace. Though people were buying less wine, there were more buyers because so many had entered the market in previous years. Wine prices certainly softened during that period, but they did not tumble, and within a couple of years they had rebounded well past their previous high-water mark.

I'm not trying to imply that wine is immune to weak economies. However, investment-grade wines have certain properties that can insulate them from the worst of the bad times. When the going gets tough, the tough rarely forsake their wines. In more than fifty years combined in the wine business, my father and I have found that wine prices can go down during a recession but volumes tend to stay constant. People never seem to stop drinking. Although they may delay getting larger-ticket items like cars and houses, even expensive wine is a relatively low-ticket luxury that many people refuse to give up. Since most people who own investment-grade wines can more than afford to hold on to their collections during recessions, you don't generally see fire sales of these when good times go bad.

Today, the prime mover of wine prices is the global growth in wealth. From Shanghai sushi shops to caviar bars in Moscow, discretionary dollars are flowing through the world's emerging economies, with many of those dollars—well, yuan, rubles, and rupees, really—earmarked for Western-style luxury goods, including the finest of wines. This new trend was apparent during the 2005 Bordeaux futures campaign, when wine buyers gathered to buy the new vintage when it was initially released to the market. And 2005 marked the first vintage in which Asian buyers, who had historically been leery of putting money into futures or prerelease wines, entered the market in significant numbers.

The additional demand far outstrips the supply of an asset already in relatively low—sometimes extremely low—production. The greatest French wines are fully planted and have no room to expand; many châteaux's vineyards press against one another or stop at natural land breaks such as streams and rivers. Production that has not increased for decades will effectively be the same centuries down the road. The 10,000 cases produced today—while sounding like a relatively large lot—will increasingly be spread more thinly across an ever-growing class of consumers outside North America and Europe who now have or soon will have the means to afford these wines. This huge increase of new buyers, then, is making investment-grade wines harder to buy, yet easier to resell. Basically, if you own it, buyers will come.

Microeconomic Factors Moving Wine Prices

Along with the macroeconomic factors are the microeconomic dynamics that are driving wines prices higher and have nothing to do with the global economy but everything to do with local wine-makers.

■ **Low Crop Yields:** Starting in the 1990s, winemakers embarked on a trend to make wines that were more concentrated and flavorful. They did so via crop reduction, meaning they reduced the number of grape clusters on each vine so the remaining grapes could flourish. The result was wines that were higher in quality and, because of the lower production numbers, rarer. That, in turn, supported increased prices for the wine. Case in point: Château Cheval Blanc.

Back in 1989, much of the château's production went into its first wine, the eponymously named Cheval Blanc, which at that time retailed for $50 to $60 per bottle. The remaining production was earmarked for the château's second label, Petit Cheval, priced at $15 to $20 a bottle. Under new ownership, starting in 1998, Cheval Blanc increased the quality of both its first and second wines through rigorous crop selection. The result: 50 percent of the château's production went into Cheval Blanc, the rest declassified for use in Petit Cheval, and in doing so, the château increased the quality and the intrinsic values of both wines, pushing the price for Cheval Blanc to $165 a bottle while Petit Cheval jumped to $80. They winery had more than doubled the price of its flagship wine by reducing the production by almost half and more than doubled the price of its second wine while simultaneously doubling its production, generating more revenue than ever. Today, Cheval Blanc's good vintages are released at more than $600 per bottle and the 1998 is currently trading at over $1,000 per bottle with a 96-point score from Robert Parker in his Bordeaux book.

■ **High-End Wines That Drink Young:** Also during the 1990s, advances in winemaking technology led to the trend of designing high-end wines that "drink young," meaning the wines do not require the same cellaring time that many older wines require.

Early-drinking wines exit the market at a faster pace because people consume them, causing their values to climb in proportion to their increased rarity. Wines that drink younger price-appreciate quicker and create a client base at a faster pace. These wines are also easier for the reviewers to understand since they don't have to guess what they would be drinking like in the future; they already taste great upon release. Wines that drink young garner higher scores upon release, which, in turn, makes them more highly coveted, which ultimately drives their prices higher at a quicker pace.

Twenty Years of Bordeaux Pricing

OK, so macro- and microeconomic factors push and pull at wine prices. How have prices actually moved in the wine market?

Consider the charts below. These are price histories for cases of wine in a hypothetical cellar made up of ten-case lots of a variety of good-vintage Bordeaux, ranging from First Growths to Fifth Growths, and all of these wines are considered to be First- and Second-Tier IGW (in an upcoming chapter, I'll explain more about the growths and price tiers).

I'm focusing on Bordeaux here and throughout much of this book because, well, Bordeaux in large part *is* the wine market. Though other styles of wine command investors' attention—particularly Burgundy, Sauternes, and others—the bulk of the world's wine investors spend the bulk of their time and money buying, cellaring, and ultimately selling Bordeaux. The 1986 data in the chart on page 18 come directly from my father's book, published in 1981, while the 1997 data are the average case prices of wine sold at auction that year by the New York auction house Sotheby's. The 2007 prices were the average prices for the same cases available for purchase on the Internet.

What you should note here is that the dollar value of the 220 cases in this fantasy cellar would have almost doubled by 1997—a fairly respectable 7 percent annual return. Take a look as well at what occured to the same virtual cellar over the next ten years as the world began to view wine as a liquid asset and as global wealth exploded and demand for top-notch wine soared. The cellar's value is up more than 500 percent, an annualized return of more than 19 percent a year. That's good money. The Standard & Poor's 500-stock index during the same period was up only 4 percent.

If a collector had purchased this cellar back in 1986 and stored these cases over the ensuing two decades, the dollar value of the cellar would be up nearly 1,000 percent, an annualized gain of 12 percent a year. And how did the S&P 500 perform during this time, amid the so-called super bull market, one of the most vaunted periods ever in U.S. stocks? It gained about 10 percent a year. Wine won, and it never had to endure the same degree of trauma that buffeted the stock market during the 1987 crash, the Asian currency crisis, the Russian debt crisis, the near meltdown sparked by the failure of Long-Term Capital Management (all in the 1990s), the terrorist attacks of 2001, and the most punishing bear market since the Great Depression.

But why is this happening? Why is it that what began in prehistoric times as simply a way to create a fermented drink from grapes has turned into such a tradable commodity? And perhaps more important, will it continue?

Truth be told, wine was a commodity even in its earliest days.

By the first century B.C., Roman soldiers had arrived to colonize Burdigala (what is now Bordeaux), and they soon set about growing the beverage. They found the land so amenable to grape growing that they set up shop, planting vineyards and making wine, which they traded with Rome. By the 400s, Romans so fancied Bor-

Bordeaux Price Appreciation: 1986 to 2007

QTY*	YEAR	WINE	SCORE**	1986 CASE PRICE
		1ST TIER		
10	1953	Margaux	98 RP	$4,500
10	1959	La Mission Haut Brion	100 RP	$3,600
10	1959	Lafite Rothschild	100 RP	$4,800
10	1961	Mouton Rothschild	98 RP	$5,000
10	1975	Cheval Blanc	90 RP	$600
10	1982	Ausone	95 RP	$990
10	1982	Cheval Blanc	100 RP	$1,200
10	1982	Haut Brion	99 WS	$800
10	1982	La Mission Haut Brion	100 RP	$660
10	1982	Margaux	100 RP	$900
		2ND TIER		
10	1961	Palmer	99 RP	$5,000
10	1975	Cos d'Estournel		$380
10	1975	Ducru Beaucaillou		$420
10	1975	Léoville Las Cases	93 RP	$420
10	1975	Lynch Bages		$320
10	1982	Cos d'Estournel	96 RP	$480
10	1982	Ducru Beaucaillou	95 RP	$640
10	1982	Grand Puy Lacoste	96 RP	$380
10	1982	Gruaud Larose	98 RP	$240
10	1982	Léoville Las Cases	100 RP	$550
10	1982	Lynch Bages	94 RP	$360
10	1982	Pichon Lalande	100 RP	$500

* Cases of a dozen 750ml bottles   ** Highest review scores received during this time period.
RP: Robert Parker score   WS: *Wine Spectator* score

1997 PRICES	2007 PRICES	'86 PORTFOLIO	'97 PORTFOLIO	'07 PORTFOLIO
$5,000	$54,000	$45,000	$50,000	$540,000
$6,000	$42,900	$36,000	$60,000	$429,000
$6,000	$46,800	$48,000	$60,000	$468,000
$7,525	$30,420	$50,000	$75,250	$304,200
$1,295	$3,876	$6,000	$12,950	$38,760
$2,000	$10,140	$9,900	$20,000	$101,400
$4,500	$18,000	$12,000	$45,000	$180,000
$2,050	$9,588	$8,000	$20,500	$95,880
$4,070	$10,788	$6,600	$40,700	$107,880
$4,300	$18,184	$9,000	$43,000	$181,840
$6,980	$35,100	$50,000	$69,800	$351,000
$600	$2,340	$3,800	$6,000	$23,400
$450	$1,416	$4,200	$4,500	$14,160
$1,000	$1,560	$4,200	$10,000	$15,600
$420	$1,872	$3,200	$4,200	$18,720
$1,500	$6,000	$4,800	$15,000	$60,000
$800	$3,828	$6,400	$8,000	$38,280
$1,200	$3,180	$3,800	$12,000	$31,800
$1,500	$5,580	$2,400	$15,000	$55,800
$2,400	$7,788	$5,500	$24,000	$77,880
$1,200	$4,980	$3,600	$12,000	$49,800
$2,400	$8,988	$5,000	$24,000	$89,880
		$327,400	**$631,900**	**$3,273,280**

deaux wines that Emperor Diocletian condemned the vineyards and had the vines burned, fearful of the competition. Four hundred years later, the vineyards returned, and by the twelfth century, Henry Plantagenet—more commonly known as Henry II, King of England—requested that the claret, as the British called Bordeaux, be shipped across the Channel for the benefit of the British aristocracy.

By the eighteenth century, wine began to move past its commodity status when those British aristocrats with a predilection for claret realized they could subsidize their consumption by buying cases of wine, then holding back extra stock for resale at a later date and a higher price, the very cornerstone of investing. Buy today that which will be worth more tomorrow. Wine as investment was born, though, truthfully, at this early stage the Brits weren't necessarily acting as investors as much as they were simply looking for a cheaper way to afford next year's supply of drink.

1919–2008: A Truncated History of Wine in America

While British aristocrats have long had a love affair with French wine, the red, white, and blue has had a schizophrenic relationship with the grape. Associated with religious ceremonies and the poor immigrants of southern European nations, wine was never seen as much of a beverage in the States. Sure, Thomas Jefferson was a legendary wine connoisseur—America's first—touring French wine regions and having cases from his favorite châteaux shipped back home. But he was an exception to the American palate that alcohol made from grains—wheat, barley, hops, and corn—was the drink of choice for this great nation. Give us our beer, our Kentucky bourbons.

Indeed, when the grape phylloxera, a sap-sucking insect with a distinct taste for grapes, brought the French wine industry to its knees in the mid-1800s, row upon row of vineyards cropped up across southern California to meet the demand for wine, though, ironically, little of that California wine remained in the States. Consumption here was negligible, which was just as well, since most of the juice ended up in Europe.

Then along came the Eighteenth Amendment to the Constitution: Prohibition. The law of the land forbade the commercial production and sale of alcohol. However, in a bone thrown mainly to the large Italian-American population, the head of a household could legally produce 200 gallons of wine annually for personal consumption. And just like that, Americans had a newfound love of wine. During the decade of temperance that ensued, wine consumption in the United States actually increased, even though commercial-grade wineries withered on the vine.

Then, like a good Bordeaux gone bad, consumption plunged.

Congress repealed Prohibition in 1933, and beer and spirit sales soared. Wine was back to its traditional role as a marginal means of getting on a good high. It was during this period that my grandfather moved the family into the liquor business. Once the Twenty-first Amendment repealed Prohibition in December 1933, he was one of the first people standing in line at City Hall and received Liquor License no. 4 from the New York State Liquor Authority. In early 1934, Dave's Liquors opened on Madison Avenue and Thirty-third Street in Manhattan, where it operated for over six decades. In the 1930s, beers and spirits carried the business. Wine was a novelty at best, certainly not a big seller.

My dad, William Sokolin, took over the business some twenty years later and purposefully moved the company toward the sale of high-end wine, convinced that in a market saturated with liquor joints, he could differentiate the business and bring to it a level of sophistication by refocusing sales on the best wines in the world. He spent his career effectively teaching the growing lot of wealthy New Yorkers about quality wines. So much did he learn himself along the way about the wine market and price movements—everything from prerelease wine sales to the price escalation of classic vintages—that he wrote America's first guide to wine investing in 1987 and is widely credited with coining the term "investment-grade wine." While he was arguably the country's most bullish proponent of wine as an investment, even he is awed by the degree to which prices in the wine market have moved.

Fine-wine prices have simply exploded. As I write in late summer 2007, the Liv-ex 100 Index, which tracks price movements of 100 investment-grade wines and is the wine industry's version of the Dow Jones Industrial Average, is up 45 percent in the first seven months of the year. That follows a nearly 50 percent gain in 2006.

But those are just statistics. The real color of what has been going on with wine prices comes from the stories of individual wines and individual buyers.

More than forty-five years ago, a wealthy banker purchased from D. Sokolin futures for ten cases each of 1961 Mouton-Rothschild and Pétrus for $100 and $120, respectively. This banker grew irate with my father for charging him that extra $20 per case for the Pétrus and in a fit of frustration decided to return all but one case. More than thirty years later I traveled to this man's house to reclaim that last case of Pétrus. He had never cracked it open and was reselling it to us. During my time at his house, this gentleman lamented his rash decision to return the wine because of a quibble over $20 a case. The reason for his fretting: That one case of 1961 Pétrus was worth $120,000. Who could ever have predicted that had he kept the entire lot, this man's twenty-case purchase, totaling $2,400 in 1962, would be worth over $2 million in 2007?

In pinching pennies to save $400 (the 2007, inflation-adjusted equivalent of about $2,700), he had forsaken a multimillion-dollar gain. Obviously, he couldn't have known that this would ever occur, and, in fact, very few people at that time looked upon fine wine as anything other than a fairly pricey fruit juice with psychotropic side effects. Only since the early part of this newest millennium has wine emerged as a true asset class.

The Growth of Wine as Investment

Wine has been a tradable commodity since the Stone Age and an investment since the eighteenth century. But only with the rise of the Internet and the explosion of global wealth has wine emerged as a viable investment easily traded among everyday investors, meaning those who aren't professional wine merchants.

A big part of that growth in the United States has been thanks to the emergence of wine auctions online, the legalization of wine auctions in New York State in 1993, and a Supreme Court ruling in 2005 that allowed wineries to ship across state lines. Prior to 1993, New York's wine merchants had lobbied successfully for years to keep wine off the auction block because they feared competition from the auction houses. While other cities did sell wine at auction, New York, because of its population density and the huge numbers of wine connoisseurs and collectors, drew attention to the wine-auction market as never before. New York rapidly grew into a global magnet for wine auctions, sparked in large part by all the dollars that flow freely through an economy fueled by high finance and seemingly unquenchable consumer spending.

Indeed, through the first six months of 2007, some $90 million of wine went to the auction block in the United States, up from $14 million for all of 1993. It's not just the sheer volume of dollars being thrown at fine wine that shines a spotlight on the market. It's the cork-popping prices that individual lots routinely command at auction that has grabbed the attention of investors who might never have considered wine as a potential asset. In 2007, for instance, a case of DRC Romanée-Conti 1985, a stellar wine among Burgundies, sold at auction for $237,000, while a forty-two-bottle lot of Screaming Eagle, a highly coveted California cult Cabernet, sold for $130,900, well in excess of estimates of just $50,000 to $80,000. And a jeroboam of 1945 Mouton-Rothschild—from the private cellar of Baroness Philippine de Rothschild, the château's owner, no less—sold for an astounding $310,700. Media reports of these gargantuan prices shine a light on the investment possibilities of wine among investors, who suddenly see that rare wine can, indeed, produce fabulous returns.

The proliferation of these auctions is certainly helping to boost the wine market. Live auctions are held several times a year by big-name houses such as Christie's and Sotheby's. Though such auctions typically occur in the biggest metropolitan centers—New York, Chicago, Los Angeles, and San Francisco—much smaller auctions are held all over the country many times a year at high-end wine stores and through smaller auction houses. Making it all the more convenient for investors, bidders don't need to be in attendance to participate. Nowadays, you need only a high-speed Internet connection to bid from home or at work—or in a hotel room on vacation, for that matter.

Many, many more wine auctions happen twenty-four hours a day in the ephemeral world of cyberspace, though wine investors certainly need to be careful about the wines they buy online and whom they buy them from. Sites have popped up all over the Internet that have made investment-grade wine widely accessible to collectors and investors who, because of their remote location, would otherwise rarely, if ever, attend a major wine auction.

Combined with changes in federal law, the Internet has given wine investors access to wines they would never find locally. In 2005, the Supreme Court erased one of the last vestiges of Prohibition, striking down as unconstitutional the long-standing state laws that prohibited wineries from shipping wine directly to consumers in other states. Now wineries can ship directly across state lines, though not all wineries ship to all states. Of particular interest to wine investors is that this legal reversal means consumers in Missouri or Montana can buy directly from California wineries the Cabernets that have become cult favorites among collectors and connoisseurs—assuming, of course, you can get onto the waiting lists, which can stretch for years.

All of this has dramatically expanded the popularity of wine as an investment, not only drawing in huge new flocks of investors but also providing them the access to the world's greatest wines that they've never before had and the tools necessary to research their investments, though they might never even taste the wine they want to own.

Perhaps this bit of data from *Wine Spectator*, one of the leading wine-industry publications, sums it all up: By 2008, "Americans will drink more wines than Italians for the first time ever, and will trail only France in terms of overall wine consumption."

2

THE MECHANICS OF WINE INVESTING

W all Street has its growth and value investors and its technical and fundamental traders, each group defining the system of beliefs by which an investor invests. Over the years, I've come to classify wine investors into three main types: technical, collector, and casual. All ultimately have their eye on profit; they just get to that point by entirely different means.

■ **Technical:** These are the active investors, the wine buyers who own wine specifically as an alternative asset class and who value a wine collection as part of an overall portfolio. They scrutinize vintages and scores. These investors might not drink that much wine, and the wine they do buy is hands-off, meaning they have no intention of cracking open the case. They'll just set it aside, properly stored, of course, in their own wine cellar or in a rented cellar, awaiting the day consumer demand begins and the price surges. These investors generally invest in only the wines that have been most sought-after for decades and that have dependably appreciated over time.

■ **Collector:** These are the passive investors, largely buying wine for the sheer enjoyment of drinking it. More often than not, though, they're buying more wine than they need, specifically expecting that the wines they're buying will increase in value over time, helping fund future purchases of wines to imbibe. Because these investors realize that fine wines historically do rise in value, they might take a flier on a few wines they don't intend to drink, a speculative play, really, and maybe with a wine more expensive than they'd ever consider drinking. Success in this arena often leads passive collectors/investors to become much more active investors, even as their passion for collecting and enjoying wine grows.

■ **Casual:** These are the accidental investors. They're wine lovers who buy what they love to drink, laying in several cases at a time. Only one day they realize their bottles and cases are worth many hundreds, if not several thousands, of dollars each, and the thought of pulling the cork on something that valuable causes queasiness. Instead, they toy with the idea of selling the wine or holding onto it even longer to see how high the price might go. These people are "investors" only in name and aren't active in the market to any real degree.

Determining what kind of wine investor you are will help you map your path through the world of wine. If you are a technical investor at heart, then you're not going to care whether you personally think a highly rated wine tastes highly rated or not. You're going to buy solely with the intention to sell.

If you're a collector/investor, you're probably going to want to invest in wines that match your definition of "good," because you'll want to enjoy what you own. And if you're singularly a collector, your only interest in the investment side of wine will be to measure the value of your cellar, possibly just for the fun of it, possibly just to sell off some of your collection when prices reach such a level that you can't stomach the idea of opening a bottle that could fund a month or two of mortgage payments.

Regardless of what classification you most identify with, the perfect wine investor has a few characteristics of his or her own. They tend to be investors who:

■ Don't expect initial public offering (IPO)-type returns, but also don't want IPO-like risks. While wine has its own IPO-like market—the Bourdeaux futures market, which we'll get into in a bit—wine prices don't move in ballistic missile–like trajectories as IPOs on Wall Street can. They move at a more measured, more sustainable pace when headed higher. And on those rare occasions when they're headed down, the fall is typically modest, so that you don't face the same sort of flameout that can wreck a young stock.

■ Expect bondlike security but with greater profit potential. Just as buyers of U.S. Treasury bonds, for instance, know that if they hold their bond to maturity, they're guaranteed to get back their principal, owners of the finest wines—particularly from Bordeaux and Burgundy—are almost equally assured that they will recoup their principal when the wines are mature and ready for consumption. Certainly, wines don't pay a stream of income for holding them, as do Treasury bonds. Instead, the investment return comes from the price appreciation the wine generates, based on the variables—pedigree, vintage, etc. Depending on how those variables stack up, wine can generate greater profits than an investor would otherwise earn from holding bonds.

■ Understand that while wine is a liquid, wine investments are fairly illiquid. While wine prices historically track higher, they don't do so on a set schedule and they don't do so overnight. You cannot expect to buy cases of Latour or Le Pin one day and see their prices bump higher the next. Wine typically requires a minimum holding period of five years before profits accrue. I'll explain more about holding periods in an upcoming section on how to buy Bordeaux futures and back-vintage wines. In short, you need to consider wine a long-term investment, if for no other reason than that investment-grade wines literally take time to mature. It's in the maturation that the return on investment takes place.

In wine investing, timing is more important than ever. The marketplace has become more efficient, and an increase in buyers has made it more competitive. It's best to buy wines early, as soon after their release as you can. Likewise, it's best to sell at the peak of publicity, when a monster score is unleashed or a score upgrade is published. Wines are produced and most reviews are published on a regular schedule, so it is good to know what you are looking for and to be ready to respond to the market.

Throughout this book, you will come across eleven rules—I call them Sokolin's House Rules. These are designed to keep you on track when it comes to buying investment-worthy wine. While I encourage you to buy and consume whatever wines you enjoy, whether they're worthy of investment or not, when it comes to the wines you want to own specifically for investment purposes, there are some rules you need to know. Here are the first five:

Rule 1: Stay Current on Wine Reviews and the Latest Releases

Later in this book we will spend an entire chapter talking about the profound effect that the small group of wine critics and their reviews has on the investment-grade wine market. For now, you simply need to know that they do. And because the leading critics hold such sway, serious investors need to stay up to date on reviews of and commentary about wines, regions, châteaux, and vintages.

This doesn't mean you need to track every wine coming out of every châteaux in every region during each vintage. If you couldn't care less about Tuscans or Burgundy is beyond your budget, no worries. Just focus on the critics who move the market in the region in which you're interested—Robert Parker and James Suckling in Bordeaux, for instance, or James Laube in California.

If you don't have the time, or aren't certain you've seen all the pertinent reviews, talk to your wine merchant. If this is a merchant through whom you funnel a lot of your trading, he'll be eager to send this information to you in a timely manner so that you can capitalize on opportunities that arise.

Rule 2: Rely Only on Reputable Sources

From newsletters and magazines to websites, e-mails, and blogs, more sources of wine-investment information are available now than ever before. That's both good and bad. For while you will undeniably find a trove of data necessary for making informed investment decisions, you'll also find a lot of blowhards touting what to buy and when to buy it, though you can bet that such recommendations are proffered to benefit the supposed oracle posting this news and not you. But regardless of all the hyperbole you will assuredly stumble across in your research, what you ultimately purchase must come from a trustworthy supplier.

Wine is a physical product, not an ephemeral investment like shares of stocks or bonds or mutual funds that, in many cases, exist only as book-entry notations somewhere or, more likely today, digital bits stored on some computer server. Wine, therefore, must be cared for. That's where a reputable merchant comes in. Being a wine merchant myself, that might sound self-serving. After all, you can troll any number of wine-auction sites online today and find a plethora of highly rated investment-grade wine to buy, some at what seem to be ridiculously cheap prices, given the vintage and the brand. All I'll say is: Be careful.

Not all of this wine you'll find has been stored properly, despite the assurances, promises, and pinkie swears of the seller. When you go to sell your investments one day, you will have no way of proving provenance, which I'll get into in a moment. So what you end up doing is buying high-grade wines at lowball prices, only to find that future buyers balk at your bottles and cases because you can't prove that your wine is well sourced. You will have to sell your wine at prices well below the market, assuming anyone wants your bottles after all. There goes your investment.

The best merchants will help you with all aspects of wine investing from procuring the best prices (which doesn't necessarily mean the lowest prices) to verifying your purchases upon receipt. They will manage your buying records, store your wine professionally, and eventually help you remarket your portfolio when you want to take some profits. Many have access to the wine-futures market and will help you nab the cases of the new vintages you want to own.

Rule 3: Buy Wine Futures and Prereleases

The best moment to buy wines is generally while the first sales are taking place, as either futures or prereleases, and we'll dive far deeper into this a bit later. This is the moment when prices will likely be the lowest on the most coveted, investment-worthy wine.

Bordeaux futures prices are announced each summer, generally two years prior to the date when the wine will actually make it onto store shelves. Other collectible wines are offered as prearrivals, after they have been bottled but have not yet shipped from the wineries.

Many wine merchants make a business in futures, as do some local liquor stores and specialty grocers that stock fine wines. To the degree that you can, buy these futures and prerelease wines and then store the bottles properly, either at home or in a professional storage unit (again, more on both of these options to come). The caveat with futures and prerelease wines is that your holding period is generally a decade or more, since it takes that long for new wines to mature into a drinkable state. That's when all the connoisseurs and collectors begin to emerge, looking to buy the stock you own.

Rule 4: Buy Only Wines with a Proven Provenance

This ties in with Rule 2. A wine's provenance is essentially its winery of origin, its path from one owner to another, and the treatment the wine has received at every stop on its journey. Basically, you want to be able to show your buyers that the wine you're selling is pristine.

I can have a 95-point-rated Ducru Beaucaillou with impeccable provenance and records proving that it has been properly acquired and stored, while you can have a 100-point-rated Mouton Rothschild with sketchy provenance that you've been keeping in your closet for the last five years. My Ducru will outprice your Mouton by a long shot. Condition and provenance are the fundamental factors here.

End consumers paying huge dollars want the best assurances possible that when they pop the cork, a bottle of wine is going to taste as it is supposed to. They don't want to have to pour $1,000 or more down the drain because the wine was improperly stored and now tastes like vinegar. For that reason, they are going to buy wines from sellers who can prove where the wine came from and that it has been stored properly. The wines without provenance will sell at sharp discounts, assuming they sell at all. Those wines certainly will not be seen as investment grade.

As the wine-investment market matures and the value of collectible wines soars, a wine's provenance has become an increasingly important determinant in its value. Or, in some cases, a fatal flaw, because if provenance is ever in question, the value of your investment shrivels like forgotten grapes.

Ideally, wines should be shipped in refrigerated containers and stored in a temperature- and humidity-controlled environment during the entire course of their lives. The fill level can be indicative of the temperature at which a wine was stored, and the label condition can be a sign of whether or not a wine was professionally stored. Consumers of high-end wines are savvy enough to know this and to look for signs of a wine's mistreatment.

How can you be assured of your wine's provenance? If you buy in the futures market, or if you buy directly from the winery, as you can with many wines from California, Australia, and Burgundy, you will have perfect provenance. You will be the first owner, and you will want to keep your purchase order or receipt as future proof of this fact when buyers question your wines' past.

If you're buying on the secondary market, you must seek out this proof. Reputable wine merchants source their wines professionally, buying from wineries and vineyards and *négociants* directly, or personally visiting the cellars of investors and collectors from whom they buy to feel confident about a wine's provenance. As such, you can feel fairly confident that a respectable merchant is dealing in wines with an impeccable provenance.

When buying from other collectors and investors, the process is a bit more uncertain. Unless you can visit the cellar and inspect the records and the wines yourself, you're buying on faith. Sometimes you'll be OK. Sometimes maybe not.

Now a word about fakes. With big wines commanding such big dollars, it's inevitable that someone somewhere is going to try to pass off a less expensive wine for a substantially more expensive wine. And none of the criteria mentioned so far will help you spot a phony. After all, aside from the difference between reds and whites, you can't tell one wine from another by looking at the contents in the bottle.

I'll never forget the time years ago when we opened a box of 1982 Lafleur, worth some $18,000 per case at the time. The Day-Glo photocopied labels were a dead giveaway. I calmly called up my supplier and told him they didn't look right, that I was going to return the shipment, and that he would have to make good on my order. It wasn't a problem. We've been trading with each other for some twenty years, and a parcel of fake wine wasn't going to end our relationship. In all likelihood, he returned the cases to his own supplier for a refund. The moral is that fake wine is not your problem, as long as you catch it quickly and if you have a good relationship with your supplier.

The question you face, of course, is how to spot a fake. Again, if you're buying from the wineries directly or from merchants that make a big business in the futures market, you've got nothing to worry about. Your wine is what it is. In the secondary market, look at the corks. They are particularly hard to fake. This is why you will oftentimes see cut capsules on particularly fine, particularly expensive wines. It's the previous buyer's way of ensuring as best they can that the wine is as billed. The cut capsule reveals the producer's brand imprinted on the cork. This does not significantly devalue that bottle (especially not if it's part of a case or multiple-case lot). It simply adds a degree of confidence to the transaction.

To deal with fakes, many high-end wineries are now using high-tech fraudproof labels to discourage this crime. But always remain vigilant so that you don't fall victim to fake wines that can sharply devalue your porfolio.

Rule 5: Invest for the Long Term

Wine is not a trader's game in the purest sense. In other words, you're not going to sit in front of your computer for a few hours during the day buying cases of Lafite-Rothschild for $9,700 and moments later selling the same case for $9,800. Wine, unlike stocks and currencies, is not a day-trading game. It is the quintessential long-term investment.

After all, if you're buying in the futures market, you'll have to wait two years before you even see your wine and another eight years or more while it matures. And if you're buying in the back-vintage market, the biggest price gains tend to accrue to those investors who snap up high-scoring wines about five years before the bottles mature and restaurants start listing them on wine menus.

If you can't invest for a minimum of five years, then you really should not be investing in wine. Though they dependably trade higher over time, wines don't always appreciate along an even curve. Thus, if you plan to hold for a very short time before trying to sell, you could be highly disappointed if the moment you seek to exit is the moment that wine values have temporarily stalled for whatever reason.

Here's the caveat to all that I just wrote: There are times when wine investment can be a short-term game, particularly right after a new issue of *Wine Advocate* or *Wine Spectator* arrives. But for the most part this means beating everyone else to the merchant first or owning these wines before a big score is published. You might do that a few times—possibly out of sheer luck—but you won't reliably be able to do that, so short-term trading isn't likely to make you a fortune in the wine market. Long-term investing, however, does have that potential.

How Big a Wallet Do I Need?

Let's be clear: Investment-grade wine is not cheap.

At the highest end in particular, cases of top-flight investment wine run up near $10,000 in the futures market. And no one calls just one case of wine a portfolio. So at the very least you're looking at a sizable outlay necessary to amass a cellar of IGW.

Indeed, if you have the funds to build a blue-chip portfolio of IGW, you can spend between $75,000 and $100,000 a year buying just a single case of each of the ten most prestigious names in Bordeaux.

That said, you don't have to tailor your investments exclusively to cases that cost $10,000 a pop. Numerous IGW trade for a few hundred dollars a case. Indeed, with the same $10,000 you'd spend on one case of First Growth wine in the futures market, you could buy a dozen or more cases of investment-worthy wine with a bit less pedigree. The brand might not be as revered and the critical reviews might not be as lofty, but at the end of the day these are still well-heeled wines with the same investment-grade characteristics, and they still have a long history of price appreciation over time.

Just as folks saving for retirement plunk $4,000 or so into an Individual Retirement Account every year, wine investors without exaggerated means could likewise pull a few thousand dollars out of their income stream annually to buy futures for highly rated, yet lower-tier Bordeaux, and over time build a very nice portfolio of investment-grade wine.

Drunk on Profits: Integrating Wine into Your Portfolio

These days, almost every conversation I have with long-standing clients includes that moment where I hear the sigh and I know the lament is coming. If only they had bought more of some particular wine—not because of the joy they had drinking it but because of the profit they realize they could have made had they laid in a case or two extra to sell later. Chastened by the experience, many have begun increasing their purchases, earmarking some of their money for a portfolio of wines designated solely as investments.

And why not? Wine's profitability has steadily increased over time, and investment-grade wines generally "produce comparable returns to equities and bonds over the long term with less volatility, because the market is largely unaffected by economic issues like higher interest rates," according to James Miles, founder of the Liv-ex.

The downside is, of course, that, cases of wine are somewhat illiquid, a key risk in the event you need your money immediately. Nor do all investment-grade wines appreciate as expected. Some stagnate in value, and there are some instances where the value of wine can slip, especially when the wine is moving past its prime. The worst drop yet recorded on the Liv-ex 100 was a tumble of more than 6 percent in one month—though to be fair, the index recovered that lost ground within the year.

There are a few risks unique to wine: breakage, theft, and spoilage. Drop a bond, and the worst that happens is you throw out your back bending over to pick it up. But the bond itself has lost no value simply by hitting the floor. Drop a bottle of '77 Château Ausone— and, by the way, that's 1877—and you will literally watch nearly $8,000 disappear.

Lose a bond or stock certificate—or be robbed by an unscrupulous broker—and there are procedures you can follow to replace the instrument. But come home from a week's wine-tasting tour of Napa or Burgundy to find your cellar bare, and you're out tens of thousands, maybe even hundreds of thousands, of dollars of wine that will be nearly impossible to recover and possibly never replaced.

You might think your shares of stock are rotten because the price has fallen or remained flat for years. But wine can literally turn rotten if the bottles are not stored properly and the corks are allowed to dry out, crack, and shrink, letting air seep in and spoil the drink.

Those are very real risks with wine, but they're manageable risks that we'll address later. The bottom line is that, based on the mounting evidence that fine wine is, indeed, an alternative investment class with measurable risks and returns, news stories in London's *Financial Times* and in *The Wall Street Journal* have recommended that investors diversify their investment portfolios with collectible wine. Academics and wine-fund experts alike have shown that portfolios consisting of fine wine have a higher expected return per unit of risk. In English, this effectively means that for the same amount of risk, you generate a higher return, or, conversely, for the same level of expected return you assume less risk. Either way it means that wine is not only good with a meal; it's also good for diversifying an investment portfolio.

3

DEFINING INVESTMENT-GRADE WINE

What Makes an IGW?

Around the world, roughly 50,000 stocks trade on the various markets and exchanges. Not all, however, are worthy of investment. Wine is no different. Indeed, the world is awash in wine. If you circled the globe, you'd stumble across tens of thousands of wine producers. Some are huge, publicly traded wineries pumping out millions of bottles a year that cost just a few dollars at the local mini-mart; many are tiny, family-owned estates barely able to produce a couple hundred bottles a year that sell for hundreds, if not thousands, of dollars.

Amid this sea of vino float less than 250 vintners producing the world's premier wines. In the late 1980s, at a time when the wine investment market was still in its infancy, my father recognized this exceedingly limited set of wines that make for potentially good investments. Investors pay attention to these fine wines because only they possess the rare ability to improve with age and to dependably increase in price for decades after they're bottled. Unlike the vast majority of the world's total wine production, which is produced largely to be consumed fairly quickly and at fairly mundane prices, investment-grade wines (IGW) can ultimately command significant premiums over their original release prices. This is where investors congregate.

Approximately 90 percent of the world's IGW is produced in Bordeaux, in western France. The remainder comes largely from France's Burgundy, Rhône Valley, and Champagne regions; from California; as well as a few notable exceptions from other regions, including Australia, Spain, and Italy. Though this book covers investment opportunities throughout the world's significant wine-producing regions, the primary focus is Bordeaux because it is such a force in the market, representing the highest-volume, most accessible, most liquid, and most profitable wine region anywhere. Moreover, Bordeaux is the region most tracked by reviewers, the region on which most of the professional wine investors focus the bulk of their cash and energy, and the region with the best-established and consistent trading history, stretching back centuries.

No matter where they're from, IGW are purposefully built to age, and they're often not as good to drink when they're young as they are when mature. With some, two decades or more of aging is required before an IGW hits its prime, but by then these wines are typically in short supply because starting about ten years after the vintage is harvested, consumers begin popping them open. A trend has begun in recent years in which restaurants and the new consumers from Asia have no compunction about popping corks on status-symbol IGW (called "infanticide" by wine connoisseurs, who loathe this practice). The effect: an accelerated decrease in the IGW that are available years later, when these wines are coming into their prime.

When IGW first move into their window of maturity, their prices start to spike. This is the point at which end consumers and collectors willingly pay up for mature, perfectly stored wines that they can enjoy now. This is the point when the world's high-end restaurants begin listing these finally-ready-to-drink wines on their wine list, and at rich prices. This is the point when demand begins pushing the price for classic wines higher and, in a wonderful little

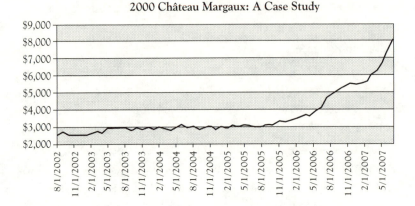

2000 Château Margaux: A Case Study

freebie for investors, when consumption begins taking increasing numbers of this limited-production asset out of circulation.

The end game of a wine investor, then, is to resell one's stock to those end consumers after the asset has matured and increased in value. That's how many of the wine funds operate and how they target returns of about 15 percent annually. They invest in cases upon cases of IGW that are just about five years from maturing, knowing that once the wine is about ten to twelve years old, consumers, collectors, and restaurants will begin pulling corks. That five-year period can represent some of the most rapid price appreciation a wine will see. Consider the graph above, the price chart from Liv-ex for a case of the 2000 vintage of Château Margaux, one of Bordeaux's top châteaux.

You don't need an advanced degree to see what happened here. The 2000 vintage was released into the market in late summer of 2002 at approximately $3,000 a case, a price around which the wine traded until the summer of 2005. At that point—five years after the harvest and five years before the first bottles of this Margaux would ideally be opened—the price began a noticeable uptrend, nearly tripling in value by the summer of 2007. As 2010 draws nearer, there's a very strong likelihood this trend will continue.

Along with time, IGW demand that two other criteria be present: score and longevity.

1. Score: The wine needs to possess a very high score from one or more of the leading reviewers. In this case, "very high" means the wine must have at least a 95 and preferably an even higher rating. Investors concentrate almost exclusively—maybe "fixate" is a better word—on wines that score at least a 95. Anything below 95 may be a very good wine, and some have the ability to earn higher, investment-grade scores as they age, but not many are considered classic IGW. We have an entire chapter coming up on critics and scores, so for now just know that score plays a defining role in determining which wines are investment worthy.

2. Longevity: Were it not for the inherent ability of investment-grade wines to age for decades, time would not be a factor in price appreciation. In their reviews wine critics generally express longevity as "anticipated maturity"—and not all wines have that. The reason is that not all wines age well and not all wines are meant to be aged. The longer a wine's expected ability to age, the more price-appreciation potential it's likely to demonstrate over the long term. Think of it in terms of Microsoft in the early years. Investors paid huge premiums (defined in this instance as a high price-earnings ratio) to own a piece of the tech giant's longevity, its rapidly growing income stream. But Microsoft grew into the price and kept moving higher as the company continued to demonstrate its ability to age well.

In the simplest of terms: If a wine hasn't garnered a high score, then it won't be in demand. Likewise, if a wine doesn't have the inherent ability to age, then it is, by definition, a wine you drink today, since it won't be any good years from now and because of that, no one will be looking for cases of it tomorrow at higher prices. Wine critics typically award the highest scores to those wines that are not only delicious now but also promise to improve with age over a long period. If a wine doesn't have *both* of those characteristics, then there's not much point in holding it as an investment.

Do You Need to Be a Wine Expert to Pick an IGW?

Touring California's Napa Valley on holiday, you stumble upon a new boutique winery that's peddling a Cabernet that you proclaim the best you've ever tasted. You load up on cases, expecting that one day the world will share your affection for this limited-production wine, that the cases will appreciate in value dramatically and pay for your child's college tuition—or at least a semester or two.

Trusting your own palate, however, is not a smart path to investment success. Many investors have lost big money relying on their personal sense of taste to choose their next great investment.

You may think you know what greatness tastes like, and you may be right. Or you may be wrong. Either way, the millions of wine enthusiasts outside your little sphere of influence, as well as the buyers who stock their bars and restaurants with the best wines, have no clue who you are. If the wine you love never earns high ratings by a respected reviewer, then it's not likely it will ever turn out to be a good investment because it's never going to generate much in the way of returns for one simple reason: no demand. Even if you own the last known case, what's your exit strategy if no one wants that wine? To be perfectly blunt, your opinion means nothing—and that's good. You don't need to be a wine expert to survive as a wine investor. With all of the information and services now available online and in the wine industry periodicals, it doesn't take a top-rated sommelier or viticulturist to inform you.

Factors That Drive the Price Appreciation of IGW

Every investment arena has a set of criteria that savvy investors rely on to determine whether an asset is a buy or a sell at any given moment and the likelihood of that asset appreciating in value over some time frame. After all, the only reason to put your money at risk in any investment is to generate some level of acceptable return on that investment.

Let's look at the six criteria for analyzing wine as an asset:

- points
- vintage
- longevity
- pedigree
- back-vintage premiums
- trading history

Points

The more the merrier.

Just as with nearly every major sport except golf, he who has the most points wins. In the modern world of wine, the number of points awarded by critics on a scale of 1 to 100 is everything. The score that a wine receives is the first factor a wine investor should consider, since the eventual buyers of your investment will be almost purely points driven. That's particularly true with the 100-point wines. There is something about the notion of perfection that compels consumers to dig a little deeper into their pockets to experience a 100-point wine.

With a numerical score, wine critics are offering guidance beyond a wine's taste. They're judging along a commonly understood scale of the hallmarks that define greatness, such as longevity and flavor complexity, in comparison to its peer group and based on a consistent set of standards. As a wine investor, this is a fact you need to remember: **Every investment-grade wine has received a score of between 90 and 100 points from one of the four most important wine-reviewing publications.** And most of the wines that are truly investment grade have a minimum score of 95 points. (Remember: A later chapter will detail what you need to know about wine reviewers who make the investment-grade wine market.)

High scores keep established brands trading at higher price levels and can put a wine on the map even if the winery has no history, a fact particularly apparent among the so-called cult Cabernets coming from California. Case in point: the 2003 Scarecrow from

It Was a Very Good Year

BORDEAUX	BURGUNDY	CHAMPAGNE	SAUTERNES
1961	1945	1971	1967
1982	1947	1976	1971
1986	1962	1982	1975
1989	1964	1985	1976
1990	1969	1988	1983
1995	1971	1989	1988
1996	1978	1990	1989
1998	1985	1996	1990
2000	1990	1999	2001
2003	1993		
2005	1996		
	1999		
	2002		
	2003		
	2005		

California's Napa Valley picked up a score of 98 from Robert Parker, the highest rating he has ever awarded a new-release California Cab. The wine's price tag quickly shot up from roughly $100 a bottle to nearly $1,000 on the rating alone, given that it was the winery's first vintage ever.

Vintage

Speaking of vintage . . . just as certain names carry great weight, so too do great vintages. They can be so widely lauded for their superiority that the vintage alone is powerful enough to move prices higher for wines that, if they scored the same rating in a nonfamous vintage, would otherwise sell for less.

As such, the market's perception of a wine's vintage is crucial to its potential price appreciation. In regions where there is significant vintage variation from year to year and a high density of pedigreed wines, such as Bordeaux and Burgundy, the savvy wine investor should stick with the great years, since end consumers will naturally gravitate toward wines from these particular vintages. It's not unusual to overhear a restaurant customer asking the sommelier what 1982 Bordeaux the cellar might be hiding. In this case, what château the wine hails from is almost irrelevant because the 1982 vintage was such a blockbuster year for Bordeaux.

Vintages judged to be "great" by the critics are those that not only produce wines of the highest quality across the board but also produce wines that will age the longest. Although longevity can be crafted into a wine by a skilled winemaker, the weather conditions of a growing season often have a greater effect in the creation of long-lived wines.

The chart above lists the top-rated vintages of the postwar period for Bordeaux, Burgundy, Champagne, and Sauternes.

Longevity

Everyone wants a long life. Wine lovers want the same for their best bottles of vino. After all, the longer a wine can survive in the cellar, the more years an oenophile has to enjoy a collection.

For a wine investor, then, the wines with the greatest longevity have the most time to increase in price. If a highly rated wine, for instance, is expected to age well for more than forty years, imagine the heights to which its price might potentially climb as the supply dwindles over the decades and the demand increases.

Longevity is a major factor critics consider when rating wines. The wines estimated to live the longest effectively generally garner the highest scores. Scores of 99 and 100 usually indicate that extreme longevity is likely, though this tends to be less so with some New World wines, which we'll get into in a later chapter.

But there is a downside to longevity for investors. Interest in some wines can stagnate for years until the wine is mature enough to drink and consumer interest perks up. Critics can be of some help here; they routinely include in their reviews an anticipated maturity date that can offer you some guidance. Savvy wine investors should pay attention to these maturity dates because consumers certainly do. As wines approach the point when consumers will begin to demand a particular wine/vintage combination, you might find some relative bargains in the bin—high-scoring wines that are just about to mature but that are off the radar screen at the moment for whatever reason. You'll have an opportunity to pick off these wines just as they're about to become drinkable and their price is about to move.

Know, though, that anticipated maturity dates aren't set in stone, just as the scores aren't. Back in early 1992, ten years after the 1982 vintage was harvested, Robert Parker rated the '82 Lynch Bages for the first time, awarding it a respectable 92-point score, estimating that the wine would be drinkable through 2007. If you paid attention to only that first review, you'd be thinking right now, in 2008, that this particular Lynch Bages is past its prime. And you'd be wrong.

A year later, Parker's score rose to 93 and the wine's longevity had extended to 2010. By January 2000, the last time Parker scored the '82 Lynch Bages, the rating had ratcheted higher yet again, to 94, and the wine's estimated longevity had extended even further, to 2015. For investors, such a situation can present opportunities. Pay attention to the movement of longevity expectations, and you can cherry-pick the market, snapping up wines that, based on critics' reevaluations, are aging better than expected. Demand for—and prices of—those wines will undoubtedly grow. Indeed, in the five years ending in July 2007, list prices for that '82 Lynch Bages steadily climbed from $1,750 to more than $4,800 a case, a more-than-respectable 22 percent annual rate of return.

Pedigree

Think about Coca-Cola for a second. It's so much more than just a sugary brown beverage. It's a slice of Americana, a shapely green bottle in roadside ads painted on the side of faded buildings from Portland, Maine, to Portland, Oregon. It's teaching the world to sing. It defines part of our collective conscience. What we're talking about here is Coke's history, its brand loyalty, the goodwill that has amassed in Coke's customer base over the decades. All of that melds into an overall market perception of what Coke stands for, which, in turn, creates demand that, at times, can be instinctual rather than conscious.

This concept factors into wine pricing, where it is known as "pedigree," the ancestral lineage of a château. Particularly in Bordeaux and Burgundy, some wines are so weighty they can override a point score simply by dint of the name on the bottle.

At the Paris World's Fair in 1855, a temporary classification system was devised as a way to help determine which French wines would be exhibited to the world's visitors. The wine brokers of the day established this system based largely on the prices various Bordeaux typically commanded in the marketplace, supported by perceptions at that time of each wine's relative quality. Today, that temporary system—the Classification of 1855—is a permanent feature of the French wine market and has come to define the ideals of greatness in wine. The 1885 Classification plays a critical role in the prices that many Bordeaux can command to this day just because of their name.

Wines with a lofty pedigree carry an intrinsic value that transcends their reviewer scores. For instance, a mediocre vintage of Château Pétrus, one of the most perennially alluring wines of Bordeaux, can command substantially more money than the highest-scoring vintage of a neighboring château with a less dignified pedigree, for the sole reason that it is a Pétrus and the world is chockablock with wine connoisseurs who collect Pétrus because of its pedigree. Case in point: the 1990 Montrose, a 100-point Parker-rated wine from the Médoc region of Bordeaux—a region home to some of the most renowned names in French wine: Lafite Rothschild, Latour, Mouton Rothschild, and Margaux. The '90 Montrose can be had for less than $700 a bottle. Add $400 to the price and lower the rating to 94, and you can pick up a '99 Pétrus. Even a 89-rated Pétrus from 1978 can cost more than that Montrose with the perfect score.

Burgundy's Domaine de la Romanée-Conti's pedigree was established over 100 years ago, and all wines from this hallowed estate sell for huge dollars, even in the very worst of vintages. The most expensive wines from what Burgundy's insiders know as "DRC" can trade for $250,000 per case, though the ratings might peak only at 95 points.

It's all driven by pedigree.

And by no means is pedigree confined to France. There are some New World wines as well that have developed a version of pedigree—albeit without the storied history dating back centuries. The acclaim they command both drives demand and allows them to trade for prices higher than what their scores might otherwise warrant. California's Opus One rarely receives a high reviewer score, yet because of its pedigree—the oenological marriage of California's Mondavis and France's Rothschilds—it opens at premium prices and trades higher over time thanks to a rabid fan base that keeps returning. Opus is a prime example of how some New World wines are capable of attaining pedigree in twenty years or less. I'm going to cover this more in an in-depth chapter on Bordeaux later in the book, but for now you need to know that pedigree works largely on a tier system, in which wines with a higher pedigree, but maybe a lower score, can typically command more money than a higher-scoring wine with a lower pedigree. My father first identified these three price tiers twenty years ago.

■ **First Tier:** The most expensive and famous investment-grade wines from each region. This is generally the smallest tier and the easiest to learn about, since you will probably have heard of many of these names. First-Tier wines have virtually no price ceiling over time, because the industries' biggest collectors and investors routinely chase after them. Over the past half century, these have been among the most profitable wine investments.

■ **Second Tier:** The second-most-expensive group of wines, usually constituting a larger pool of wines, many of which sport names that are famous among wine collectors. The most attractive feature about Second-Tier wines is that they always seem like a good value when compared to their First-Tier peers, which works to steadily drive their prices higher as First-Tier wine prices escalate. Their upside, though, is limited at some point.

■ **Third Tier:** These are the up-and-coming overachievers, in addition to the revamped older estates that are making far better wines today than ever before. Third-Tier wines must have higher scores to justify investment, largely because they don't carry the cachet of First- and Second-Tier wines. Savvy investors, however, can often get the most out of investing in Third-Tier wines, since some do become more popular and leap into the Second Tier, dramatically improving their price performance characteristics.

Back-Vintage Premium

Eventually, all wine investors—even those who buy strictly in the futures market—become back-vintage traders when it comes time to sell. As noted above, investment-grade wines are far more desirable when they've got a little age on them. The market pays up for highly regarded wines that are ready to drink today, particularly wines from a widely lauded vintage.

The premiums these wines receive relate back to maturity and, at some point, scarcity. A wine that's ready to drink now is far more appealing—far more valuable—to an end consumer than is a wine that still needs several years in the bottle before its full force is on display. That chart a few pages back on the '00 Margaux speaks to this fact. For five years, no one paid much attention to the wine; its price movement was as flat as week-old Champagne. That had nothing to do with Margaux or the vintage—both, in fact, are stellar. It's simply that supply-demand balance. There has been little demand for the supply up to this point. But as the day draws nearer to when the '00 Margaux will be ready for consumption, the price of what is now a back-vintage wine has begun to move. Demand is kicking in, in anticipation of the arrival of 2010, when those first bottles will be opened and consumers will begin requesting this particular Margaux.

In 2005, the wine market was turned on its head because some châteaux released their futures at prices higher than their own high-scoring, back-vintage, and inherently more valuable wines already on the market. For Americans, the strong euro played a hand in this, but it was due mostly to the châteaux's steep price increases in the futures market. But if you follow this through to the logical conclusion, the back vintages will likely catch up. They have to. Economically, the current situation makes little sense. Wine in the barrel, while rated, is nevertheless a question mark. These wines are rated along a range, say 98 to 100, meaning they could come in at 100 when the first bottle tastings occur . . . or they could come in at 98, still a fine score but a possible disappointment to those gambling on 100.

But let's assume the wine does receive a 100-point rating when it finally makes it into the bottle. At that point, consumers still have another five or so years to wait before they're able to drink this stuff. In the meantime, there are 100-point-rated vintages from the same châteaux already available at prices below that of the younger wine. You can see where this is leading: Consumers thinking, "Hmm. Can't drink that '05 yet; too young. But hey, look at this! The '95 is available and it has the same score. And it's cheaper! I'll take that one, please."

What happens next? Consumers consuming a limited supply of a rare asset. Assuming economists do not alter the laws of supply and demand, the consumption of the back vintages will continue to sap the market supply, pushing the prices up, most likely beyond those for the recent, younger vintages.

The message: There's opportunity for buyers of collectible, back-vintage investment-grade wines.

Trading History

Would you throw money at a stock just because it's a good company? Of course not. That's not investing; that's betting on red or black and hoping your color comes up a winner. Instead, you want to know the price of shares in relation to the company's earnings and where that ratio has trended over time.

To gauge whether a wine's price is worthy of entry at some given moment, you need to compare prices of the same wine in vintages of comparable stature and with comparable reviewer scores. For example: the 1982 and 2000 Bordeaux vintages are considered two of the very best in modern history. In mid-2007, the 100-point Parker-rated 1982 Lafite Rothschild was priced at up to $14,500 per case, a third more expensive than its 2000-vintage sibling, also carrying a 100-point Parker rating. True, the 1982 was already drinking well by 2007 and the 2000 vintage still had a few years to mature before consumers would be clamoring for it. But that's sort of the point: At first blush, the 2000 Lafite still has legs, given its 2050 maturity window and considering that another 100-point Parker-rated Lafite—this one from 1959—sells for upward of $45,000 per case. Consider, too, that there are only five 100-point Lafites in history to date, and you can see why there's plenty of room for price appreciation in the 2000 vintage.

Using past price records for a particular wine as a measure of its future potential is a decent rule of thumb, but with today's rising release prices it could mean missing opportunities. The wine market has been experiencing such a tremendous boom that it seems price records are being broken almost daily, yet wine prices remain buoyant.

What if you'd used past trading history to gauge whether or not to buy a prestigious Hamptons beachfront property during a real estate boom? Common sense might have warned you away when the price reached what seemed like oxygen-deprived levels. But in hindsight you'd see that a complete metamorphosis was recalibrating what most had come to expect as a "normal" real estate market. Hamptons real estate at the highest end tripled in the past decade because of the tremendous creation of wealth and the incessant demand among the wealthy for a Hamptons address. The escalating high-end real estate had the effect of dragging lower-end mansions along for the ride.

Likewise, the global clientele for rare wines hasn't flinched at rising Bordeaux prices and thus have skewed the trading histories that most had defined as normal in the fine-wine market.

But where normal no longer exists, you often find opportunities as an investor. I've begun seeking out older vintages of particular wines that are trading below the price of the younger wines from the same château. This upside-down trading history indicates that so much attention is focused on the latest supervintage that otherwise excellent, high-scoring wines can get overlooked. Yet, as I noted earlier, these higher-priced new releases have the propensity to pull up the prices of the older wines. My clients and I have profited handily from trading in the similarly rated, back-vintage counterparts of the stratospherically priced new releases.

4

_____

HEARD IT THROUGH THE GRAPEVINE

The Scores, the Critics, and How the Two Move Wine Prices

very investment market imaginable has its analysts, the people charged with ferreting out the good from the bad from the ugly for investors eager to keep pace with changes that always seem afoot. Be it the person tracking home builder stocks for Merrill Lynch, the "experts" on corporate debt at Standard & Poor's, the local realtor writing a newsletter on housing prices, or even the self-proclaimed master of yens and euros on a currency-trading blog, investors in every conceivable asset class can find someone to turn to for some sort of useful—or useless—analysis.

Wine, too, has its analysts, known as "critics," and their main aim has not so much to do with investing as with telling consumers about the quality of the wines they'll find on their store shelves. Their numbers are huge. Publications the world over employ all manner of reviewers to spill a bit of wine and then spill a bit of ink describing in mellifluous terms whether the latest bottling efforts from Bordeaux or Western Australia are really worth the time to hunt them down. The vast bulk of the analysis, though, is generally useless to investors.

Not to be churlish, but all these reviews that all these publications combined print do not have an effect on the wine-investment market at large. Sure, a particularly saccharine review in a local food and entertainment section might spur you to nab some new Rhône the next time you stop by the local liquor depot, but so what? The rest of the world does not see this review. The review doesn't move the price of the wine or dent the supply/demand balance outside the relatively small sphere of influence of some random publication.

Thus, the rest of the world does not care.

But that's not to say critics have no impact. They do. And it is undeniably gargantuan. It's just that this ability to sway the market in one way or another is limited to an exceedingly small, elite group of critics who command worldwide attention when they speak . . . well, when they write, actually.

They are oenology's Four Horsemen—Parker, Tanzer, *Wine Spectator*, and Meadows—the world's leading entities of wine criticism, whose musings and palates have the unique ability to turn a little-known wine into a market darling in the time it takes to peel a grape. They can send prices soaring—or sinking—in less than fifty words. The thing is, while those four names stand out, they generally don't stand alone. Though he originally made a name for himself on his own, Robert Parker is now backed by a team of reviewers he employs to help him rate the ocean of wine that he alone couldn't possibly make time for. James Suckling, a star in Bordeaux for the *Wine Spectator*, doesn't cover California, where it's his colleague James Laube whose reviews carry weight. Whatever the case, the scores and reviews awarded by this foursome—or, more broadly, their publications—represent what has come to be the most critical factor in the price of an investment-worthy wine. The Bordelais who run the châteaux often seethe at the power these critics wield, and they routinely disagree with their assessments, but the unassailable fact is that a 99- or 100-point score from any of these guys, and a wine is golden. A 90 and above, and it's an investment. Anything less and, while still possibly fantastic, a wine is generally just another bottle to drink with a meal.

Indeed, these days the score a wine earns from a respected reviewer is the most important determinant in the wine's price. As such, anyone who aims to invest in wine must be familiar with the Four Horsemen, and that means subscribing to some or all of the periodicals for which they write. At the very least, you need access to the ones that exert influence over the wine region or regions you're focused on.

The critics' game works exactly as it does with analysts on Wall Street: The earlier you act on new information, the larger your profit potential. Their words have been magnified by the impact of the Internet. As recently as the 1990s, the wine market was a relatively lethargic beast, slow and unresponsive to big scores, upgrades, and new reviews. The postal service was the communication medium of choice, and consumers had time to read and cogitate on the information before reacting. When they did get around to it, they'd find the market hadn't really done much with the information to begin with.

In the 1990s, I'd see a wine tagged with a 100-point score and the price would barely react, assuming it reacted at all. Sure, prices would continue to move higher over time, but that was largely a function of pedigree, demand, and the continual supply shrinkage from consumption. The price action today, though, is almost instantaneous, a function of the high-tech nature of digital life. Just as it is when some publicly traded company announces blockbuster earnings and the stock immediately surges higher, a similar surge ripples through the wine market within minutes of a respected critic awarding some wine a huge score. Stock-market investors rush to own a particular stock; wine lovers and investors rush to own particular bottles. In both instances, each investor is reacting to the same emotion: fear of loss. They know that others have received this information and that they must react quickly or lose this opportunity. So they act on their impulse to buy, and, well, the prices move up quickly.

Today, the reviewers' critiques scamper around the globe at the speed of electrons, and consumers who read about the latest vintage and the dramatic upgrade of some wine produced by a little-known Fourth Growth château scurry to scour wine-buying websites from Los Angeles to London, looking to grab cases where they can find them at the best prices they can find before everyone else drives the price higher. Blogs, meanwhile, disseminate information on the fly, and wine prices change frequently based upon what the reviewers say—or don't say, as the case may be. As a direct result of this critic-meets-Internet world, the wine market is larger, more active, and substantially quicker on its feet, meaning investors must react faster or miss opportunities that can be short lived.

The critics' weapon of choice is the 100-point system I've referred to several times, so let's look at how it works in investor terms.

And Your Point Is? Wine Scores and Their Impact on Wine Prices

There is a lot of wine sloshing about the world.

In 2006 alone the global wine industry produced some eight billion gallons, from a Nebuchadnezzar of the best Bordeaux to a box of private-label White Zinfandel down at the local super-megamart. That's enough for every human on the planet to consume a gallon of wine . . . and you'd still have nearly 1.4 billion gallons remaining. The thing is, though, there's a gulf separating the best Burgundies, Bordeaux, Super Tuscans, and Spanish Riojas from that box of White Zinfandel, and that gulf is quality. Anyone with a passing interest in wine knows that box of White Zinfandel is going to pale in comparison to the finest Burgundy. But the comparison grows substantially more fuzzy when you're trying to choose among the hundreds or even thousands of selections at a wine merchant's shop. What you need is some sort of ranking system, something to immediately resonate with everyone who encounters it, the application of which is instantly self-evident. Enter Robert Parker and his 100-point rating system.

For decades, British reviewers dominated wine criticism, led in large part by the British magazine *Decanter*, where, as with other UK-based wine publications, critics have historically relied on a five-star rating system to score wines. Despite its longevity, though, that system has never gained traction outside of Europe. The reason: Five stars provides too broad a scale, effectively lumping all wines into quintiles, thereby implying that an unquestionably flawless wine is in the same category as a generally fine, though certainly not great wine.

A Maryland lawyer previously unknown in the wine world, Robert Parker came along in the late 1970s and revolutionized wine criticism—and ultimately the entire wine market—by popularizing the inherently simple, inherently obvious 100-point scale published in his then-slender newsletter, *The Wine Advocate*. American consumers immediately gravitated toward this scoring system because it fit the frame of reference they had been trained to understand since their very first elementary-school test scores. The farther away from 100 you get, the worse you're doing. Simple.

More important to the wine market was that a 100-point scale allowed for a dramatically different level of specificity and differentiation than five stars ever could. As in the classroom, a 100 is a job well done; an 85 obviously needs some work. A 65 is an utter failure. To the absolute consternation of European wineries, particularly the French Bordelais unaccustomed to such stark differentiation and the unvarnished truth with which this middle-American nobody applied his scores, the market quickly adopted Parker's scale as the new benchmark in wine reviews.

And with good reason. Walk into any wine shop or even stroll the aisles or major supermarket chains, and you're overwhelmed by choice. Bin upon bin of California wines. Row upon row of French wines. Aisles devoted to Spain and Italy and Australia, and smaller partitions reserved for wines from Germany, New Zealand, and

South Africa . . . and Hungary, Greece, Chile, Argentina, Portugal, Turkmenistan—the list stretches to nearly seventy wine-producing nations, according to the United Nations Food and Agriculture Organization's 2005 data. Then, just to mix up the fun, you have a bewildering array of varietals to consider: Cabernet Franc, Chardonnay, Grenache, Malbec, Merlot, Petite Sirah, Tempranillo—roughly three dozen in all. There are red and white wines and blush. Sweet and dry wines, and dessert wines, too.

How could any consumer possibly have a clue about which wines are decent, beyond the names you already know and trust? Sure, you can experiment through trial and error, grabbing new and random bottles with each visit to your local wine merchant. Some will be good. Some delicious. Some you'll take one sip and dump the rest in the sink, along with the $20 or $40 or $100 you spent on that bottle. Parker's revolutionary yet elegantly simple scale solved the uncertainty of buying wine.

Under its original guise, the 100-point system was designed to help flustered consumers better navigate all those many choices at the wine shop. Over the years, however, the scores have effectively been usurped by investors and collectors, who use them to plot their buying activities. Collectors want the high-scoring wines for their cellars, and consumers want high-scoring wines to impress friends, family, business associates, and others. Investors know this and, so, logically snap up the investment-grade wines, fully expecting to resell them one day to those consumers and collectors.

To be considered investment grade, wines must have at least one reviewer, preferably more, and a score of between 90 and 100 points. But there's a lot that changes from the low end of the scale to the high. Wine scores function almost like a Richter scale, where each progressive number represents seismic activity ten times more powerful than the previous number. Though wine prices don't generally move by a factor of 10 with each numerical increase, the concept is similar. Essentially, wines that register a 95 are substantially more valuable than those that hit 90, yet they can't compare to wines that touch 99 and 100. Here's a prime example of how wine scores affect the market for two wines of identical pedigree and vintage: The 1990 Château Margaux, a First Growth Bordeaux, was trading at about $1,200 a bottle in late summer 2007, while bottles of the equally famous First Growth Château Lafite Rothschild from that same 1990 vintage fetched just $700. The only difference: the scores. The Margaux carries a perfect 100; the Lafite, a still-respectable but less impressive 92.

You might rightly ask yourself, "Why not invest only in 100- and 99-point wines?" That can be a fine strategy, albeit an expensive one. In pursuing that path you limit your profit opportunities. Other stops on the scale are worthy of investment, too, and give you the chance to acquire lower-cost wines that have the ability to grow equally well, sometimes faster, in percentage terms. After all, it's easier for a $500-per-bottle wine to double in price in a given period than it is for a $4,000 bottle. Even at $1,000 a cork, a tremendous number of buyers still exist. Far fewer are willing to spend $8,000, thereby limiting the upside potential or, at the very least, markedly shrinking your customer base.

Throughout my career, I've observed that there are four distinct point ranges between that 90- to 100-point span defining investment-grade wines. Let's examine how this 11-point range affects the wine market.

■ **100 Points:** These are pedestal wines. So rarely do 100-point scores show up that when they do arrive they capture the attention of wine buyers the world over. By my estimate, just 220 individual wines have thus far earned 100-point scores from one or more of the top four critics in the thirty or so years that the critics have been active. Given the volume of wine produced annually, those 220 wines show you just how unique a perfect score is. Wines that reach the century mark are potentially the best wines for investment because the perfect score generally indicates longevity and, thus, an extended period over which the price will appreciate. Of course, depending upon your budget, the price of entry could be prohibitively steep. But if you have the means to invest in this universe, 100-pointers have historically demonstrated that they lack a price ceiling, meaning there has yet to be a limit beyond which no wine trades. Price records continually go up for the centenarians.

In February 2007, Sotheby's put up for auction wines from the private cellar of Baroness Philippine de Rothschild, the current owner of Château Mouton Rothschild. Included in the lot was a jeroboam of the 1945 vintage, a 100-point wine from one of history's most highly acclaimed vintages. The last jeroboam of '45 Mouton sold for $57,360. Given the exquisite provenance of this jeroboam—the baroness's private cellar—expectations were that the bottle could hit $150,000 before the gavel fell.

Final price: $310,700.

I know collectors who purchase 100-pointers from regions that produce wines they don't even enjoy drinking. They do so simply for the investment value, which adds to the ultimate frenzy that swirls around these rarities. In fact, I have a client who has created a trust fund for his children made up solely of wines rated 100 points.

■ **99 Points:** Many people might think that to differentiate between 99 and 100 points is quibbling. But it's no different from quibbling over, say, the New England Patriots going 18–1 or winning a perfect nineteen games. One point makes all the difference in the world.

So wine collectors quibble.

The 99-point effect is strong on wines, almost as strong as 100 points. Wines that receive a 99 from the right reviewer can trade up higher than their points should otherwise warrant because of expectations that, at some point, this wine will improve with age and be upgraded to 100 points. It does happen. In 1995, the '82 Pichon Longueville Comtesse de Lalande, from a superb vintage all around, had a 99-point Parker rating. Five years later Parker bumped the wine up to 100. (By the same token, though, scores can tumble, as befell the '82 Margaux, which started life as a 99-point wine but by 2000 had fallen to 94.)

For investors there's a notable difference between 99 and 100: cost. The 99-rated wines are generally more affordable, relatively speaking, and can produce larger percentage gains for the investor. The 2000 vintage of Château Lafite Rothschild, a 100-point wine, is priced at nearly $1,500 a bottle. But step down to the 99-point Château Latour, and the price slips to $995, a third less than the Rothschild simply because of one little point.

Make no mistake: 99-point wines are stellar wines. And even if reviewers never add them to the list of centenarians, these wines perform admirably as investments. Just as a 100-point wine has a certain aura among wine drinkers, so too does a 99. It's *that close* to perfection, and it's cheaper. Again, there is a relatively small number of buyers who will spend more than $300,000 on a jeroboam of '45 Mouton or $8,000 for a bottle of '47 Cheval Blanc. But there's a plentitude of buyers who will readily spring $375 for a bottle of 99-point Léoville Las Cases.

■ **95–98:** This is as low as the world's most serious wine collectors will typically stoop. Generally, young wines in this range are priced at a steep discount to the 99- and 100-point oenological stars. For example: While a 100-point, 2003 Ausone fetches about $2,300 a bottle, a 98-point Cos d'Estournel commands $200, and the 95-point Branaire Ducru is available for just $65.

As vintages age, wines in this range have an ability to trade up to extremely high price levels, though never as high as their 99- and 100-point compatriots. A case of 1990 Lafleur, rated 97 points by Robert Parker, currently sells for more than $24,000 a case—a price range we generally associate with 99- and 100-point wines.

Perhaps the most important fact is that the market of end consumers chasing 95- to 98-point wines is immense. Not everyone can afford perfection, but millions of consumers can afford greatness, and wines scattered amid this point span are routinely regarded as great. The irony: As all those über-wealthy investors and connoisseurs push the prices ever higher for the world's greatest bottles, the knock-on effect puts upward pressure on this group of wines as well, a nice little benefit.

■ **90–94:** A tricky area for investors, this is the terroir of the up-and-comers. The wines you'll find lurking in this range trade for relatively low prices and, over time, have the potential to pull down higher, more valuable scores as they age. A brief example: the '04 Batailley, a wine rated 90 by Robert Parker in the summer of 2007, which costs less than $40 a bottle. According to Parker's review, the Batailley is the "sleeper of the vintage," and the '04 vintage "marks the renaissance [of a château] that is displaying strong signs of moving into the big leagues. Anticipated maturity: 2009–2025."

You could read that and surmise that, given the expected longevity this wine possesses and the florid description Parker uses to depict the château's reemergence as a winemaking force, this Batailley should age well and possibly improve its score along the way. So might it be a wine that you buy a few cases of and cellar for ten years or more? If nothing else, a growing legion of customers is fed up with paying for perfection and chasing highly rated wines ever higher, yet they're still seeking high quality. This point range tends to indicate that a particular wine will likely age well but that it can also "drink younger," both potentially good signs for investors since this kind of quality creates demand—though, again, not the same level of demand you find with wines rated 95 and above.

With pedigreed wines, like a Lafite Rothschild or a Pétrus, this range lends an added thrill to end consumers who aren't points obsessed and who find excitement in being able to affordably tuck into a bottle of one of the hallowed names in wine. There's also a trend with these lower-rated, highly pedigreed wines in which the new breed of Asian buyer often bases their purchases on brand names, not yet as dialed into the reviews and scores. As prices of the most highly rated wines escalate, these lower-point, high-pedigree wines could rise with the tide, although you should certainly exercise caution with this strategy.

In short, there is a clear, direct relationship between the points a wine receives from a critic and the price that wine can ultimately command in the market. Let's get to know the folks wielding the scores.

Robert Parker: The Rise of Modern Wine Criticism

Robert Parker's devotion to unadulterated truth won him a loyal, albeit small following early on in the United States. His 100-point scale framed wine criticism in a language the average wine fan could inherently understand. But it was 1982 that put him on the map as a force in the high-end, often archaic world of Bordeaux.

That year, he enthusiastically asserted that the '82 vintage was destined to be one of the greatest in Bordeaux history. Had he been just another voice in the crowd, you might not know his name today as anything other than another wine reviewer. But, importantly, his call went counter to the opinions of the day's top critics, who as a group largely panned the vintage. Parker bucked the wisdom of the world's accepted experts, and history awarded him his glory.

Today he is regarded by much of the wine-speaking world as a celebrity in his own right. *The New York Times* once referred to Parker as "the most influential wine critic in the world," while others label him the single most important critic in any field. His sphere of influence is so large, in fact, that he can almost single-handedly set the prices for each Bordeaux vintage and for almost every important wine from the 1800s to the present. He once was quoted as saying that his job came with immense pressure because his reviews impact the economic well-being of France, year after year. In kind, two French presidents have awarded him the two highest presidential honors for achievement in France, the Legion of Honor and the National Order of Merit, making him one of a tiny handful of foreign recipients.

In truth, this wine-grading business is wildly subjective. There are no concrete standards as in, say, grading an astronomy exam. The moon is what the moon is. But wine is never what it appears to be, beyond its obvious status as a liquid. Where one reviewer tastes hints of plum, another tastes crème brûlée. One rates a wine a pleasant 93, another insists it's a masterful 99. That's the way the world spins; some like green, some like blue, side with whom you wish.

Parker's legion of fans side with him because he knocked wine off its pedestal and brought a once-haughty corner of gastronomy down to the level of the everyman. He democratized the market by evaluating wines' quality regardless of pedigree. His reviews swayed buyers and, in that process, forced wineries—centuries old, in some cases, and stubbornly hewing to outdated customs—to rethink the notion of quality. He has shocked the storied and staid French wine industry by expressing irreverence for some of Bordeaux's most famous names, at times criticizing entire decades, such as the 1970s, as limp, mediocre attempts at winemaking. Likewise, he has praised underdogs for improving their quality and giving wine lovers something to smile about over dinner. In doing so, he has reshaped the landscape of investment-grade wines, bringing into the fold names formerly excluded from the club, such as Châteaux Pavie, La Mondotte, and Larcis Ducasse.

Along with his fame have come the critics who insist that because of Parker's powers to define the wine market, to move prices, and to steer consumers in one direction or the other, winemakers have begun creating wines to appeal particularly to his palate, which leans toward dark, concentrated, high-alcohol reds. Critics, therefore, complain with some credibility that Parker has caused a stylistic homogeneity now endemic in many of today's finest wines. They call it the "Parker Effect."

For his part, Parker contends he is responsible for nothing more than elevating the overall quality of wines by penalizing those who fashion overcropped, diluted, substandard wine marketed as liquid sunlight behind the banner of a famous château's crest. The homogeneity that some perceive, then, could simply reflect winemakers stepping up to improve what was a flawed product to begin with. Until Parker came along, no one had the gumption to tell the winemaker that his wine fairly well sucked.

From a merchant's perspective, it's easy to see the effect: a wine market easily segmented into "AP" and "BP" wines—"After Parker" and "Before Parker." While he certainly didn't invent the art of wine tasting or wine criticism, Parker certainly standardized the language and the rating system. The fundamental descriptors he brandishes in his reviews—oaky, vegetal, herbaceous, backward— came from one of his mentors, Émile Peynaud, author of *Le Goût du Vin: Le Grand Livre de la Dégustation (The Taste of Wine: The Science of Wine Appreciation)*. Parker simply organized the language in a way that was formulaic, accurate, and consistent for consumers who wanted to know the difference between a Pétrus and a Pavie without having to spend a fortune figuring it out themselves. Though it all begin with a small newsletter, Parker's brand today extends to websites, blogs, and books. All of these move the market, yet they don't always reflect identical ratings and reviews, a fact that an investor must be aware of.

For some thirty years, the success of Parker's *Wine Advocate* was based on the cult of personality that developed around him. However, there simply weren't enough days in a week for him to taste the ever-increasing number of fine wines produced in the world. So he has hired an entire team of reviewers to cover specific territories.

Let's start with his publications before we meet his team:

The Wine Advocate: This launched an industry. Though a newsletter in name, *The Wine Advocate* is more than a quarter inch thick and runs to eighty-four pages of tiny type. Spartan when it comes to production values, the bimonthly *Advocate* is nonetheless crammed with data, scores, reviews, and commentary that drive the market.

The two-week period after *The Wine Advocate* hits mailboxes is possibly the most critical period in a given wine's price trajectory. This is when Parker's latest scores make it into print and when buyers see the numbers for the first time. A highly rated new wine can see its price spike almost overnight. A wine that earns an upgraded score and effusive praise will surge in value as merchants reprise their stock in preparation for the onslaught of demand they know is coming. Consumers, merchants, and investors rip open *The Wine Advocate* and run their finger along the column of scores, a viticultural scavenger hunt for high-scoring wines to snap up as soon as they can find a stash to buy.

Robert Parker Online: Parker's website, erobertparker.com, is content rich, loaded with an abundance of features including a searchable database of prior reviews and ratings. For casual wine collectors and wine lovers who prefer to read in a hard-copy format, rather than on a computer screen, they can keep up on the great new vintages and boutique wines that might impress dinner-party guests with just a subscription to the printed version of *The Wine Advocate*. Serious subscribers would be well-advised to subscribe to the website or to the newsletter and the website.

Beyond scores, reviews, and a database of old ratings, Parker's website is also home to chat boards, his "unofficial" reviews of wines during dinner tastings, and, among other offerings, an online wine-certification course. Those unofficial reviews are possibly the most intriguing bit of content for investors. They're posted as part of what Parker labels *The Hedonist's Gazette*, an account of the wines tasted informally during various dinners. They are, in effect, tasting notes, albeit notes posted under innocuously titled entries such as "Dinner Chez Parker" or "Rovani's 40th Birthday." At the bottom of every gazette posting, Parker lists the wines tasted that night and offers an informal score, meaning this is not an official rating, just his take on the wine in a real-life setting.

Despite Parker's warning that these scores are, indeed, informal and that readers should not confuse them with scores awarded in formal, professional tastings, the wine market trades on these scores as if they were gospel. An upgrade to a previously rated investment-grade wine will move the price just as an official score would. Oddly, though, if Parker downgrades a wine in these tastings, the market pretends it doesn't exist, silently conspiring, instead, to accept the officially published—higher—score, since that obviously keeps the wine's status and price elevated. The exception: when the down-grade is severe. This can prompt merchants and investors to reassess the wine and sell it off, anticipating a possible downgrade in the future. Savvy investors, therefore, pay attention to these unofficial musings in *The Hedonist's Gazette* to possibly get a jump on the market, maybe take profits on a wine while it's still considered a valuable commodity.

They're also paying attention to *Mark Squire's Chat Board*, where professionals and avid consumers debate everything from recent vintages to stores with great deals to how much life remains in the 1961 Bordeaux. Of particular interest, though, to investors are Parker's own posts on the board; they've often turned out to be harbingers of soon-to-be published *Wine Advocate* reviews.

Parker's Books: Known as *Wine Buyer's Guides*, Parker's book-publishing efforts periodically chronicle the world of wine and his ratings. While these are fine compendiums for consumers, in general, the books aren't nearly as important to wine investors as are the newsletter and website, largely because the books contain older information.

But there is a caveat. Many upgrades, and some of the most recent scores on important investment-grade wines, show up only in Parker's books. For instance, in Parker's 2003 edition of his Bordeaux book, the 1990 and 2000 Cheval Blanc are rated 100 points, though they're rated lower on his website. Another example is the 2001 Château d'Yquem, which online is the only 100-point Yquem since 1847, an amazing sales pitch. However, in Parker's latest Bordeaux book, both the '75 and '76 Yquems score 100 points as well. Thus the books provide a huge edge to readers who notice the ratings anomaly.

The reason for this quirk: Because of his publisher's copyright, Parker hasn't been permitted to include in his online database the updated scores and notes based on retastings that he does for his books. The books, thus, can still be of value for the serious wine buyer.

Team Parker

Once upon a time, there was Robert Parker the man. Today, there's Robert Parker the ratings conglomerate.

Simply put, the world has too many wine regions for one reviewer to review effectively. To that end, Parker has all but cloned himself, adding a team of reviewers in 2006 to help him handle the reviewing demands of the high-end wine market. While he still runs the show for Bordeaux, California, and the Rhône—his pet project—he has largely passed the spittoon for Burgundy, Champagne, Italy, and elsewhere.

The question the wine world wonders is whether a Parker rating will carry the same weight if it's not Parker's palate behind the points. Or is the Parker imprimatur so ingrained in modern wine culture that Parker the score is more relevant now than Parker the man? To this point, the Parker brand hasn't been diminished by his use of surrogates to rate and review wines, but it is still relatively early in the process.

These are the faces of Team Parker:

NAME: Robert Parker
PERIODICAL: *The Wine Advocate*
IGW REGIONS: Bordeaux, Rhône, and California
SINCE: 1978

BOOKS: *The World's Greatest Wine Estates: A Modern Perspective; Bordeaux; Parker's Wine Buyer's Guide: The Complete Easy-to-Use Reference on Recent Vintages, Prices, and Ratings for More Than 8,000 Wines from All the Major Wine Regions; Wines of the Rhône Valley; Burgundy: A Comprehensive Guide to the Producers, Appellations, and Wines*

NAME: David Schildknecht
IGW REGIONS: Burgundy and Champagne
SINCE: 2004

Schildknecht is Parker's newest Burgundy critic, and although it's too soon to tell his preferences, he has a merchant background and has a good sense of the market forces that affect wine. Because of the clarity with which he writes, his industry experience, and, of course, his ties to Parker, his reviews are likely to become a force in the market.

NAME: Antonio Galloni
(formerly wrote *Piedmont Report*)
IGW REGIONS: All regions of Italy
SINCE: 2006

Parker has traditionally been a fan of the Piedmont region's Barolo wines. So, too, is his new specialist Antonio Galloni, who has years of experience reviewing Piedmont wines in his own newsletter. Galloni's early reviews for *The Wine Advocate* have been marked by a high degree of technical skill. His market impact remains questionable at this point, but, again, the tie-in with Parker and Galloni's own expertise should marry well for investors interested in the Piedmont wines.

NAME: Dr. Jay Miller
IGW REGIONS: Spain, Portugal, Australia
SINCE: 2006

Dr. Jay Miller, a former child psychologist and a longtime friend of Robert Parker, has a background in wine retail, and his reviews have appeared on Parker's online *Hedonist's Gazette* for years. He has recently been charged with reviewing wines from the regions noted above. Miller's market impact was recently put to the test when he pronounced the 2004 vintages of several Spanish wines as the best in history, awarding five wines a score of 100 points—no Spanish wines had previously been rewarded a 100-point score, let alone five in one vintage. The market immediately responded to his reviews, driving the price of 2004 Clos Erasmus to $400 per bottle at the time of this writing in 2007, whereas the 1990 and 1992 vintages of this very wine, rated 91 and 93 points respectively, were trading at $30.

NAME: Mark Squires
IGW REGION: Portugal's Dry Wines
SINCE: 2006

Mark, formerly the forum leader on Prodigy's Wine Forum, authors the popular Wine Bulletin Board on erobertparker.com. In 2006, he began covering Portugal's dry wines for *The Wine Advocate*.

NAME: Neal Martin
(formerly writer/webmaster of wine-journal.com)
IGW REGION: "Critic-at-Large"
SINCE: 2006

Neal Martin was hired by Parker to add a youthful and more European sensibility to *The Wine Advocate*. Martin was the founder and writer of the influential wine blog wine-journal.com, and his notes have been added to the Parker database. Martin is known to brandish his youthful irreverence with glee. However, he evinces a preference for very mature wines, which is uncommon for his age group.

An Ode to Motor Oil . . . and Fruitcake

You can't read a Robert Parker review without wondering: What in the world has this guy been putting in his mouth?

He has developed a lexicon built around tastes that aren't normally in the memory banks of the average reader. He uses words and phrases to describe wine that seem at times oddly out of context or just plain confusing. Like, well, "going dumb." How does a wine go dumb? In Parker's world, a dumb wine—one that doesn't taste good—has essentially lost its drinkability, even if temporarily, during the aging process.

Other words that routinely show up in his sometimes purple prose: "crushed rocks," "massive," "muscular," and "brooding." Some wines are "backward," others "forward-drinking." There are "precision" and "purity," "viscous" and "chewy," and "soft." And that's a very small sampling.

To get a feel for how Parker prose reads, consider his florid take on a 100-point, 1947 Cheval Blanc.

1947 Cheval Blanc	100 Points

What can I say about this mammoth wine that is more like port than dry red table wine? The 1947 Cheval Blanc exhibits such a thick texture it could double as motor oil. The huge nose of fruitcake, chocolate, leather, coffee, and Asian spices is mind-boggling. The unctuous texture and richness of sweet fruit are amazing. Consider the fact that this wine is, technically, appallingly deficient in acidity and excessively high in alcohol. Moreover, its volatile acidity levels would be considered intolerable by modern-day oenologists. Yet how can they explain that after 47 years the wine is still remarkably fresh, phenomenally concentrated, and profoundly complex? It has to make you wonder about the direction of modern-day winemaking. Except for one dismal, murky, troubled, volatile double magnum, this wine has been either perfect or nearly perfect every time I have had it. . . . Having a 1947 Cheval Blanc served out of an impeccably stored magnum three times over the last three years made me once again realize what a great job I have. The only recent Bordeaux vintages that come even remotely close to the richness, texture, and viscosity of so many of these Right Bank 1947s are 1982 and 1990. Last tasted 10/94.

—Robert Parker, *The Wine Advocate*

Wine Spectator

Founded in 1982, *Wine Spectator* magazine has grown into the most widely circulated wine publication on the planet, unmatched by any other wine periodical. It reaches more than 400,000 subscribers and 2,000,000 regular readers. With such a following in print, it's little wonder that winespectator.com is the most heavily trafficked wine site on the Internet.

The biweekly *Wine Spectator* wields enormous influence in the wine market, producing more wine reviews than any other publication. Those reviews have recently begun to carry even more weight, gaining on Robert Parker. The magazine's reviews are based on blind tastings to isolate the wine and negate the label as a potential influence. In doing so, *Wine Spectator* has established consistency over the past twenty-five years, and its reviewers have developed the highest degree of credibility in the wine market.

Although his name doesn't resonate as loudly as Robert Parker's, James Suckling has come into his own as a world-renowned reviewer. His criticisms, combined with the breadth of *Wine Spectator*'s reach and reputation, have helped define and move the Bordeaux market. Formally trained as a journalist, Suckling started tasting in-barrel Bordeaux more than twenty years ago and has become so highly skilled at this esoteric art that his annual Bordeaux reviews are must-read, much-anticipated reports among consumers and investors.

He camps out in Bordeaux for five weeks annually during the futures rally and is the first to publish reviews in real time on his blog. He understands the vagaries of rating young wines and he scores them accordingly, sometimes with as much as a five-point spread, such as 95–100, which irks some detractors, who carp that such an overly broad range is unhelpful.

James Suckling is a major mover and shaker in the Bordeaux futures market, and he has become a driving force in the market for Italian wines. He is almost single-handedly responsible for creating today's Brunello craze. A testament to his power in Italy: his reviews have greater impact on consumers and the market than do Parker's.

But just as Parker isn't alone at *The Wine Advocate*, Suckling isn't flying solo at *Wine Spectator*. James Laube has become a key reviewer of California wines, while Bruce Sanderson takes on Burgundy. Though both are the second horse in their respective fields, their reviews nevertheless can ripple noticeably through the market.

NAME: James Suckling
IGW REGIONS: Bordeaux and Italy
SINCE: 1981

BOOKS: *Vintage Port: The Wine Spectator's Ultimate Guide for Consumers, Collectors, and Investors*

Along with Parker, Suckling is the most influential force in the Bordeaux marketplace and the single most influential critic of Italian wines.

NAME: James Laube
IGW REGION: California
SINCE: 1983

BOOKS: *Wine Spectator's California Wine; California's Great Cabernets: The Wine Spectator's Ultimate Guide for Consumers, Collectors and Investors; California's Great Chardonnays: The Wine Spectator's Ultimate Guide for Consumers, Collectors, and Investors*

James Laube is God's gift to the California wine industry, and his reviews of California wines can affect that market as potently as do Parker's reviews of wines from this region.

NAME: Bruce Sanderson
IGW REGIONS: Burgundy and Champagne
SINCE: 1992

Bruce Sanderson recently replaced Per-Henrik Mansson as the chief taster of Burgundy, so older *Wine Spectator* reviews of Burgundy will display Mansson's name. Nonetheless, Sanderson's pronouncements can carry as much weight to the vast *Wine Spectator* readership as a *Burghound* or Tanzer review can to buyers who do not subscribe to the magazine.

NAME: James Molesworth
IGW REGION: Rhône
SINCE: 1997

James Molesworth has been working for *Wine Spectator* for over a decade and has finally earned his wings to be the magazine's judge of Rhône wines.

NAME: Harvey Steiman
IGW REGION: Australia
SINCE: 1984

BOOKS: *Wine Spectator's Complete Wine Tasting Kit; Wine Spectator's Essentials of Wine: A Guide to the Basics; Harvey Steiman's Kitchen*
Harvey Steiman is a very active writer of books about wine and food. A *Wine Spectator* staffer for more than two decades, he is now its official taster of Australian wines.

Unlike Parker's *Wine Advocate*, which publishes just six issues annually, *Wine Spectator* publishes eighteen issues a year. As such, the sheer volume of reviews can cause the market to focus on the latest, greatest scores, along the way losing interest in favored wines from the previous issue. *Wine Spectator*'s main effect, therefore, is the rapid and immediate wine sales spurred by the latest issue to hit newsstands or, more likely, mailboxes. The wines awarded high scores start selling immediately. For that reason, investors who decide to build a position in a featured wine, especially those named to the magazine's annual "Top 10 Wines of the Year," must act with haste. These wines quickly trade higher.

That quick impact, however, also creates selling opportunities for investors who happen to already own the wines that pick up a big rating. The sales wave created by *Wine Spectator*–induced demand can serve as a good chance to take profits and reallocate some of your capital in other wines you might be eyeing.

Winespectator.com

As with Parker's website, *Wine Spectator*'s most current reviews are first printed in the hard-copy publication, migrating online at a later date. As you might expect with the world's most heavily trafficked wine site, this one offers a jeroboam's worth of data and useful features including:

■ *Wine Spectator* **Insider:** Here subscribers sign up to receive a free newsletter e-mailed every two weeks and are given sneak peeks at pending reviews. That's precious inside dope. While this isn't 007 "for your eyes only" information, anytime you can gain even a slight jump on other investors, you've got an edge. Wines reviewed include back-vintage retrospectives, as well as new releases.

■ **Auction Index Search:** This is a feature of the site's Wine Collecting & Auctions section, where subscribers can sign up for free newsletters that offer investment advice. Just type the wine of interest into this search engine, and it will decant the latest auction results for the past two years. In turn, you can use these auction

When Is 100 an 89 . . . or Vice Versa?

Oscar Madison had Felix Unger, Tom had Jerry—odd couples that get along oddly but never see eye-to-eye.

The chasm between *The Wine Advocate* and *Wine Spectator* has never been more apparent than it is with the 1988 Château Mouton Rothschild. This wine has been the center of a classic battle between the industry's two most influential wine voices.

Wine Spectator awarded the '88 Mouton a coveted 100 points. Parker dished out a withering 89. In the world of investment-grade wine, such a wide span for a top-flight wine is fairly rare, and the 11-point gap is the difference between a rock star and a backup singer in a cheesy lounge act.

So what is it? Fish, fowl, or something different?

At this point, it looks like a draw.

Despite its 100-point rating from *Wine Spectator,* this Mouton has never traded at the levels achieved by any 100-point Parker-rated Mouton. Yet it has never traded down to the level of typical 89-point Parker-rated Bordeaux, and it sells in much higher volumes than any 89-pointer could hope to.

The *Wine Spectator* score—along with the château's name—clearly spurred sales, but Parker's tepid take on this tipple clearly depressed prices. In the final accounting, investors might read this to mean that Parker's scores drive pricing, while *Wine Spectator*'s move a large number of cases and entice drinkers to pull corks.

And what happens when the two are in agreement? Well, there's nothing stronger for investors. Parker's score solidifies the value of the wine, and the *Spectator*'s impact on sales creates rapid scarcity . . . a very profitable combination.

prices to compare against retailer prices as you analyze your investments.

■ **Editors' Blogs:** Twelve blogs posted by a cross section of regular contributors, who include château owners, collectors, restaurant chefs, and well-known *Wine Spectator* critics, giving the reader a good perspective of what is happening in the business. Some of these blogs actually contain point scores that cannot be found anywhere else, which you can use to your advantage.

■ **Wine Spectator School:** Offers online courses at reasonable rates and lots of free wine education materials.

Stephen Tanzer's Wineaccess.com

That's Stephen Tanzer. Although, to be clear, he's not Russian.

By the mid-nineties Tanzer's *International Wine Cellar*, established in 1985, began to demonstrate that it had some stroke in the market. Because his scores tend to be lower and his hyperbole less hyperbolic, consumers and merchants began to accept his reviews as not only authoritative but also sober. The market began to believe that "If Tanzer likes it, it's got to be good!"

He is widely considered one of the toughest wine reviewers, whose commentary can be as cutting in its accuracy as it is alienating to a novice unfamiliar with his lexicon. Whereas Parker's reviews have a sense of excitement, exuberance, and downright lust for the wines, and whereas *Wine Spectator* connects with the public on a mass-market, easy-to-digest scale, Tanzer shies away from these approaches, using a more technical wine jargon that connects better with experts than with beginners.

Though he writes about all wine regions, Tanzer is best known for reviews of Burgundy and Rhône, and investors routinely buy on his reviews but sell on Parker's scores. Savvy investors take notice of Tanzer's infrequent high scores as a clear sign to hold such wines in their portfolios. Then, if Parker comes along and gives the wine a high score, this can be a good time to sell, as his comments have such a massive impact on the market. A profitable strategy to use with Tanzer: check out his reviews, which are often published before the others. His higher-scoring entrants will give clues as to higher reviews that could follow from his peers.

NAME: Stephen Tanzer
IGW REGIONS: All
SINCE: 1985

BOOKS: *The WineAccess Buyer's Guide: The World's Best Wines and Where to Find Them;* Food & Wine *Magazine's Official Wine Guide*

Allen Meadows, aka *Burghound*

It seems somehow apropos that a retired banker would become the de facto wine expert to the world's richest men. Allen Meadows's first trip to Burgundy came nearly thirty years ago, in 1979, and he has been visiting the region and the domaines every year since. The bulk of those trips, though, were done as collector, not wine reviewer. Indeed, during his early forays into France, Meadows was serving as a corporate chieftain for companies the likes of mortgage lender Great Western Financial Group.

But with the launch in January 2001 of his premier issue of *Burghound* newsletter, Meadows became a wine critic—and one who has quickly gained respect and a following among buyers of ultra-high-end Burgundy. Thus, while he's the baby of the bunch in terms of his time on the wine scene, he has emerged as Burgundy's most influential reviewer, despite his relative lack of exposure in comparison to the other key reviewers. *Burghound* offers the most detailed insights into Burgundy wines, particularly among the priciest, rarest segment of investment-grade wines, namely *Grand Cru* and *Premier Cru* Burgundy. Though Burgundy represents a small fraction of the overall wine business, it is the most exclusive sector, populated by some of the industry's most elite collectors and domaines. Burgundy fans tend to be *intense* aficionados with extremely deep pockets to fund their fascination. Because the supply of each *cuvée* is so small, there seems to be no price that is too high for one of the über-wealthy. Even if some buyers miss the first two or three waves of buying, money is still no object to them and prices soar into the stratosphere.

In the days following La Paulée, a Burgundy wine-tasting soiree held yearly in a different global locale and dubbed "The World's Classiest BYOB Party," five guys sitting at a table with Meadows can easily drive the price of the glitziest Burgundies up by 25 percent.

Significant price appreciation a few days after a pricey wine dinner? A few managing directors from an investment banking firm can inadvertently corner the market on back vintages because five guys with significant buying power who love the same rare wine at the same time have been known to have an effect on prices and supplies of certain rare items.

NAME: Allen Meadows
IGW REGIONS: Burgundy and American Pinot Noirs
SINCE: 2001

Simply put, Burgundy's most important critic.

Burghound.com

It's hard to imagine that anything in the wine world can be as cryptic as Burgundy—and Burgundy can be inscrutably cryptic—but *Burghound*'s website makes no attempt to demystify the *sanctum sanctorum* of the wine world. This website is as un-user-friendly as the region, where you can have 100 wines named "Gevrey-Chambertin" produced in any given year. Nevertheless, Burghound .com is highly recommended for serious Burgundy investors.

In fact, Meadows discourages people from subscribing to the hard copy version, charging an extra fee for it. An online subscription offers access to his back issues and to his searchable database.

Burghound is arguably the least commercial wine critic. He does not accept advertising dollars, as does *Wine Spectator*, and he awards lower scores than any of his peers. For instance, he called the legendary 1962 La Tâche "one of the greatest wines of my lifetime," yet he gave it only 99 points. Indeed, Burghound is known for such daunting standards that he has been dubbed "Mr. 90 Points," which for him is a big score and potentially worthy of your investment. The 90-point score, which Burghound awarded to the 1993 Dominique Laurent "Ruchottes" Chambertin, equates to the 94 and 96 points that Parker and *Wine Spectator* gave to the same wine, respectively. Because he is the first and last word in Burgundy in the United States, and because supplies of these wines are typically Lilliputian, snatching up the bottles he blesses with high scores—as soon after publication of his reviews as possible—is all but guaranteed to earn you a profit.

Little known about Burghound is that, in addition to his position in Burgundy, he has quietly built a name in U.S. Pinot Noirs as well. A Pinot that is "Burghounded" with a good score carries the same cachet as a California Cab that has been "Parkerized." Both wines have been anointed by the wine gods, and, thus, the buyers follow.

5

WHERE TO BUY

Finding Reputable Sources

Despite modern technology, the rise of the Internet, and the emergence of advanced winemaking capabilities, buying wine today is not so different from the way it has always been. Consumers buy from a winery, a wine merchant, or an auction house—the three main avenues for buying investment-grade wine—and the cases are either shipped to you directly or you walk out of the store with your wine in tow.

The Internet, however, has made the process markedly different in two aspects: you're no longer limited to shopping locally or required to travel to the wineries and auction houses to buy or bid. Nor must you even have your own cellar to properly store your portfolio.

Now you can reach out to merchants and auctioneers and the wineries themselves on a near-instantaneous, global basis. Moreover, you can sell off your portfolio far more easily than in the past. Fine-wine merchants and auctioneers located online will be glad to visit your cellar or to take delivery of your wine from a professional storage facility for sale or auction. And speaking of professional storage facilities, you even find online nowadays a host of wine-storage operations scattered around the country that are in the business of providing the perfect climate for your portfolio to age in.

In effect, then, wine investing today is not that different from buying shares of stock on E*Trade or Fidelity.com: you can, if you choose to, buy, store, and sell your wine without ever laying a hand on any bottle that you own.

Nevertheless, the wine market is rich in idiosyncrasies that don't always translate to other asset classes. As such, you need to understand certain facets of this business so that you'll be prepared for what you confront. I'll detail these in the order in which you will run up against them: buying, storing, valuing, appraising, and, ultimately, selling your portfolio of wine.

Buying Wine and Understanding Wine Prices

It's probably apparent to you at this point that you're not going to find IGW at the local Wal-Mart Supercenter. You're probably not going to find it available at most general-interest, chain-store supermarkets, though you will occasionally discover a few worthy bottles at specialty grocers, some of which have knowledgeable wine buyers on staff who are snapping up fine wines in the futures market. And in the event you do locate a few bottles at some local liquor store or grocer, you have to be concerned about provenance. Wine doesn't like bright lights, or a dry atmosphere, or temperatures well above 55 or 60 degrees—and how many stores do you know that operate moist, cavelike retail centers just to keep a few bottles of wine happy?

In short, if you're buying wine as an investment, you have to buy from places that make a business in investment-grade wine. The three primary venues are specialty wine-retailers, auction houses, and the mailing lists of certain wineries, particularly those in California and Australia.

The Retail Market

The word *retail* may suggest shopping malls and corner stores, but in the wine business, retail typically refers to the large wine merchants who do the bulk of their trade on the telephone, on the Internet, and via e-mail. Serious retailers of investment-grade wines have robust websites and large subscriptions to their e-mailed offers and printed catalogues.

Through these retailers, you can often participate in the futures market and find a broad selection of back-vintage wines. Some offer onsite storage facilities—for a fee—if you don't want to take delivery of your wine, and, instead, want it professionally stored in climate-controlled facilities with redundant power sources. The better retailers understand wine from an investor's perspective, not just from the consumer's point of view. They will be able to address your questions and offer an assessment of a particular wine's investment potential or point you in the direction of a better investment idea.

Again, my aim is not to necessarily direct you to any particular retailer. But out of a sense of fairness, I will tell you that all you need do is search the Internet and you will find an abundance of online wine shops. I won't vouch for any except my own, since I have no clue how the others run their business. Some, I can tell you, have gone out of business through the years, so beware of whom you're dealing with.

You also need to be aware of wine pricing. In the stock market, the price of a share of stock is transparent; you know exactly what the price is at any given moment, and, aside from differences in a broker's commission, where you buy or sell that share will not impact your cost. Wine pricing is less clear. You can visit twenty wine retailers in person or online and come away with twenty different prices. So it pays to shop around. Just remember, though, as an investor you want to build a relationship with just a few retailers, since they will be the ones who provide you access to some of the best IGW they come across. While it's fine to hit the lowest price on occasion, you don't want to build a portfolio by focusing solely on low price and by buying from scads of retailers. You will effectively lock yourself out of the best opportunities in doing so.

Know, too, that what is supposedly available might not be what's *really* available or what fits your wants. For instance, you might find on some wine retailer's website a great price for a particular wine; then you place the order online, only to find that the price is not for a case but for the last bottle the merchant is trying to unload. Prices are always in flux, and most websites are not up to date because merchants don't spend their days continually changing prices. Nor do most resellers stock large volumes, and inevitably the cheapest wines you find will be in the smallest quantities.

To get an accurate picture of what wine is available and in what quantities, you need to call. While I certainly advocate purchasing wine online, you shouldn't do so unless you first talk to an actual human being on the other end of the phone line, especially in the initial stages, when you might be trying to build a relationship with the merchant.

This leads us to another set of rules. Remember, I noted in an earlier chapter that there would be a set of 11 Sokolin House Rules to help you become a better wine investor. Well, here are rules six, seven and eight:

Rule 6: Develop a Good Relationship with a Reputable Merchant

Because wine is a delicate, perishable product, you would do well to put as much effort into developing a relationship with suppliers as you do into hunting for the lowest prices. You will almost assuredly realize larger profits down the line, even if you do pay more for that case of Lynch Bages than you would have if you bought it from some random person selling it online.

You will have problems reselling wines of suspect provenance. Self-serving or not, you are simply better off investing through reputable merchants who stand behind what they sell. The greater the degree of professionalism in your merchant's shipping and storage methods, the more valuable your wine.

Rule 7: Have a List of Questions to Ask Your Merchant

With a few simple questions, you can weed out lesser suppliers by showing a wine merchant that you are an educated investor. The answers provided will give you insight into whether this is a wine merchant you want to be dealing with.

- Do you have a temperature- and humidity-controlled store or warehouse? The answer should be yes. Wine allowed to over-heat, or corks allowed to dry out, can result in wine going bad. And bad is not good when you have thousands of dollars invested in cases of undrinkable wine.
- Is there any area where wine is stored in your facility that is *not* set at 55°F? The answer should be no, for the same reason as above.
- Are you able to e-mail me a digital summary of all of my purchases with the shipping status and estimated arrival times for my wines? Yes should be the answer, which shows you the merchant has an efficient process for managing your records and can let you know when your wine will arrive. The last thing you want is a case of wine sitting at your front door cooking in the afternoon sun.

Rule 8: Don't Buy from Too Many Merchants

The idea of scoring the lowest price available on every wine purchase is so alluring that there are some investors and collectors who will purchase from fifteen different merchants. The truth is, the investment-grade wine market is inefficient and immature. Unlike the stock market, where the price of IBM stock doesn't change whether you're using Merrill Lynch or Fidelity as your broker, you will routinely find lower prices on investment-grade wine from one merchant to the next.

The best-priced IGW is often sold prerelease, just after bottling but not yet shipped from the winery, or, as with Bordeaux, in the futures market, when the wine is still in the barrel, up to two years prior to bottling. Most IGW are sourced offshore, and it can take weeks, months, or even years after your purchase for wines to ship. Unless you have a receiving department and a clerk to keep track of everything, physically organizing your purchases can become time consuming and labor intensive. What begins as an interesting exercise in finding the lowest-cost supply of some particular vintage can ultimately turn into a real pain as you track international wine shipments that aren't always moving in a timely manner or in the right direction.

Moreover, with so much time lag between purchase and eventual shipment, it's easy to lose track of who sold you what, particularly if you're buying the same wines from multiple vendors. I see this all the time in clients with multiple vendors; they can't sort out who sent them what, and when a wine is bad they don't know whom to turn to. Some merchants go out of business between the time you ordered and the time the wine is shipped; some lose your documentation; some you might forget about.

Confining your purchases to a select few sources, even if they aren't always the cheapest on every wine you want, benefits you in several ways. First, you don't have to worry about which supplier sent what. You'll pretty much know it was this one or that one. More important, when you spend all your investment dollars with just a few vendors, instead of spreading your dollars around in dribs and drabs here and there, you become a bigger fish to those few merchants. That's important in your ability to gain first-look access at the best inventory and better deals than the smaller players will ever see. In the end, it benefits you to concentrate your spending in just a few places, rather than fervently chase the lowest price through numerous merchants.

The Pros of Buying Wine Through Retailers

CONVENIENCE: You can place a wine order from your computer at any hour of the day from a retailer who is allowed to ship to your state. Not all retailers or wineries are allowed to ship to every state, but that will be laid out on each merchant's website. Some will have ways around whatever restrictions exist. A winery in California, for instance, might have the ability to ship to a middleman in a third state who has the ability to forward the wine on to you.

GUARANTEES: The more reputable merchants will take back wines that are bad or turn out to be fakes. That reduces your risk, since you won't typically find that guarantee when you buy at auction.

LOW STRESS: You're buying from home, in your pajamas if you wish. The stress of investing doesn't get lower than that. Plus, you have time to fully research what you want to buy, and you can always call the merchant to discuss the merits of your planned purchases. And you always know the cost going into the transaction, so you will never pay more than you expected.

The Cons of Buying Wine Through Retailers

PERCEIVED HIGHER PRICE: Because you're dealing with a retailer, you assume you're paying retail prices, but you are, in effect, overpaying. While that's true in some cases, particularly with local retailers who face little local competition, that's not so much the case on the Internet. Competition is so widespread these days that you can always find fair prices somewhere.

LIMITED SELECTION OF RARE BACK VINTAGES: Most retailers are in the business of retail. They're not repositories of the world's rarest or most highly prized wines. That's the role that investors play, actually. So while you will occasionally find old, rare wines that a merchant gets as part of buying a collection from an investor, you won't find an abundance of the rarest wines readily available in the quantities you might want as an investor with the exception of a handful of retailers like my company.

The Auction Market

This is where you will find some of the rarest inventories of fine wines become available for resale. Because of that, auctions attract some of the world's most astute investors and, particularly, collectors.

Like retailers, auction houses are all over the Internet. They range from the well-known auctioneers such as Sotheby's to smaller, online-only wine-auction firms that have cropped up in recent years.

Auctions can be an interesting, albeit much more complex, way to buy wine. You must navigate several issues that can drastically raise the price of your purchase beyond your expectations. Novices often forget, for instance, that auction houses assess a commission of between 10 and 20 percent of the total value of a winning bid to both buyer and seller. Win a coveted case of Latour for $10,000, and your cost is actually as much as $12,000.

Moreover, prices posted online or in the catalogs are not necessarily *the* price. Generally, the price displayed is the accepted opening bid or possibly the reserve amount, the price the wine must fetch at auction or it won't be sold. The real price—the so-called gavel price—is likely to be higher, sometimes markedly higher, determined by the auction process. That process often results in a phenomenon known as "paddle fever," in which bidders get so wrapped up in the action—and so intent on winning a particular lot they've had their eye on—that they push prices higher than you anticipated. That can sharply raise your cost of entry if you're one of those bidders. Indeed, record highs are set at auction specifically because of paddle fever, generally expressed as a bidding war. A retailer who started an auction company once told me that certain wines he'd had difficulty selling in a retail setting sold for much higher at auction because of paddle fever.

It's a good idea to make a phone call to the auction house and learn how to calibrate listed prices versus what you can expect to pay; that way you can more appropriately gauge the real cost you'll likely have to pay to win the lot. Ironically, the principal attraction of auctions is the generally misguided prospect of buying very rare wines for below their real market value. Wine collectors, in particular, are a savvy lot, and they're not about to let some precious rare wine go at a ridiculously cheap price. More likely it will sell for above its preauction estimate.

The better auction houses will provide you with information about the wines' provenance, critical to establishing their real value. Nevertheless, buying at auction is caveat emptor, because the "buyer beware" policies of most auctions leave you little recourse if any of the wines you buy is bad.

Before buying at auction, you need to become conversant with wine prices, educate yourself about auction processes, and prepare a game plan. Auctions move fast. You need to know what you really want to bid on and what might be of interest in the event that what you really want is ultimately priced out of your league. You also need to be certain that you're paying a fair price; you don't want to get so wrapped up in the process—paddle fever—that you overpay for the wine, thereby sapping whatever return you hoped to generate on its future resale.

The most disciplined approach to buying at auction is to place your highest bids on the books, in which case you don't have to be physically present at the auction and paddle fever won't apply. The advantage: You'll never overpay. The disadvantage: You may be outbid frequently.

The Pros of Buying Wine at Auction

ACCESS TO RARE WINES: Many old and rare wines go to auction specifically because of paddle fever. Investors and collectors know that auction-goers are likely to bid up the wines in their efforts to win the lot.

POTENTIAL FOR LOW PRICES: Yes, you can occasionally find some bargains at auction, particularly in cases that are incomplete. Those prices are generally cheaper, though that also means your price at resale may be lower, too, since investors and collectors generally like trading in round lots, complete cases of a dozen bottles.

EXCITEMENT: There's nothing like the activity of a wine auction in full swing. The staccato bursts of the auctioneer's calls, the seemingly nonchalant paddle twitches as the price of a rare case of Mouton-Rothschild climbs ever higher. The sound of the gravel smacking the podium and the boisterous clapping when "*Sold*" echoes through the room as another record price falls. It's a heady atmosphere equal to the hedonistic pleasures of the wines that make it to the auction block.

The Cons of Buying Wine at Auction

CAVEAT EMPTOR: You cannot always be certain that what you're buying is what you think it is. The auction can perform its due diligence, but if bad wines or, worse, faked bottles of the best wine make it into an auction and you win them, there's not much you can do. Auction houses routinely impose "buy at your own risk" policies.

LABOR INTENSIVE: You can spend a great deal of time researching what you want to bid on at auction but then go to a dozen auctions and still lose in every case to buyers who are willing to pay more.

HIDDEN COSTS: The commissions and paddle-fever potential can sharply alter the price of ownership for certain wines you want.

The Mailing-List Market

Small boutique wineries, particularly the producers of California and Australia cult wines, operate mailing lists and allow only those on the list to buy their wines. These are wines that are generally in very limited production, usually just a few hundred cases a year.

These mavericks use this distribution model because the standard wholesaler distribution route is not ideal for wines with such miniscule productions. Get on the list for a highly desirable wine, and you're golden. Wines from names like Screaming Eagle and Harlan can soar in value by hundreds of dollars per bottle on the secondary market just days after they're released to their fans on the mailing lists.

The problem: getting your name on the list to begin with. Access to the most coveted lists is closed to new members for years at a time. Wine collectors and investors are forever asking me how to get their name on one of these lists. My answer: Give to charity and hope karma's kind to you. The stark reality is that there are no backdoor ways onto these already filled lists. Worse, the waiting lists are often longer than the official membership list. The only time openings occur is generally when current members fail to buy their allotted amount of wine for three or more consecutive years. This mailing-list approach, then, serves an interesting goal for wineries: It effectively assures sellout demand for their product in years when the wines aren't as great because investors and collectors want access to the bottles in years when the wines put up monster scores.

If you really want to invest in cult wines, the best opportunity you'll have to get onto mailing lists is to tour California's wine country—or Australia's, if you care to venture down under—and stop in on the new boutique vineyards that spring up all the time. That way you're one of the pioneers, able to get onto the list before the wines are discovered by the critics and everyone from Miami to Mumbai is e-mailing the winery with a request to join the mailing list that will let them buy next year's wine.

The Pros of Buying Wine Through Mailing Lists

PERFECT PROVENANCE: No one can question your wine's history if you can show them the original purchase order and bill of lading from the winery. That's bulletproof provenance—although they could raise questions about your storage, but that's a topic we'll address in a few pages.

EASY PROFITS: Many of these cult wines are so highly sought after that once you're on a mailing list, you can buy your allotment of wines each year—often no more than a six-pack, maybe a case—and immediately sell them to other investors or collectors at a huge profit, generally 50 to 100 percent higher than your cost.

The Cons of Buying Wine Through Mailing Lists

WAITING LISTS: Waits of five to ten years are not uncommon, and such a wait can be interminably long.

OBLIGATORY PURCHASES: You may not want to buy the bad years and would rather funnel your investment dollars those years into more productive wine assets. But for the most part you can't without risking your ability to buy these cult wines in the years when everyone wants the high-scoring bottles.

6

PICKING PROFITS

Two Central Wine-Investment Strategies

There is no other market quite like the market for investment-grade wines. With a limited quantity of an asset that for centuries has been in high demand, this demand increases as the world's wealth expands, and through consumption, each bottle in each vintage grows increasingly limited by the day. Just imagine if the stock market worked in similar fashion.

One day you buy shares in a company like, say, Google on the Nasdaq Stock Market. Every day Google is making its business better, yet every day a few of Google's shares are permanently removed from the marketplace. Sooner or later you reach a point where only a handful of Google shares remain, and everyone who knows anything about the company and its business wants to own those shares and a piece of Google's profit stream. It doesn't take much imagination to figure out that the investors who own those few remaining Google shares will be able to price them very high because of the demand. Nor does it take much imagination to know that the investors savvy enough to have bought the shares at the earliest prices, and patient enough to hold them for the long haul, are the ones who reap the most stunning gains.

This is exactly what happens in the wine market. Every year

investors have the opportunity to buy into wines' initial public offerings—the new vintage—at the cheapest prices the wines will likely ever see. As the consumption period begins and bottles start evaporating from the market, prices move higher, ultimately reaching some point decades later where only a handful of a particular wine or vintage remains and investors who own that remaining supply can all but name their price.

What we're talking about here is the wine industry's futures and prerelease market, and the back-vintage market that ultimately emerges years later. Both represent two distinct investment opportunities, each with their own unique strategies.

Futures: Looking Ahead

Anyone familiar with futures contracts in the financial markets, which allow you to buy a commodity such as a bushel of wheat or a barrel of oil at a predetermined price at some point in the future, will understand the premise behind wine futures. Under this system wine buyers negotiate to pay predetermined prices for cases of wine that will be delivered in the future.

The key difference between buying wheat and oil futures and buying wine futures is that wheat and oil trade continuously between buyers and sellers, and the prices can fluctuate wildly from hour to hour, day to day, year to year. Bordeaux futures tend to trade just once, when the original buyer buys the contract, and the prices historically don't fluctuate much. In fact, they generally stay flat for most wines and go up over time for the premier wines. This has been the case in every futures campaign for the past twenty-five years, with the exception of the disappointing 1997 vintage. That failure stemmed from low-quality wines that the châteaux had overpriced to begin with, the combination of which killed investor demand.

Bordeaux futures, known as en primeur sales, emerged centuries ago as a way for the châteaux to improve their cash flow. Château owners would harvest their grapes, ferment and barrel the juice, and then, about six months later—well before the wine was ready for delivery—they'd sell their unfinished wine to merchants. This let the wineries generate income off the current year's vintage and apply the money to the needs of raising next year's grape crop. For merchants, these presales allowed them to acquire in-demand wine at favorable prices, without having the responsibility of storing it for a couple of years.

This quirky approach to sales has now become a kind of theater in Bordeaux. When the futures market opens each spring, France is palpably atwitter with anticipation and activity. For three weeks during March and April each year, thousands of critics, journalists, and wine merchants from Alaska to Kazakhstan descend on the châteaux for so-called barrel tastings, in which château owners pull unfinished wine from the barrels to provide the first taste of what the year's effort has produced. Though the wines won't be bottled for another eighteen to twenty-four months, and while they won't be drinkable for several more years, the world of wine awaits this annual carnival like partyers await Mardi Gras in New Orleans. The reports and reviews that emerge will shape consumer interest and drive prices when the futures contracts ultimately go on sale several weeks later. Then the excitement starts all over again. The less significant châteaux begin announcing their prices in May, while the intensely watched First Growth châteaux join the party in late June or July. Some châteaux have more than a score of family members, all of whom must agree on release price. Multiply this by hundreds of châteaux, then factor in the egos, the familial rifts, and the inevitable financial squabbles, and you begin to see not only why it takes several months to do something as simple as price a bottle of wine, but also why the wine-futures market is filled with so much high drama.

Futures are released by the châteaux through their négociants in *tranches* (literally, slices), enabling the châteaux to optimally capitalize on the value of their products. Early tranches can be limited to as little as fifty cases at a time. When a tranche sells out, the price is raised and another tranche goes up for sale. This is the châteaux testing the market to reap the greatest possible profit. Dribbling out tiny amounts of the most-sought-after wines in stellar vintages is also a way to rapidly drive prices up, and to whip consumers into a frenzy—an art the Bordelais have mastered.

In effect, the futures market is wine's version of an initial public offering, the first chance investors have to invest in a particular wine or, more broadly, a particular vintage. It is common for futures prices for wines from châteaux such as Pétrus, Ausone, Lefleur, Latour, and others to move markedly higher off their initial offering price once consumers hear from critics that some vintage has turned out exceedingly well or that some château has performed nothing short of a miracle in coaxing greatness from its plot of grapes.

In general, buying wine en primeur represents the greatest potential profit for investors, though it also entails some risk and requires the greatest amount of patience since you'll have to wait a couple of years before you even receive the wine, and then you'll have to properly cellar the wine for several more years to let it age before consumer demand ramps up. Still, futures prices are most likely the lowest price you will ever see on some of the most-sought-after wines, particularly during the most-talked-about vintages.

Collectors, connoisseurs, and merchants who buy in the futures market do so to lock in prices now on the wines they want, knowing the price will likely increase once the wine is in the bottle and on store shelves. Investors who buy in the futures market do so because they expect that certain wines will earn high scores from reviewers and critics once they're bottled, and that will drive consumer demand and propel the price higher. The benefit for investors is that buying wine futures gives you full control of your wine's history—a crucial factor when it comes to proving your wine's provenance and obtaining the best possible price at resale.

How to Participate in the Futures Market

You don't just show up at, say, Château Latour in the spring, knock on the front door, and whip out the checkbook to negotiate a futures contract with the winemaker.

The futures process is centuries old and still archaic and highly fragmented in many ways. There is no central Wine Futures Exchange in downtown Bordeaux where you go to interact with buyers and sellers. You have to go through wine merchants in the United States and Europe, and even then it's not any old merchant who will have access to contracts for every available wine. The biggest players, though, will generally have access to the most widely sought after futures from the most popular châteaux.

If you want to invest in Bordeaux futures, alert your merchant of your interest well ahead of time. This way you will have a better shot at adding to your portfolio the assets you really want and not be stuck having to root and scavage among the leftovers, hoping to find an overlooked gem.

I'd just as soon you log on to sokolin.com to buy your Bordeaux futures. However, despite the fact that we pioneered this business in the States and we have deep ties to Bordeaux, making us a key source for wine collectors and investors, the fact is that these days you can find a handful of respectable online retailers making a business in selling Bordeaux futures.

But I offer this extreme caution: Beware of whom you deal with. A Colorado company bilked investors and collectors out of a collective $13 million in a wine-futures swindle, in which the owner of the online wine retailer was using the money not to buy wine futures for his customers but to remodel his house, buy cars, and travel, among other uses.

For investors, purchasing futures from the most reliable sources with the closest ties to Bordeaux—even if the price is a bit higher—is of utmost importance. Every year, especially in the best vintages, I see investors get burned looking only for the lowest prices. The wine-futures market differs from traditional commodity markets in one crucial way: the timing payments. Invest in corn futures, and, assuming you actually want to take physical delivery of the commodity, you pay for those bushels of corn when they're delivered. The corn grower, the farmer, assumes all the risk up to that point. With wine, you pay for your purchase up front, eighteen to twenty-four months before the wine will be delivered. You take on the risk.

I have seen too many situations in futures where merchants have lost customer receipts, forgotten to order the wine, or gone out of business before the wine is even bottled. Some orders just never show up, even though the merchant is still in business. And there sits the investor who never receives his wine and may not be able to recoup a refund from a merchant who's no longer around.

Investment-grade wine futures have become such a big-money business that merchants have to function at the level of an investment bank to manage all the money and contracts and ordering that the process demands. Your best bet: Stick with retailers with decades of experience in this business of selling wine futures. At the very least, they have proven through their own longevity that they have the resources to survive and to manage their customers' books of business effectively. You absolutely want to know that the merchant selling you those futures will be in business two years later to make good on the transaction. You might pay a little more for the futures contracts you want, since the weakest newcomers to the merchant business are the ones underpricing to the wine business, but you'll have greater faith that your transaction will ultimately be completed.

In this chapter, there are a few sample portfolios of what I consider to be smart 2005 Bordeaux investments. I've included three portfolios, one for each price tier, and my predicted prices for the next five- and ten-year periods. When my father put his initial Bordeaux price predictions on paper in 1987, people laughed at what they saw as irrational bullishness, though they used an entirely different bull-related phrase to express their disbelief. My father's predictions, however, turned out much too low for what history has ultimately witnessed in the investment-grade wine market.

Futures Investment Strategies

Essentially, there are two ways to play the futures market, meaning there are two ways to exit with a profit. After buying futures contracts, the first opportunity to exit your position is when the wine is delivered. At that point, the wine is almost three years old and now has a score and one or two key reviews (more on both in a moment). If the scores are particularly high and the reviews particularly effusive, investor and collector demand will assuredly already exist and the price almost certainly will be higher than what you originally paid twenty-four months ago. Once you have your wine in hand, you can turn around and sell the physical cases of wine to other investors or to collectors. You will likely do this through a merchant, since that's where most investors and collectors go to be assured of a wine's provenance, or its traceable history from winery to current owner.

This is the moment for short-term investors to get out with a good profit and put those proceeds back to work in the current year's crop of futures contracts. Otherwise, you're entering the long-term-investor arena, because after this initial spike, the wine's price will flatline for another five to seven years as the bottles rest in cellars awaiting their debut.

The second chance to get out—the chance for long-term investors to finally realize some profits—comes after those five to seven years pass. That's when wine is just about to hit its consumer phase. Bordeaux in particular generally requires a good decade of aging after it first goes into barrels as fermented grape juice. As those ten years draw to a close, fine restaurants the world over begin to debut these wines on their menu. Now consumer demand drives the market and prices once again move higher as increasing numbers of bottles are consumed and leave circulation.

In theory, there's a third strategy for futures: trading contracts with other investors before the wine is delivered. This happens with futures contracts at the Chicago Board of Trade and the New York Mercantile Exchange every day. You wake up to a hurricane in the

Dave Sokolin Price Predictions for 2005 Bordeaux by Tier

WINE	R. PARKER SCORE	2008 CASE PRICE	2013 EST. PRICE/CS.	EST. 5-YEAR GAIN	2018 EST. PRICE/CS.	EST. 10-YEAR GAIN
1ST TIER						
2005 La Mission Haut Brion	96–100	$7,800	$15,600	100.0%	$30,000	284.6%
2005 Mouton Rothschild	93–95	$7,200	$12,000	66.7%	$20,000	177.8%
2005 Haut Brion	96–100	$9,600	$19,200	100.0%	$32,000	233.3%
2005 Lafite Rothschild	94–98	$9,600	$17,000	77.1%	$30,000	212.5%
2005 Cheval Blanc	96–100	$9,600	$19,200	100.0%	$32,000	233.3%
2005 Margaux	98–100	$10,800	$20,000	85.2%	$35,000	224.1%
2005 Latour	96–99	$10,800	$18,000	66.7%	$30,000	177.8%
2005 Ausone	98–100	$36,000	$50,000	38.9%	$80,000	122.2%
		$101,400	**$171,000**	**68.6%**	**$289,000**	**185.0%**
2ND TIER						
2005 Léoville Poyferré	92–95	$1,150	$1,800	56.5%	$3,600	213.0%
2005 Lynch Bages	90–92	$1,200	$1,800	50.0%	$3,600	200.0%
2005 Léoville Barton	94–96	$1,500	$2,400	60.0%	$4,800	220.0%
2005 Montrose	94–96	$1,500	$2,400	60.0%	$4,800	220.0%
2005 Pape Clément	96–100	$2,350	$3,600	53.2%	$5,000	112.8%
2005 Cos d'Estournel	94–96	$2,650	$4,200	58.5%	$8,400	217.0%
2005 Ducru Beaucaillou	95–97	$2,700	$4,000	48.1%	$8,000	196.3%
2005 Larcis Ducasse	96–100	$3,000	$5,000	66.7%	$7,000	133.3%
2005 Troplong Mondot	96–100	$3,000	$5,000	66.7%	$7,000	133.3%
2005 Léoville Las Cases	94–96	$3,600	$6,000	66.7%	$10,000	177.8%
2005 L'Angélus	96–99	$4,500	$6,500	44.4%	$10,000	122.2%
2005 Pavie	98–100	$4,500	$8,000	77.8%	$16,000	255.6%
		$31,650	**$50,700**	**60.2%**	**$88,200**	**178.7%**

WINE	R. PARKER SCORE	2008 CASE PRICE	2013 EST. PRICE/CS.	EST. 5-YEAR GAIN	2018 EST. PRICE/CS.	EST. 10-YEAR GAIN
3RD TIER						
2005 Du Tertre	91–93	$450	$900	100.0%	$1,800	300.0%
2005 Faugères	91–93	$500	$1,000	100.0%	$1,800	260.0%
2005 Prieuré Lichine	90–92	$580	$1,200	106.9%	$2,400	313.8%
2005 Duhart Milon	90–92	$600	$1,200	100.0%	$2,200	266.7%
2005 Sociando Mallet	92–94	$600	$1,200	100.0%	$2,400	300.0%
2005 Beychevelle	92–94	$650	$1,200	84.6%	$2,400	269.2%
2005 Pavillon Rouge	91–93	$950	$1,800	89.5%	$3,000	215.8%
2005 Grand Puy Lacoste	93–95	$1,000	$1,800	80.0%	$3,600	260.0%
2005 Lascombes	94–96	$1,080	$1,800	66.7%	$3,600	233.3%
2005 Czalon Ségur	94–96	$1,100	$2,200	100.0%	$4,400	300.0%
		$7,510	$14,300	90.4%	$27,600	267.5%

Caribbean, and you buy oil futures on the expectation that the storm will disrupt Gulf of Mexico production and send the price of a barrel of oil higher, making your contract worth more money. But then the hurricane veers toward Honduras and the gulf is spared any destruction; recognizing that no production disruption means oil prices will reverse course, you quickly jump back into the market to sell your contracts while you still have some profit in them.

That practice doesn't flow across to wine futures. Necessary exchange mechanisms are not in place to transfer ownership or twelve cases of Château Le Pin from an investor in Butte, Montana, to a buyer in Sarasota, Florida, who then turns around and resells to another investor in Boonton, New Jersey. Once the futures contract is sold, merchants—who are not in the business of wine investing—don't have the time to continually change their internal records to indicate that next month those twelve cases of Le Pin are now going to New Jersey instead of Montana.

So, until the day arrives when contracts can easily be sold multiple times between investors and collectors, the contracts you buy have no value to anyone but you, and you'll have to wait until the wine is delivered before you can monetize your futures.

The Scores That Drive Futures Prices

While we're talking about wine futures, you should at least begin to understand the role that wine scores play in the contracts' prices. Most IGW, particularly Bordeaux-still-in-the-barrel, are tasted and reviewed by critics several times long before the wine ever sees the inside of a bottle. Their first tastes come during that frenzied period each spring when the barrel tastings occur for the new vintage. From that initial swirl around the palate, respected reviewers determine just how good, mediocre, or blah a wine is in particular and a vintage is in aggregate. They quantify their impression in a score that ranges between 1 and 100, though in practice you rarely see anything below 50—and at 50 you're essentially drinking pond water filtered through grass clippings. That score is then reported in the various outlets through which they publish their reviews, be it their own in-house newsletters or a newspaper like London's *Financial Times*.

At this stage of the process, determining just what a wine will be when it grows up is hard. After all, the wine still has two or three more years in the barrel and another seven or eight in the bottle before it's ready to drink. As such, critics typically assign a score that spans a range of points—usually two to five points, depending on the critic—and enclose those points within parentheses, such as (95–100).

This is a reviewer's way of noting that a wine is still young and that a lot can happen between now and the time it's listed on a restaurant menu. If all goes well, the critic is effectively saying with this bracketed score, this wine's ultimate tally could hit the top end of the range . . . and at the very least it possesses characteristics that should earn it a score at the low end. Again, though, this is a best guesstimate, an art form based on years of grading young wines and then resampling them several times over many, many years to determine just how well they've matured since the first barrel sample.

Wines with a 100 in their range make investors and collectors giddy. That triple-digit number blinks like a Las Vegas marquee so bright that it all but blinds investors from seeing the two-digit potential. They bid up the futures contracts for those wines, assuming the 100 is a done deal. But buying a young wine in the futures market and hoping it scores that 100 is, to use a craps analogy, betting on the come. If the gamble pays off, great; your wine's value will pop as consumers the world over rush to own the latest 100-pointer.

If, however, the wine ultimately arrives bearing a score in the middle or low end of the range—or if it comes in below expectations, as does happen—your investment will drop in value or, in the best case, will be dead money. Lower-tier wines that fail to live up to potentially big scores will likely see their prices slide. The wine will still be magnificent and will be an IGW, but the disappointment of not being quiet good enough to "ring the bell" will have sharp repercussions on wines that do not routinely play in the elite sandbox. In contrast, if a top-tier wine that was expected to hit 100 doesn't, the market isn't nearly as punishing. The wine's price certainly won't surge, but it isn't likely to soften much either. It will just hang around its current value for several years until consumer demand kicks in and starts gulping down the bottles.

The Vintage of '05: The "Bordeaux Effect"

Nature kissed western France in 2005. The growing season that year was extraordinarily dry, though never brutally hot. Light rains sprinkled the Médoc, Pomerol, St.-Émilion, and Graves regions in August, and some slightly heavier rains moistened the ground in

September. But even well into October the countryside remained relatively balmy and dry. The result: With cool nights and dry days, château owners were in no rush to harvest their grapes, giving the fruit the perfect opportunity to effectively build character.

When they finally did get around to picking their grapes and fermenting the juice, the owners knew they were part of something amazing. The reviews confirmed what they'd already come to believe: 2005 was a very special year, indeed. The praise was so widespread and so sweetly effusive it bordered on sycophantic. Consistency reigned throughout the region. Châteaux from First Growth stalwarts down to Fifth Growth also-rans had produced some of the greatest wines their vineyards had ever seen.

And with rare exceptions, futures for the class of 2005 were priced equal to, and often dramatically higher than, older vintages had ever been. For instance, when Château Latour was released, futures prices fueled by a Robert Parker rating of 98–100 ran to $800 a bottle, almost $10,000 a case, for wine that wouldn't be drinkable until 2015 at the earliest. For that same price, though, you could buy the legendary 100-point 1982 Latour, which was already drinking quite well—and you didn't face the risk that the final wine might come in at a 98 rating instead of 100. For the first time in history, the market for 2005 Bordeaux futures no longer put a premium on older, more desirable, ready-to-drink wines.

The chart on the next page compares examples of 2005 futures prices against retail prices for older vintages from the same estates. These prices were all as of June 2006, when the 2005 futures prices were announced. By the way, I chose these five particular vintages for a reason: They're each widely lauded as some of the absolute best vintages in modern history.

How did it come to this?

It all started in 1990.

The château owners of Bordeaux that year seethed as customers and merchants reaped the lion's share of the profits on their wines in the aftermarkets. Cases of top Bordeaux were quickly trading hundreds of percent above the original release prices set by the

2005 Bordeaux Futures Prices vs. Back Vintage Prices in Mid-2007*

	2005	2003	2000	1990	1986
Lafite Rothschild	$700	$550	$550	$400	$550
Margaux	$800	$600	$700	$700	$450
Léoville Las Cases	$315	$200	$325	$300	$400
Cos D'Estournel	$200	$200	$150	$200	$170
Pichon Lalande	$140	$125	$200	$150	$200

* Bottle prices

châteaux. The Bordelais wanted a bigger piece of what they recognized as the real market value of their annual efforts.

The Bordelais also despised what they regarded as the Johnny-come-lately California cult Cabernets that were releasing their wines at astronomical prices. Oh, the insult! Here were their own legendary châteaux with centuries of tradition, and some snot-nosed little boutique winery that, were it a person, wouldn't even be old enough to drive, is selling limited-production Cabernet at prices double that fetched by the grandest of the First Growth Bordeaux. This, the Bordelais determined, must change. They surmised—correctly—that if a Screaming Eagle can command such a high price, then so, too, can a Bordeaux.

So it was, then, that in 1996 the First Growth châteaux of Bordeaux doubled the release price for the 1995 futures to $120 a bottle. Thus began the era of ever-escalating futures prices.

By 2000, the trend was in full bloom. When fulsome reviews labeled the first vintage of the new millennium the "vintage of the century," the château owners took full control of their market, abandoning traditional pricing history. First Growth Bordeaux futures were released at $235 per bottle, which was astonishing at the time. When the next great vintage emerged just three years later, the Bordelais once more pushed their prices higher, this time to $275 per bottle, effectively squeezing from their grapes increasing profits to match what they saw as increasing demand, not just from their historical customers, the end consumers, but from these new creatures the Bordelais were now beginning to understand. Investors, seeing the macroeconomic trends at play, had begun to move into the wine market with profit, not the "compelling perfume of black fruits" or "powerful, unctuous flavors," as their only motivator.

And then came that magical '05 vintage to completely warp the scale.

Thus, in the span of about fifteen years, Bordeaux producers had radically redefined the futures market and radically altered the economics of buying, collecting, and investing in wine. Many collectors and investors questioned whether the astronomical gains could continue now that futures prices had reached such dizzying heights. The market provided the answer: As prices increased, customers not only bought in, they bought out—as in, everything they could find from the '05 vintage on back. The 2005 futures campaign had shifted upward what the public was willing to pay for just about every IGW.

Moreover, the client base had grown exponentially, and, given the huge returns that were accruing to wine investors, new buyers flooded in. In years past, a few thousand American and European collectors would each amass multiple-case lots of all the First Growth names like Latour, Mouton Rothschild, Margaux, and others. But because of the focus on a string of great vintages—2000, 2003, and now 2005—distribution spread across the world in smaller lots to buyers in Asia, Eastern Europe, and South America. Everyone was competing for every IGW he could find, snapping up not only futures but cases of back-vintage wines as well, catapulting prices for older Bordeaux past the futures prices, which, weirdly, made those futures prices suddenly look inexpensive again, validating their original high prices and, in a benevolent if not demented cycle, pulling up futures prices even higher.

So, despite having raised their futures prices by 300 percent, the top-rated châteaux had correctly predicted what the market would bear, and investors, collectors, and consumers willingly drank it up. Outside Bordeaux, this seismic shift allowed premier wine producers all over the world to ratchet their prices upward, as well—the "Bordeaux Effect."

The question that investors in particular and the broader wine market in general now must ask is whether '05 was a beautiful fluke or a permanent revaluation. In the shadow of 2005 lies the unheralded '06 vintage, widely regarded as subpar. Nevertheless, the top Bordeaux released their futures at prices comparable to those of a year earlier. Is it now that because of investors' actions and emerging-market wealth the world's best wines are worth more, regardless of the vintage and score? Or is a shakeout in the offing for futures prices? Given that the vintage is so recent, it's too early to answer that question. But savvy investors would be wise to pay attention to how this question ultimately is answered—how wine prices for '06, '07, and beyond move in comparison to their original release prices. You don't want to find yourself having paid so highly in an overly bullish futures market that your returns are impaired for years to come, though in my opinion 2005 marked the dawn of a new era in Bordeaux wine prices.

Old Is New Again: The Back-Vintage Market

The phrase "old is new again" fits the investment-grade wine market perfectly. New wines are released with every vintage, only to lie in cellars for years, if not decades, undisturbed and all but forgotten. And then one day, they emerge dusty and older. Consumers and connoisseurs enjoy them for the first time. Old has, in effect, become new again.

You'll recall from an earlier chapter the fact that professional wine investors, the managers who run wine-investment funds, typically buy wines that are about five years away from debuting on restaurant menus. They are investing in old wines, what the industry calls "back vintage."

When the new wines are introduced every spring, the previous year's bottles are suddenly back vintage. In fact, every wine other than the current vintage is, by definition, part of the back-vintage market, regardless of whether it's a year old or centuries old. As you might imagine, then, the back-vintage market, backed by millennia of wine production, is the oldest, largest wine market in the world. While there are a couple hundred IGW available each year in the futures market, there are thousands upon thousands of IGW trading as back-vintage wines.

How to Participate in the Back-Vintage Market

Unlike futures, which are available almost exclusively through merchants, you can buy back-vintage wines from numerous sources. That doesn't mean you should, only that you can. Aside from merchants—both reputable and questionable—you'll find a variety of auction houses and online wine-auction websites that offer a nearly unlimited supply of back-vintage wines from all the key grape-growing regions.

For my money, I'd stick to reputable merchants with whom you can build a long-term relationship and auction houses such as Sotheby's that inspect wine cellars, research provenance, and vouch for the authenticity and pedigree of the wines you win. The reason: You face risks when you're not the first person to own a particular case of wine, as you are when you buy in the futures market.

Premier back-vintage wines are the playground of the nefarious. With the ability of relatively low-cost computer printers to spit out high-quality knockoff labels, the criminally minded easily replicate the world's greatest wines, at least on the exterior of the bottle. But that's often enough to fool investors inexperienced at spotting fakes. Then, when you go to sell your portfolio, a merchant or an auction house spots the faked label or otherwise questions the authenticity of the wine, and the value of your investment crumbles. Indeed, a Florida billionaire paid more than $500,000 for five bottles of claret from Château Lafite and Brane Mouton—the predecessor of Mouton Rothschild—from vintages in the late 1700s purportedly owned by Thomas Jefferson. Only the FBI and officials at Monticello, Jefferson's Virginia estate, say there is no evidence that America's third president ever owned the bottles, meaning their real value may be just 1 percent of their cost.

Outright crime isn't the only risk you confront. You have to worry about the white lies in which a merchant of questionable morals or a shady member of an online wine-auction site insists the case of 1990 Château Latour has been properly cellared since delivery, even though the seller has had the case sitting atop a refrigerator for the last decade and has no clue where the previous owner stored the wine.

In short, when you're a back-vintage investor, you must be certain that the sellers you're buying from are reputable and stand behind the wine they're selling. Otherwise you could end up with investment-grade wine that isn't worthy of your investment.

The Back-Vintage Strategies

As with futures investing, back-vintage investors generally have two primary strategies to pursue:

■ Buy relatively young wines—those about five years from being opened for the first time—and cellar them until the wines begin to appear on menus, at which point you sell them off to monetize the profits, then reinvest the proceeds in another batch of IGW about five years from hitting its consumer phase.

The wine-investment funds that pursue this approach do so with the expectation that the cases they buy will generally double in value over the five-year holding period, an annualized return of about 15 percent. So far, the investment funds have fared well with this approach, but as a group they are fairly young and have had fair winds at their back because of the stellar vintages and the dramatic influx of new buyers from emerging markets. If a string of lackluster vintages piles up or demand drops because of global economic reasons, the returns could soften—though IGW prices will still be likely to move higher, just at a slower pace.

With this strategy, you don't have to concentrate on the highest-rated wines from the greatest names in Bordeaux. Indeed, many Second through Fifth Growth wines rated in the 95-to-97 range do exceedingly well with this strategy. Their prices are much lower in comparison to the premier names, so the base of consumers is substantially larger, meaning more bottles pulled out of circulation, ultimately making it easier for the price to double.

■ Buy much older back vintages that are already drinking well. With this strategy you're largely focusing on either the best wines or the greatest vintages, or both.

In focusing on the best wines, you essentially concentrate your buying on the châteaux with the greatest pedigree (you'll learn those names in the chapter "Bordeaux and Beyond"). Unless the reviewer scores are atrocious—and with the most pedigreed wines, that would basically be below 90—these are the wines that have a demonstrated history of increasing in price, if only because of the brand name printed on the label.

Or concentrate your buying on wines with the highest scores—99 and 100—regardless of name. Because so few peers exist at this altitude, and because demand from collectors is effectively limitless, these wines historically perform well as investments.

Or concentrate on the greatest vintages. Wines from the vintages every connoisseur knows by heart—1947, 1982, 2000, 2005, etc.—are always in demand among consumers and collectors. With this approach, you can spread your dollars across just about any IGW you can find with a score of 95 or higher from a respected reviewer.

Or you can play what might best be labeled the value approach. Concentrate on wines that are at least a decade old, with scores of 93 or 94, but that have begun drinking very well based on updated reviews. You're looking for wines with scores that are on the ascent in consecutive reviews, betting that the wine will continue to improve with further aging and that future reviews will push the score to at least 95. At that point, the wine is officially an IGW and its price will likely reflect that improvement in quality.

How Big a Wallet Do I Need?

This answer depends on your particular approach to back-vintage investing.

If you follow the strategy of investment funds and buy young wines before they reach their consumer phase, you can spend several hundred to several thousand dollars per case, depending upon which wines you buy. Lower-tier wines, and those with scores of 95 and 96, will price at the lowest end of the spectrum, while First-Tier wines—the premier names like Margaux, Latour, Rothschild, and others—and those with scores of 97 and 98, will price much higher. If you invest in First-Tier wines that carry huge scores of 99 and 100, you can expect to pay multiple thousands of dollars per case.

But again, you don't have to own the highest-rated premier wines to make good money in wine investing. Fifth Growth châteaux such as Lynch Bages and Pontet Canet routinely fare well as investments, so much so that wine-investment funds are regularly in the market snapping up investment-grade cases of these wines because they know that demand for value-priced, high-scoring Bordeaux is nearly limitless.

If you opt to invest in older back vintages already drinking well, your cost of entry can climb dramatically. Remember, these are wines that already have at least a decade of cellaring behind them and consumers are already demanding these wines, so the amount of competition you face in buying them is elevated. The biggest costs you will face—easily thousands of dollars per case—will come from buying the highest-scoring back vintages of First-Tier wines. Demand rarely wanes for these 99- and 100-point all-stars.

IGW from great vintages can vary in price, but they generally start in the $2,000-a-case range and rise like a mountain from there. In fact, the effect on your pocketbook is a bit like climbing Mount

Everest: the higher the tier or the higher the score, the greater the pain you'll feel in your wallet.

The cheapest way into the back-vintage market is through that value approach I mentioned—buying wines rated just below IGW status that are drinking well and are moving higher on the point scale. You can still buy into some of those for less than $1,000 a case. But remember: There is risk associated with this strategy. If the wine climbs no higher, never accumulating enough points to reach IGW status, your wine's price isn't likely to do terribly much over time. It will likely retain its value, meaning you won't nec-essarily lose money, but it won't continue to rise in price on an IGW-worthy score, limiting or erasing your potential return on investment.

We've reached the last of Sokolin's 11 House rules. These final three deal with quantity and quality.

Rule 9: Buy Standard-Sized Lots

If you've ever bought bonds, you know that a so-called round lot is ten bonds. This is the standard trading unit in which investors gen-erally transact. You can certainly buy fewer than ten bonds—you can buy one, if you wish—but the pricing usually isn't as good, meaning you pay more to buy that one bond and you receive less when you sell. The reason is that the bond-trading industry is built to trade in a standard lot size, and any time you break up a round lot you're creating a so-called odd lot, which is more difficult for a bond trader to get rid of. If a bond buyer wants a "round lot," that is, a standard lot of ten, and you're selling an odd lot, the buyer will have to find another odd lot or break another seller's round lot.

Wine, too, trades in standard-size lots—cases of a dozen 750-milliliter bottles, the standard-size bottles you find at the local wine shop. Non-case sizes are also called odd lots in the wine business, or sometimes they're more colorfully named "broken cases." The only single-sized bottles that trade as a standard unit are the specialty, large-format bottles, such as jeroboams, Methuselahs, and others, and particularly old and rare 750ml bottles for which a single case may no longer exist. However, when originally released from the châteaux, magnums are packaged in wooden cases of six, while double magnums come in cases of three. To the degree that you can, then, invest in standard-size lots. They will be easier to trade and be more valuable to your buyers than a single 750ml bottle.

Indeed, the highest-bidding collectors and resellers purchase in large quantities. They want to own multiple cases, because to the wine trade and to auctioneers, a twenty-case lot of a collectible wine is extremely attractive. It garners much more attention than a smaller lot does, and it has more credibility, which, in turn, makes the collection more valuable. When I am offered cellars with large case quantities, my concern about the wine's storage history is diminished. Who would buy in five- and ten-case lots and not protect that wine? Nobody. Large lots are easy to trade because there's substantial interest in them and substantial competition from merchants, potentially making your cases worth more.

There is substantial lack of interest in a single bottle of 2003 Latour, no matter how fine the vintage. And there's very little competition from merchants looking to buy that single bottle. They'd much rather buy a full case or multiple cases to resell. And while you can often find odd lots or broken cases at a discounted price, you will end up reselling at a discounted price as well, unless you can build a case-sized lot from multiple odd lots.

Rule 10: Buy Large-Format Bottles

Mathematically speaking, a magnum of wine is the equivalent of two regular-sized 750ml bottles of wine, a simple one plus one equals two equation. Economically, it's more like a one plus one equals three. Because they are far rarer than 750ml bottles, magnums often trade at much higher price levels than bottles of the same wine from the same vintage. In 2007, a regular-sized bottle of

1961 Latour sold for $5,000, meaning that two bottles would, obviously, fetch double that. Yet a magnum of the same Latour was priced at $15,000. Wine collectors love big bottles. It's an ego thing. These bottles are a dramatic addition to a dinner party, and they stand out in a cellar. Moreover, vintners don't offer large-format bottles with every vintage. That rarity factor plays a big role in the price premium, as does the fact that wine bottled in larger formats tends to age longer than wine bottled in 750ml and half bottles.

When buying Bordeaux wine futures, you can ask your merchant to contact the négociant and request that, for a small premium, your wine be bottled in a larger-format container. Many investors request that their rarest wines be bottled in magnum format, due to their potential to price-appreciate higher than regular bottles.

The premium for large-format bottles applies only to investment-grade wines. Wines that don't have the ability to age and are not collectible can actually suffer a price decline when bottled in large formats. After all, who wants to open eight bottles of White Zinfandel at one time?

Rule 11: Physically Inspect Your Wine on Arrival

You'll recall that back in chapter 2, one of the original five Sokolin House Rules I laid out dealt with a wine's provenance, its bona fides, so to speak. Rule 11 fits in with that because the physical condition of a wine can speak to its provenance—or lack thereof.

The basic professional condition criteria are the following:

■ **Fill level**—Where along the neck of the bottle does the wine reach? That's fill level. A perfectly drinkable wine might have a terrible label from being stored in a damp cellar (which isn't necessarily bad), but the fill level is the first clue to a wine's condition. If the level is low, buyers will be concerned that the cork has shrunk, allowing wine to evaporate or, worse, allowing in outside air that has spoiled the contents.

What's In a Name?

Milk comes in containers labeled quarts and gallons. Beer comes in tall boys and 40s. Wine comes in some of the most colorfully named container sizes imaginable—Methuselah, jeroboam, and Nebuchadnezzar among others. Try asking for a Nebuchadnezzar of Diet Pepsi the next time you pop into the local mini-mart. Below is a chart of wine-bottle sizes and the quantity of wine inside.

Bottle Size	Quantity	Net Contents in Bottle Quantity
Half bottle	375ml all regions	½ bottle
Bottle	750ml all regions	regular size
Magnum	1.5 liters all regions	2 bottles
Double magnum	3 liters in Bordeaux	4 bottles
Jeroboam	3 liters in Bordeaux and Champagne	4 bottles
Jeroboam	5 liters in Bordeaux after 1978 (4.5 liters before 1978)	6 bottles
Imperial	6 liters in Bordeaux	8 bottles
Methuselah	6 liters in Burgandy and Champagne	8 bottles
Salmanazar	9 liters in Bordeaux	12 bottles
Balthazar	12 liters in Bordeaux	16 bottles
Nebuchadnezzar	15 liters in Bordeaux	20 bottles
Melchoir	18 liters in Bordeaux	24 bottles

- **Capsule and cork**—Is the cork protruding or leaking and is the capsule intact or cut? The first two are signs that the wine was stored in unsuitably hot conditions and that the wine is likely cooked. A cut capsule is acceptable in a rare wine because the vintage branded on the cork is made visible and this helps to establish that the wine in the bottle is, indeed, the wine on the label.

- **Label condition**—Is the label pristine, stained, or "bin soiled"? The condition of the label can say a lot about how the wine was stored. The more pristine the label, the better for investment return because collectors—no matter if they're into wines or baseball cards—universally seek out unblemished examples of whatever they're collecting.

Unintentional shipping errors do happen, so if you do not have the time to personally inspect your wine every time a shipment arrives, you should store your wine with professionals who will verify your purchase for you for a small fee.

If a buyer can reasonably imagine that a wine is suspect because of fill level, damaged cork, torn, ripped, or soiled labels, or because you can't prove where the wine came from or that it was stored in immaculate conditions, then you don't have an investment-grade wine in that buyer's eyes. There's too much left to the imagination—and none of it is beneficial to the value of your wine.

The best strategy as an investor, in my opinion, is to develop a relationship with a trustworthy, well-connected merchant who has access to in-demand wines that have been stored properly and who also has the most up-to-date market information. You can certainly go it alone, just as millions of investors do when buying and selling stocks online through discount brokerage firms. Many of those investors do well. But wine is a far more fickle market than stocks, because wine trades on a unique set of variables. A better course, in my opinion, is to call upon an experienced advisor, a wine merchant, and to back that up with your own web-based research.

The best merchants will help you form not only an investment strategy but an exit strategy as well. It's a symbiotic relationship between customer and merchant, where the customer will buy and hold onto wines and later sell them back to the merchant at a handy profit. The merchant, meanwhile, wants to steer you toward the best wines you can afford because he's anticipating the day you'll be back in the store, ready to sell, and he can then buy back these classic vintages and resell for a bigger profit.

7

STORAGE AND RESALE

Once You Own It, What Do You Do with It?

I've used the word "provenance" many times up to this point, and by now you've undoubtedly deduced that, outside of the wines themselves, this is the single most important factor in wine investing. You can own the world's greatest library of rare wines, but if you store them in a broom closet next to the water heater, your portfolio has about the same value as that ratty mop stuck in the back corner.

Storage is everything when it comes to IGW, and every collector or investor with any degree of wine savvy will question you about your storage facility. Auctioneers and wine merchants certainly will and may even want to inspect your storage operations before they agree to buy, consign, or auction your portfolio, particularly if it's a collection of the finest of the investment-grade wines.

To that end, wine investors have two primary choices: professional or home storage.

■ **Professional storage:** While a relatively small collection can be neatly stored at home, an investor who owns larger volumes will likely reach a point where storage needs outstrip available space. Moreover, you might realize you need logistical support as well in managing the incoming and outgoing wine. That's where a professional wine-storage facility comes in.

Once largely confined to metropolitan New York and the area immediately surrounding California's wine country, professional storage facilities dedicated exclusively to re-creating a perfect wine climate have popped up all over the country in recent years. Some are bare-bones facilities absent any pomp and circumstance; others are more engaging affairs, with private tasting rooms for small gatherings and wine-storage lockers that provide a work space for collectors and investors to manage their own back-office chores, such as keeping a cellar log.

In either instance, your wines are kept in temperature-, humidity-, and light-controlled environs designed specifically to ensure appropriate aging. Additionally, when wine is stored professionally, the documentation helps establish provenance since the facility keeps records of the wines coming and going through your collection and their storage conditions.

Professional wine-storage facilities can manage every aspect of your investment, handling the chores that, once a collection is large enough, can become overwhelming. If wine in less-than-stellar condition arrives from a vendor, the storage client is immediately notified, whereas at home it could go unnoticed for months or years if you're not paying close attention to every box that arrives.

Professional storage today is relatively inexpensive, costing approximately $15–$20 a year per case. Generally, these facilities offer insurance at an annual cost of between 1 and 2 percent of the collection's value. At D. Sokolin & Co., I've found that once collectors experience the benefits of professional storage, they tend to move the bulk of their cellar there. For instance, when they discover that bottles can be shipped overnight to their vacation homes or even their favorite restaurants in different cities while they're traveling on vacation or business, the allure of a home cellar fades.

■ **Storage at home:** Despite the benefits of professional storage, almost every wine investor dreams of having a cellar at home. Even if you plan to store the bulk of your portfolio professionally, there's a certain attraction to walking into your own cool, dark cellar and seeing all those bottles resting on wooden racks.

There are many options for in-home cellars these days, ranging from refrigerated stand-alone units that can fit in a closet to full-blown, custom-designed showcase cellars to room-sized underground caves specially built with tasting rooms, mood lighting, and dramatic display racks encased in glass. You can spend a few thousand dollars to well over a million, depending on your wants and your budget. Online you'll find a vast assortment of computer-assisted design programs that help you draft plans for your cellar, then print the design and a materials list, or you can locate builders who specialize in custom in-home cellars.

The cellar must be built right, and that means an airtight, vapor-sealed, and heavily insulated room with a dedicated air-conditioning and humidifying unit to create the proper environment. And that proper environment is a temperature of between 50 and 55 degrees and a relative humidity of between 60 and 65 percent, and no light except for the brief moments you're in there adding to your portfolio or retrieving a case that you've sold. In essence, you want a place a hermit might find cozy.

The absolute no-no in wine storage: a bedroom closet, the garage, or even a basement. Those environments are often much warmer in the summer or much colder in the winter, and the air is often much drier—all very bad for wine and wine corks that expand and contract with temperatures that vary drastically. If those are your only options, then you really must go with a professional storage facility if you want to own investment-grade wine.

The Cellar Log: A Mandatory Back-Office Chore

If you do store your investments at home, make sure that you have a wine-tracking/cellar log program that you follow religiously. As their name suggests, these programs track the wines that come and go through your cellar, recording the costs, quantities, suppliers, and dates of purchase, delivery, and sale, among other items. These categories are a must. The cleaner, more accurate your records are at the time of sale, the better the provenance of your wine and the greater its value.

You don't have to spend a ton of money on one of these programs, though you certainly can. Some of them cost thousands of dollars and are based on a bar-code system that prints small labels for each bottle or case so that the program can track location within the cellar and other sundry variables. If you don't want to go to that extreme, use one of the most effective and readily available tracking tools that most people already own—a computer spreadsheet program like Microsoft Excel. All you need do is build a simple spreadsheet that tracks those key notations mentioned above. Then keep all your records as proof—the shipping labels, purchase orders, and any other documents you receive that will help you one day prove your wine's provenance.

Insuring Your Portfolio

If by chance the stockbroker you use for trading in the financial markets goes belly up, your investments are protected by a form of insurance offered by the SIPC, the Securities Investor Protection Corporation. Wine investors need something similar. After all, if anything happens to your portfolio because of theft, natural disaster, temperature-control failure, or name your reason, you'll want some assurance that you're not out tens or hundreds of thousands of dollars. And these things do happen. Hundreds of thousands of dollars of fine and rare wine were lost in New Orleans' famous eateries during Hurricane Katrina. And in 2007 a Silicon Valley entrepreneur came home from vacation to find that his cellar had been looted of about $120,000 in rare wines, including a magnum of 1959 Château Pétrus, itself worth about $7,000 at the time. Nothing else in the house was missing.

Insuring the replacement value of your portfolio is a must, especially if you store your collection at home. A regular homeowners policy isn't likely to cover fine wine since those wines were never part of the underwriting process and aren't considered germane to home ownership as are traditional household items such as furniture and appliances. Instead, you'll need either a rider on your existing policy, or, depending upon the size of your collection, a separate policy altogether that covers only your portfolio.

Such coverage requires an accurate appraisal of your collection's market value. In recent years, services have emerged that appraise wine collections for insurance and other purposes. Many wine merchants and auction houses can help you with this process or put you in touch with the appropriate companies.

Valuing Your Portfolio

This is where investors often lose their bearing. They see prices listed for a particular wine they own, and they assume that's what their wine is worth at that given moment. Maybe it is. More likely, it's not.

If you ran a wine shop and knew that based on current market conditions a case of 2004 Château Pétrus was worth about $6,000, would you spend $6,000 to buy it, knowing you could get only $6,000 for it in your store? Of course not. You'd buy it at a discount from retail so that you could generate a profit.

As an investor, then, don't expect to sell your wine to a retailer or auction house at retail prices. So the question becomes: What's my wine really worth? In general, retailers are looking to mark up the wines they buy from 10 to 25 percent.

Through an auction house, the price that you achieve depends upon the degree to which paddle fever strikes the day's crowd. But remember that you must haircut the value of your wine by upward of 20 percent to account for the seller's commission that auction houses charge. To value your collection at the auction level, contact the auction house and request historical price comparisons so that you can gauge the value of your wine based upon the prices those same wines have fetched at auction in the recent past. Pay attention, though, to the date of sale. If the last sale for some particular case of wine you have is more than a year old, chances are that price isn't terribly reflective of the current environment.

The Rich Man . . . in the Library . . . with a Wine Opener

The most ignominious end to a highly valuable, exclusive collection of Lafite Rothschild happened in New Jersey. A young man called us in the mid-1990s, responding to an ad we placed in *The New York Times* for an assembly of Lafite Rothschild library wines, wines that had come to us directly from the château's personal library of back vintages.

This gentleman was interested in wines that we had procured from Lafite's cellars, consisting of rare bottles from vintages between 1870 and 1900. Until their trip to our facility in the Hamptons, these wines had never left Lafite's cellars in Bordeaux. I personally drove the bottles to the client's large Jersey mansion, which he'd funded on his success in the business of selling weight-lifting supplements. Not only was he interested in collecting wines, but he also had a large rare guitar collection. I was excited to deliver these wines and especially to play some of his guitars.

When I arrived, I was shown around, noticing along the way that there wasn't much of a wine collection. When I unpacked the wine, I asked him where I should put it. His answer: What better place to put library wines than . . . the library?

I was astonished and dismayed. I explained just how rare these wines were, that they needed proper storage to survive, and that standing them upright, in the light, in an actual library was not how these wines should be treated.

He handed me a check for many tens of thousands of dollars and said, "Let's do it." So I reluctantly agreed.

And that's how it came to be that some very ancient, very valuable First Growth French wines met their unglamorous demise.

The Grape Escape: Selling Wine Assets

Until recently, selling wine as an individual investor could be a mystifying process, often leaving the collector/investor with few options other than hoping to find a hometown buyer willing to pay market prices for the wine, or consigning the cellar to an auction house, generally in New York or some other large city, that might be hundreds or thousands of miles away, necessitating big transportation costs and commissions for the privilege of unloading the portfolio.

Now, though, you can quickly find online a veritable vineyard of merchants, auctioneers, consumers, and other investors around the globe eager to help you monetize your portfolio. Basically, you're no longer confined to the few square miles surrounding your home. Wherever in the world there's an Internet connection, you have a potential buyer. That means a greater likelihood that you will achieve maximum prices for your wine.

The primary means of dispensing with all or part of your portfolio is through the same two channels that served your purchase needs: retailers and auction houses (you're obviously not going to resell your wines by way of a winery's mailing list).

Back-Vintage Exit Strategy

With young wines, the exit strategy is simple: When they reach their consumer phase, you sell. The five-year stretch between the time you buy and the time the wines are ready to drink often represents the greatest degree of price appreciation that many wines will see. Sure, they will continue to rise in value over the years, but the pace of appreciation will slow—unless we're talking about those vaunted wines with monster scores from major vintages . . . and if so, all bets are off. Those prices can go into the stratosphere.

With older back-vintage wines the strategy is less regimented. You essentially hold until you're ready to sell. Are you happy with doubling your money? A 50 percent gain after one year? A 500 percent gain after a decade?

Prices for these wines generally move in fits and starts, and thus it's incumbent upon you to pay attention to the value of the wines in your portfolio. You might have a 97-point Château Palmer that has risen in value with relative, albeit slow consistency. And then one day the price jumps sharply higher, maybe because of a broad revaluation of Palmer wines or because wines across that particular vintage are aging substantially better than anyone expected or because a 2005-like vintage comes along and radically shifts the price spectrum. Whatever the reason, your original investment of $2,000 is now worth $7,000 after seven years. Are you satisfied with an annualized return of 20 percent? If so, sell. If not, don't.

The point is that when you are an investor in older back vintages, your exit strategy has to fit your needs. I can't tell you to sell after the wine has doubled in price. You might think I'm being much too conservative for your appetite . . . or you might think I'm being way too risky, and you'd be much happier to sell if the wine increases by half. Only you know the price at which that little voice inside your head says, "Yep, that's a good price; time to sell." So I'll repeat myself: You must pay attention to the prices of the wines in your portfolio. That way, you'll know when the moment to sell arrives.

When you do sell, either you will go through the merchants you have already built a relationship with and who know your cellar (meaning they know the wines have been properly stored), or you will contact an auction house that makes a business in fine wines. If the auction house doesn't know you yet and your collection is of some size and your wines are of some renown, it will likely send a representative to inspect your cellar and your cellar notes (we'll cover those in a bit) so that the auction house can assure bidders of the wine's provenance.

While it's hard to say what you, the individual investor, should aim for as an investor in back-vintage wines, I can say this: In the twenty years ended in 2006, the returns for a portfolio of fine wine outperformed a variety of stock and bond indices, such as the Dow Jones Industrial Average and London's *Financial Times* Stock Exchange 100. IGW should return between 10 and 12 percent annually, and do so with far less volatility than stocks or bonds.

RETAILERS: Selling your collection of IGW back to your primary merchants can be the easiest and quickest route to resale, if only because you receive an immediate payment instead of one dependent upon the vagaries of the auction market and the fickleness of that day's crowd. Wine merchants like me are always looking for well-cellared collections of fine wines to buy and resell. Investors and collectors are the biggest and best source of hard-to-source back-vintage rare wines.

Retailers with whom you already have relationships can be a great place to start the due diligence process. Show them your collection, let them inspect your cellar and cellar log if they care to, and let them know you're looking to trim your portfolio.

The problem with retailers is that they might try to cherry-pick your cellar to grab only the lots they know will be easy to resell. You can quash that by stating that you have no interest in breaking up the inventory you're looking to sell. Choose a reputable retailer. Beware of underfunded brokers and traders who may have problems paying you.

CONSIGNMENT: If you and a wine merchant can't come to terms on a fair price for the lot of wines you want to sell, ask if the retailer will sell the collection on a consignment basis. This option still allows a retailer to augment his inventory with IGW that are regularly in demand and might get you closer to your asking price. You will not, however, receive a lump-sum payment at that very moment. Instead, your payments, minus the retailer's share, will trickle in over time as each bottle or case is sold.

AUCTION: Many of the downsides that buyers confront at auction are the upsides you benefit from as the seller. Most notable is paddle fever. It can work to your favor as you watch the value of your wines escalate well beyond your expectations. In addition, the "buyer beware" policy can work in your favor as well, allowing you to unload wines that are in less-than-perfect condition or that don't have perfect provenance.

Before selling at auction, though, be sure you understand exactly how much you're going to pay in a seller's commission. If you're selling a huge collection, an up-front payment and the minimum price per item can more easily be negotiated, although it is not uncommon for sellers to have to wait more than six months to be paid by the auction house. And you should certainly try to negotiate the "reserve price," the lowest price at which you will let the wines go. The risk here, of course, is that you might get stuck with unsold lots.

If you're selling wine in odd lots (cases that are not a complete dozen), expect that the price will immediately be discounted. It's the odd-lot syndrome endemic to most investment-worthy assets, since odd lots are less desirable and, thus, often harder to sell. Either you'll pay more to trade them, or you'll have to accept less to sell them.

Non-investment-grade wines are often priced at a steeper discount since there is far less demand. Wines in an original wood case (often denoted as OWC) that is in good condition typically sell at a premium.

Along with the major, brand-name auction houses such as Sotheby's and Christie's, you will find online a number of do-it-yourself wine-auction sites. Beware, as either buyer or seller. You often have no idea where these wines are coming from, so ensuring provenance can be nigh impossible. And as a seller, you may see the value of your wine underpriced, since others out there are discounting the fact that they don't know the provenance of your bottles and cases.

Finally, beware of anyone offering to buy your portfolio at prices inflated noticeably beyond what you know their current value to be. I've seen unwitting sellers taken in by small-time brokers claiming to have a whale-sized client willing to pay big dollars. Inevitably it turns out that the broker is just buying time in order to broker your collection at a big profit to himself and doesn't have the resources to pay for it upfront. There was never a whale on the hook to begin with, though you end up getting harpooned because if the broker can't find anyone to buy your wine, he'll walk away without losing a cent and you will possibly have missed the opportunity to connect with a legitimate buyer, who has found similar merchandise elsewhere and is no longer interested in your wines. Stick with merchants and auction houses with which you've previously had good business transactions, and you'll routinely be satisfied with the results.

One last point: You might be wondering why there's no futures market exit strategy, just one for back-vintage wines. The reason: No efficient market has emerged to allow owners of wine futures to sell their futures contracts before the wine is bottled and delivered. That means the first opportunity you have to sell the wine you buy in the futures market is when it is delivered, generally two years later—and at that point, well, your wine is back vintage.

PART II

An Investor's View of the World's Greatest Wine Regions

8

BORDEAUX AND BEYOND

Truth be told, there's no real need to venture beyond Bordeaux to be a successful wine investor. By far, the largest portion of wine buyers, wine collectors, wine lovers, and wine investors focus their energies—and their monies—almost exclusively on the wine produced along the Gironde, Dordogne, and Garonne rivers of southwestern France, just outside the town of Bordeaux.

But while Bordeaux sucks up most of the oxygen, wines from other regions of France and the world generate a great deal of interest as well. These other wines beget huge, oftentimes fanatical followings among consumers. And where you find rabid fans, you find rabid fans with lots of dollars just looking for a bottle of their favorite tipple to buy, meaning profit opportunities for the savvy wine trader.

This section, then, is your travel guide to the world's investment-grade wines. We'll start, naturally, in Bordeaux and end in the same region, with Sauternes, a sweet white wine. In between we'll spin through Burgundy, Champagne, and the Rhône regions of France and make stops in Spain, Portugal, and Italy before abandoning Europe for the New World—California and Australia.

The upcoming chapters take a look at the wines themselves and the regions they come from, and why it is that these wines, and not, say, wines from the vineyards next door have become the standard bearers of greatness among consumers, critics, and investors.

So, off we go to Bordeaux . . .

Wine's Blue Chips: Bordeaux

In numerous wine circles, Bordeaux is the beginning, the end, and the middle of any conversation about great wines and great wine investments. It *is* the wine market. The best wines from this estuarine region of France—and they are legion—have for centuries dependably improved in flavor and appreciated in price over a period that can stretch to decades. Fans of Bordeaux's greatest names have for centuries sought out the pleasure of these wines over all others because no other wine-growing region in the world makes wine with the kind of name recognition afforded Bordeaux's best châteaux. They are synonymous with high-dollar luxury. You don't need to be a literary genius to have heard of William Shakespeare, nor must you be a wine maven to have heard of such names as Lafite Rothschild, Latour, and Mouton Rothschild. They command attention just by their presence.

For centuries, the wealthy have sought to own these wines, out of their own hedonistic pursuit of pleasure and as an outward, obvious financial message to their peers: "I have arrived." Time has not dampened such basic emotions. If anything, time has intensified them because the store of wealthy consumers has only increased throughout history, and today that store is experiencing its most fevered growth ever as developing economies spin off new millionaires every day. And no matter the culture from which the *nouveau* millionaire arises, the sentiments are always similar: a desire to show the world that the mountain has been climbed.

Little wonder that the trappings of prosperity are in abundant demand these days: yachts, second and third homes, investment jewels, private jets. In the first half of 2007, sales at the luxury-car maker Bentley—where prices *start* at $170,000—hit record levels, driven in part by surging demand in China, Russia, and the Middle

East. Bordeaux's star attractions easily slide into this category. Fet-ing your guests with bottles of Latour and Pétrus and inviting them into a private cellar to sample a Lafite or a Mouton says more than your proclamations of wealth ever could. Even as top-shelf Bor-deaux grows in its traditional markets in Western Europe and the United States, the wines are finding new love in places such as Bei-jing and Dubai.

Astonishingly, a pool of what I estimate are just 118 Bordeaux châteaux account for 90 percent of the entire dollar volume in the investment-grade wine market, which includes the finest wines from every other region in the world. More amazing is that only twenty-five of Bordeaux's best châteaux account for approximately 80 percent of the dollar volume in the industry. Everything you need to know about what makes a wine an investment-grade wine you'll learn in this chapter on Bordeaux.

If looking across the coming decades you see cause to be bullish about the future, not just America's future but the global future, then you should feel pretty confident that growing wealth will translate into ever-larger numbers of people who can afford to shop at the highest end of the wine market, over time breaking price re-cords for classic Bordeaux along the way.

Because of their importance to the market, Bordeaux are the most extensively tracked wines in the world. They're coddled by vintners, hyped by merchants, and cooed over by collectors. Like college football prospects headed into the professional ranks, Bor-deaux wines are assessed on multiple characteristics by legions of reviewers, and the notes are released to a phalanx of fans, eager to drink up the news. In Bordeaux's case, the wines are rated three times before they ever reach consumers, twice before the wines are even bottled. In a market all but dictated by reviewer scores, this is yet more proof that Bordeaux is the most investment worthy of all wines.

Up until the early '90s, when prices were significantly lower, Seagram's fine-wine importing division, Château & Estate, domi-nated the distribution of most of Bordeaux's best wines simply by buying all of them in every vintage. However, in the mid-1990s, when the château release prices rose dramatically, not even this wines-and-spirits behemoth could muster the muscle necessary to maintain this strategy, and the firm lost its virtual monopoly in the Bordeaux market.

Higher prices have resulted in a more fragmented market, what some call "open source," populated by small players and multiple vendors selling the same wines in the same territory at competing prices, leaving the investor with abundant opportunities for procuring these wines.

Wrap it all together, and Bordeaux stands alone in producing the world's highest-quality, most-coveted wines in quantities large enough that the wines are readily available, a fact not true of every important wine region. All of this makes Bordeaux—the place and the product—perfect for wine investors.

The Four Keys to Bordeaux Profitability

Easy to Understand

Given its provenance, its history, and the sheer number of experts who seemingly know every grape in every vineyard, at first Bordeaux might seem intimidating. In truth, Bordeaux is quite the accessible wine region.

For our purposes as investors, however, all that stuff, while nice trivia with which to pepper a cocktail conversation, is essentially irrelevant. Wine traders need know only the names of the best châteaux and, in general terms, where they fall within the hierarchy that wine connoisseurs pay attention to. A Lafite Rothschild, one of the five First Growth châteaux, will always command more attention than a Château Pédesclaux, down among the Fifth Growths—though that's not to imply that Fifth Growths are inferior; several routinely produce desirable investment-grade wines.

So don't be intimidated by the region. It's just wine, after all.

Mass Production of Boutique-Quality Wines

The top Bordeaux vineyards have the unique ability to mass-produce wine of unmatched quality. Château Latour, for instance, can produce upward of 15,000 cases per year, and at a quality that almost always results in prices that hold their ground over the years.

This consistency, combined with enormous volumes, makes for a dependable market that allows investors to take large positions, confident that they will be able to offload their stock in the future.

Even in the most-sought-after vintages, a serious investor can collect many pallets of the finest Bordeaux. That is a near impossibility with many investment-grade wines, such as those coming out of California, where vintners often produce just a few hundred cases that are gobbled up by the lucky souls who have for many years been on mailing lists that are generally closed to new entrants.

The mass production of high-quality wines effectively means Bordeaux is a liquid market; you can buy and sell with relative efficiency and relatively quickly because there's almost always a buyer lurking somewhere at or near the current market price.

Longevity of Wines

I touched on longevity in a previous section, but it's one of the characteristics I must mention again here. Through the centuries, top Bordeaux wines have proven time and again that they possess an exceptional ability to live long lives. It is the foundation of their allure among consumers and a bedrock of their success among investors. Some fifty-year-old Bordeaux are as young and vibrant today as the day they were released. Bordeaux's amazing ability to age enables investors to trade these wines over and over again, from collector to investor to, finally, an end consumer who is happy to pay up for a rare, old bottle of the best Bordeaux.

Wine critics, wine experts, and even those with an untrained palate can identify the characteristics that make for a wine's longevity simply from tasting an immature barrel sample. Critics can predict the arc of a given Bordeaux's life cycle, the amount of time necessary to cellar the wine, the window of its peak drinkability, and its ultimate decline.

I don't mean to make it sound as if longevity is a black-and-white science with definitive, numerical variables that simply fall into place with the appropriate calculus and a handheld calculator. This is an art form. As such, these are educated guesstimates that can be off by a year—or eight. But the point remains that Bordeaux wines have been known far and wide throughout history for their proven ability to age, a characteristic that makes them appealing to investors who know the wines aren't likely to go bad quickly.

Dependable Price Appreciation

Nothing on Wall Street is guaranteed. Nothing in the wine market is guaranteed either. But the longevity and predictability of Bordeaux give collectors and investors the conviction that young wines will age gracefully and, thus, be worth more one day, and gives them the confidence to buy and hold older vintages, knowing that they will improve in flavor and appreciate in price.

Because of this predictability, economists like Mahesh Kumar, as well as individual investors, can estimate with reasonable certainty how a Bordeaux's value will appreciate over time and gauge when is the best time to sell.

This expected price appreciation doesn't occur like clockwork. As I've pointed out elsewhere, wine prices are dynamic valuations that can fall as well as rise over relatively short periods. Prices don't rise in straight-line fashion. Nevertheless, history has shown that investment-grade Bordeaux dependably trends higher with the passage of time.

Ultimately, no other region boasts so many wines that possess both the longevity of Bordeaux and the vast, well-established market for back-vintage wines.

The 1855 Bordeaux Classification:
Centuries of Branding Power

Imagine that on Wall Street a gaggle of bankers convened in a smoky chamber in the middle of the nineteenth century and over a few stogies and a couple bottles of French wine determined a list of the best companies that were to be representative of the U.S. stock market, elevating these names to a vaunted position in American financial lore.

OK, that scene didn't actually happen that way, but such a list exists—the Dow Jones Industrial Average, the compilation of America's thirty premier corporate names, arguably the most august listing of publicly traded companies anywhere in the world.

Wine's Dow Jones is the 1855 Bordeaux Classification.

This list, created for the World's Fair in Paris and based on the price hierarchy of the best Bordeaux at that time, was the prime determinant of Bordeaux prices for over 150 years. When I was a child, my father described the 1855 Classification as a contest, where everyone voted on which wines were the best. He explained that for the most part, the winners of 1855 were the winners of today. He oversimplified it for my understanding, but he was essentially correct. A lot has changed in Bordeaux over the last 150 years, but many of those original rankings have remained intact; and today they still continue to carry weight in the price hierarchy of investment-grade wines.

The 1855 Bordeaux Classification identified what were then the region's sixty-one best wines and organized them into five categories known as "growths."

- 4 First Growths   *Premiers Crus*
- 14 Second Growths   *Deuxièmes Crus*
- 14 Third Growths   *Troisièmes Crus*
- 10 Fourth Growths   *Quatrièmes Crus*
- 18 Fifth Growths   *Cinquièmes Crus*

Though more than 150 years old, the Classification is still considered by those involved in the business of growing and trading in the wines of Bordeaux to be fairly indicative of the winegrowing potential of the various estates on the list.

Winemaking technology was extremely limited in the nineteenth century, so the plots' exposure to sunlight, the characteristics of the soil, and drainage were absolutely crucial to a château's ability to produce great wine. Even today, with advanced winemaking technologies, each vineyard's soil and climactic idiosyncrasies come through in the wine's taste. These qualities ultimately distinguish the truly remarkable estates from those that are merely very good. For that reason, the Classification continues to be a prime determinant of the opening prices of many wines in Bordeaux.

Despite technical advances and the ebbing and flowing of a given château's quality and its consumer popularity through the decades, not much has changed with the Classification—the notable exception being Mouton Rothschild, which began as a Second Growth and was upgraded to First Growth status in 1973, after decades of dogged lobbying by its influential owner. The divalike Baron Philippe de Rothschild refused to accept that his wine was anything short of stupendous, once stating that prior to the upgrade, the motto of the wine was *"Premier ne puis, second ne daigne, Mouton suis.* (First, I cannot be. Second, I do not condescend to be. Mouton, I am.) It was later changed to *Premier je suis, second je fus, Mouton ne change pas.* (First, I am. Second, I was. Mouton does not change.)

When Robert Parker first arrived on the scene in the late 1970s, he argued that the 1855 Classification encouraged the higher-ranked châteaux to rest on their laurels. But the rise of his style of authoritative wine criticism spurred most of the classified châteaux to improve their winemaking. Today, the bulk of First and Second Growth châteaux do tend to qualitatively outperform wines lower in the Classification.

The Classification of 1855 precedes and in many cases transcends twenty-first-century concepts of marketing. The sheer staying power of the châteaux that made it onto the list is impressive enough, imbuing each with a brand recognition, a reputation, and an allure with few parallels in other markets. Meanwhile, the soil characteristics, known as *terroir*, which in many ways helped define the original Classification and which impart a sense of place to the wines of Bordeaux, continue to swaddle the region in as much mystique as ever, if not more, exerting a powerful force over the marketplace 150 years after it was established.

How to Read a Bordeaux Label

When you look at a Bordeaux label, you might not immediately understand it, but they are relatively uncomplicated and easy to

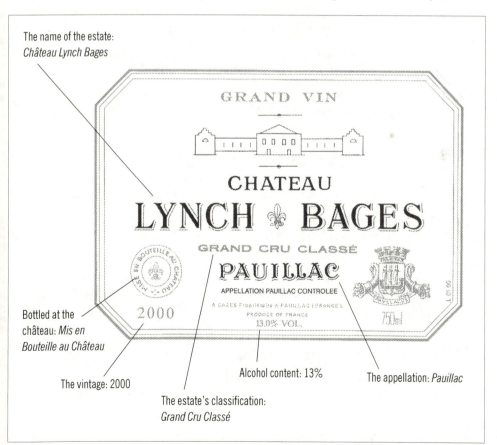

The name of the estate: *Château Lynch Bages*

GRAND VIN

CHATEAU
LYNCH ✦ BAGES
GRAND CRU CLASSÉ
PAUILLAC
APPELLATION PAUILLAC CONTROLEE
A CAZES Propriétaire à PAUILLAC (FRANCE)
PRODUCE OF FRANCE
13.0% VOL.

2000

750ml

Bottled at the château: *Mis en Bouteille au Château*

The vintage: 2000

Alcohol content: 13%

The estate's classification: *Grand Cru Classé*

The appellation: *Pauillac*

read. They tell you everything you need to know about a wine and its birthplace.

Based on what you've read already in this book, you can probably tell fairly quickly that this is the label on a bottle of 2000 Lynch Bages. The appellation indicates that Lynch Bages falls in the Pauillac, effectively the "neighborhood" in the region (in this case, the Bordeaux region) in which the grapes were grown.

In France, the *Appellation d'origine contrôlée* (AOC) laws dictate not only that all grapes must be harvested from a particular appellation in order for that name to appear on the label but also which grapes can be grown in what appellation. These regulations seek to preserve the identities and traditions of each region's wines. For that reason, Bordeaux labels don't indicate what grape varietals go into a particular bottle of wine. That's implied in the appellation's name. By and large, Cabernet Sauvignon, Merlot, and Cabernet Franc are the predominant grapes used, typically in some blend, in Bordeaux wines. Other Bordeaux varietals include Malbec and Petit Verdot for reds, while the grapes used to make white Bordeaux are Sauvignon Blanc and Sémillon.

A River Runs Through It

The wine market typically splits Bordeaux into the "Left Bank" and the "Right Bank" of the Gironde River, which meanders through the region. It might seem a geographically arbitrary division—after all, the wineries are all very close, often touching each other's borders. But in taste, Left and Right Bank wines are fairly distinct from each other because the geography and grape varietals differ markedly.

Left Bank vineyards sit on gravelly soils and are planted chiefly with Cabernet Sauvignon grapes. Right Bank vineyards sit atop mostly clay soils and are planted with Merlot and Cabernet Franc grapes. Due to the differences in soils and the ripening characteristics of the varietals, the wines from one side of the Gironde can perform measurably better than those on the other side of the river

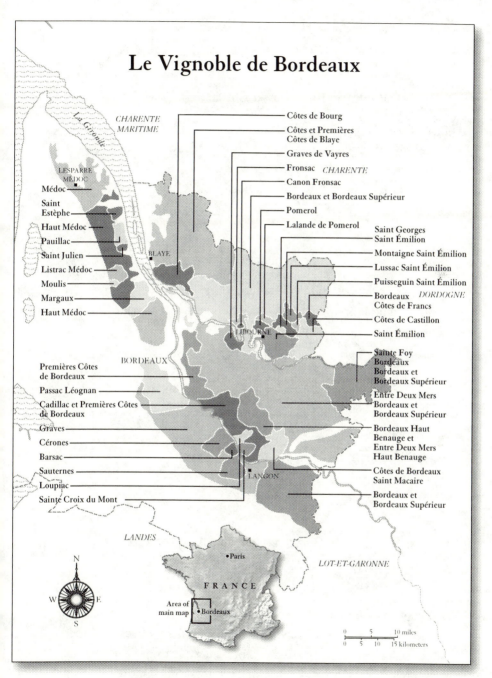

Le Vignoble de Bordeaux

CHARENTE MARITIME

La Gironde

LESPARRE MÉDOC

Médoc

Saint Estèphe

Haut Médoc

Pauillac

Saint Julien

Listrac Médoc

Moulis

Margaux

Haut Médoc

BLAYE

CHARENTE

Côtes de Bourg

Côtes et Premières Côtes de Blaye

Graves de Vayres

Fronsac

Canon Fronsac

Bordeaux et Bordeaux Supérieur

Pomerol

Lalande de Pomerol

Saint Georges Saint Émilion

Montaigne Saint Émilion

Lussac Saint Émilion

Puisseguin Saint Émilion

Bordeaux Côtes de Francs

Côtes de Castillon

Saint Émilion

DORDOGNE

LIBOURNE

BORDEAUX

Premières Côtes de Bordeaux

Passac Léognan

Cadillac et Premières Côtes de Bordeaux

Graves

Cérones

Barsac

Sauternes

Loupiac

Sainte Croix du Mont

Sainte Foy Bordeaux Bordeaux et Bordeaux Supérieur

Entre Deux Mers Bordeaux et Bordeaux Supérieur

Bordeaux Haut Benauge et Entre Deux Mers Haut Benauge

Côtes de Bordeaux Saint Macaire

Bordeaux et Bordeaux Supérieur

LANGON

LANDES

N

W E

S

• Paris

F R A N C E

Area of main map • Bordeaux

LOT-ET-GARONNE

0   5   10 miles
0   5   10   15 kilometers

from one vintage to the next, though in some vintages both sides can be astounding—or underwhelming.

Left Bank and Right Bank: Bordeaux's Geography

LEFT BANK: All the 1855 classified growths are from the Left Bank, most of which is encompassed by the Médoc region.

RIGHT BANK: Many IGW are produced on the Right Bank, though the Classification of 1855 does not apply to this area.

Appellations

Wine-growing appellations are named after their surrounding communities. The Left and Right Bank areas renowned for producing the most investment-worthy wines are:

Left Bank	**Right Bank**
Pauillac	Pomerol
St. Estèphe	St. Émilion
St. Julien	
Margaux	
Pessac Léognan	

Vintage: In Bordeaux It's All About the Year

Numbers over names. That's a rule to remember when it comes to Bordeaux.

Every year represents another opportunity for the Bordelais to do their magic with the grapes that nature has produced and the weather that has rolled across the region. And from year to year wines change because of the natural factors—the rain, the sun, the heat—that go into their growth. For that reason, vintage—or the year in which the grapes were grown, pressed, fermented, and bottled—plays a defining role in Bordeaux. The perception of a given vintage is as important to a Bordeaux's valuation as its individual score. I've watched reasonably priced off-vintage First Growth Bordeaux languish on the market, while the best vintages of the same wines climb to record-setting prices. Even the best vintages of non–First Growth wines have surged in value simply because of the year in which they were born.

Every year, *Wine Spectator* rates Bordeaux's current vintage based upon the quality of the wines as a group. Robert Parker, meanwhile, rates the specific areas or appellations within Bordeaux, since, as I noted above, a vintage that is stellar for one appellation can be mediocre or subpar for another. Below is a list of Bordeaux's most highly collectible vintages, noting the specific appellations to look for in the various years.

- 2005 (all of Bordeaux)
- 2003 (St. Julien/Pauillac/St. Estèphe)
- 2000 (all of Bordeaux)
- 1998 (Pomerol, St. Émilion—none of the Left Bank wines)
- 1996 (St. Julien/Pauillac/St. Estèphe)
- 1990 (St. Julien/Pauillac/St. Estèphe, Pomerol, St. Émilion)
- 1989 (Pomerol)
- 1986
- 1982 (all of Bordeaux, except for Graves and Pomerol)
- 1961

Bordeaux's Distribution

Bordeaux wines can command vastly different prices on release from year to year, subject to the critical acclaim of the vintage. The idiosyncrasies of this market have caused a unique system to evolve for the distribution of Bordeaux.

Châteaux sell their wines exclusively to négociants (Bordeaux wholesalers), who serve to insulate them from market uncertainties by buying mass quantities of everything that they're offered every

year. It's sort of a "use it or lose it arrangement" in that the négociants either buy their entire allotment or lose their coveted allocations. The négociants are offered wine futures, newly bottled
releases, and back-vintage rereleases.

When selling to their own customers, the négociants, in turn,
tie in less desirable wines with their investment-worthy ones. Tie-
ins can be passed along at all levels of distribution, even at retail.
Négociants and their clients who request greater quantities of off
vintages are rewarded with larger allocations of great vintages in
subsequent years. Not every négociant deals with every château,
and most of the allocations are channeled through the ten largest
négociants.

Wine as Collectible Art?

In my view, high-end merchants of investment-grade Bordeaux are
transforming from retail salespeople into a new kind of art dealer,
and London's *Financial Times* seems to agree with this view:

> It is not just life that imitates art. Fine wine does, too. Like
> the art market, the fine wine market has lately experienced a
> vertiginous run-up in prices. The 2000 Bordeaux first
> growths (Margaux, Mouton, Lafite, Latour, and Haut Brion)
> and their Right Bank equivalents (Pétrus, Lafleur, Cheval
> Blanc, Ausone) have doubled in price in the past three years,
> while the 2005s opened in the stratosphere and will almost
> inevitably climb higher still. . . . The Liv-ex 100, the wine
> world's version of the S&P 500, is up 64 percent this year.
>
> . . . Princeton University economist Orley Ashenfelter, a
> well-known oenophile . . . does not believe that the fine
> wine market is experiencing a bubble. He . . . contends that
> the La Tâches and the La Moulines have essentially ceased
> to be wines and have instead become collectibles . . . he also
> concedes that the most highly acclaimed wines have gener-
> ated stellar returns over the past 25 or so years. "My pharma-

cist collects all the first growths in each vintage and stores them perfectly but he doesn't drink them. He has often asked me if he should sell his collection and I've always said: 'Yes, the prices can't go higher.' He has wisely ignored my advice."

And, of course, if there really is a fine wine bubble and if it does eventually pop, the Latours and Lafites at least offer something that no other collectibles can claim: they can be consumed. Try eating a Picasso.

The Three Price Tiers of Bordeaux IGW

I mentioned earlier that twenty years ago my father identified three price tiers that explain why Bordeaux with a higher pedigree, but maybe a lower score, can typically command more money than a higher-scoring wine with a lower pedigree. Now's the time to explain how this works.

Twenty years ago, the number of Bordeaux producers making wines that qualify as IGW category totaled about thirty. Today, many of these names have remained unchanged, but the list has expanded to about 118, largely because the overall quality of wines being produced has increased and because the market has grown so dramatically.

My revised list of the 118 Bordeaux IGW producers is similarly divided into three price tiers. I classify the producers based on the price histories of their wines over the past three decades. As a rule of thumb, the release prices of Second-Tier wines are 25 to 50 percent of those in the First-Tier Bordeaux, and the release prices of the Third-Tier wines are about 5 to 30 percent of those of the First-Tier wines.

First-Tier IGW: The best of the best: 11 wines
Second-Tier IGW: "Super Second Growths": 26 wines
Third-Tier IGW: Rising stars: 81 wines

First-Tier Bordeaux IGW: The Best of the Best

The top eleven châteaux in Bordeaux produce some of the most sublime, sought-after luxury goods in the world, among the few purchases left that can still excite people whose wealth has provided them with anything and everything they want.

In the greatest vintages, these wines are among the few material things that money can't buy, since they are not always for sale. This only adds to their allure, as well as to their upside potential for the wine investor.

First-Tier Bordeaux consist of the most famous names in wine, and this group has probably been the most profitable sector of wine investment over the last twenty-five years. Like Picassos, Monets, and other classic masters, these First-Tier Bordeaux constantly top their own price records. No matter what absurd price a collector paid to acquire these wines in the 1980s, 1990s, and 2000s, someone else has always come along to pay even more. Thus, First-Tier Bordeaux have a solid, bankable track record. Most of them have been in favor for more than 150 years, and they show no signs of waning popularity. Like all collectibles, these wines' prices can be subject to global economic forces, but if life as we know it continues, it's a fairly secure bet that these select Bordeaux—particularly the greatest examples from the premier vintages—will continue trading at higher prices than they command today.

Like economic indicators that point out when the country is pulling out of recession, First-Tier IGW are bellwethers of prosperity. Routinely I've found they are among the first luxury items consumers demand when the economy is looking brighter, and they are the last to be disposed of during the downturns. After all, you can always go back and buy shares of IBM cheaper. But you might never again have the chance to buy the 1945 Latour. Thus, wines are not like stocks that investors dump with little emotion.

For these reasons, First-Tier IGW are among the best and most secure wines for investment. Despite all of this upside potential, though, First-Tier IGW face a constant concern that "this time, the

First-Tier Bordeaux IGW

LEFT BANK	RIGHT BANK
Haut Brion	Ausone
Lafite Rothschild	Cheval Blanc
La Mission Haut Brion	Lafleur
Latour	Le Pin
Margaux	Pétrus
Mouton Rothschild	

PRICE RANGE OF FIRST-TIER BORDEAUX IGW

Current Release Prices: $600–$3,000 per bottle
Highest-Priced Back Vintages: $1,000–$15,000 per bottle

prices can't go any higher." That, though, depends upon your time horizon.

During a trip to Bordeaux in the spring of 2006, I was complaining about the price of 2005 Latour to Thomas Duroux, the winemaker at Château Palmer. At the time we were drinking a $4,000 bottle of 1959 Latour, which was still delicious but clearly at the end of its life cycle. Thomas said that 1959s likely wouldn't be appreciating in value over the next two decades, and he asked me what price the 2005 Latour would trade at in twenty years. I considered that the 100-point wine had at least another fifty years ahead of it and that 2005 is considered to be one of the greatest vintages in history. My answer was "Higher than its current $1,000 price—and higher than the $4,000 price of this bottle of 1959!" On reflection, I think the 2005 Latour could well march toward $15,000–$20,000 per bottle by the time 2028 rolls around. More important for investors with a shorter horizon, I can see price tags hovering around $1,600 by 2013, just five years from now.

One of the Greatest First-Tier Bordeaux of All Time

I could spend 1,000 words trying to define what the perfect Bordeaux tastes like, but why reinvent the cork when Robert Parker used only the 215 words below to accomplish the same task?

1982 Mouton Rothschild   100 Points

I decanted the wine in the morning and consumed it that evening and again the following evening. It is immune to oxidation! Moreover, it has a level of concentration that represents the essence of the Mouton terroir as well as the high percentage of Cabernet Sauvignon it contains. Cassis, cedar, spice box, minerals, and vanillin are all present, but this opaque black/purple Pauillac has yet to reveal secondary nuances given its youthfulness. It exhibits huge tannin, unreal levels of glycerin and concentration, and spectacular sweetness and opulence. Nevertheless, it demands another decade of cellaring, and should age effortlessly for another seven or eight decades. I have always felt the 1982 Mouton was perfect, yet this immortal effort might be capable of lasting for 100 years! Readers who want to drink it are advised to decant it for at least 12–24 hours prior to consumption. I suggest double decanting, i.e., pouring it into a clean decanter, washing out the bottle, and then repouring it back into the bottle, inserting the cork, leaving the air space to serve as breathing space until the wine is consumed 12–24 hours later. The improvement is striking. The fact that it resists oxidation is a testament to just how youthful it remains, and how long it will last. Anticipated maturity: 2010–2075.

Robert Parker, *The Wine Advocate*

Why First-Tier Bordeaux IGW Are Increasing in Price

- The production of these wines has remained static for 200 years and cannot increase because the vineyards are land-constrained. They have nowhere else to go.
- The increase in global wealth has created a larger group of people able to afford and willing to buy these wines of limited production at any cost.

- The quality levels of these wines have improved. The best vintages of Château Latour and Margaux made today are better than any of their predecessors.
- Due to modern winemaking technology, these wines require less bottle age to become drinkable. This allows them to become scarcer sooner and to increase in value sooner.
- The reputations of these eleven estates have few rivals in this sector of the luxury-goods market.

The Effect of Scores on First-Tier Bordeaux Prices

100 POINTS: When a First-Tier Bordeaux receives a 100-point score, the effect on price is incredible, largely because between Parker and the *Wine Spectator,* only fifty-nine First-Tier Bordeaux have ever earned this top rating.

100-point First-Tier Bordeaux are the most expensive wines on the planet, and they're produced in case quantities large enough that you actually have a chance at buying a sizable allotment. These wines continually set the bar for the highest prices that other Bordeaux wines can fetch in any given vintage, and their prices can affect prices for the entire IGW market. Effectively there is no price ceiling on these wines. Every time a price level is reached, it is eventually breached.

There is an unusual collector fascination with these 100-pointers, and it's a trend worth investing in—albeit an expensive one. At the time of this writing, 1982 Mouton was selling for $1,500 per bottle, a hefty price tag for sure. Despite that, I expect it to trade up to $3,000–$4,000 per bottle by 2013. They simply know no peers, anywhere in the world.

99 POINTS: All that I said about 100-point Bordeaux pretty much applies to 99-point Bordeaux as well.

These tend not to have a price ceiling either, and they routinely trade at higher prices than their lower-ranked peers. There are very few 99-point Bordeaux wines on the market, and they, too, have

made for some of Bordeaux's most profitable investments throughout the years. Your cost basis is likely to be considerably lower than
on a 100-pointer, though your eventual exit price could be close to
that of the higher-rated wine—meaning 99-pointers can be smarter
investments.

95–98 POINTS: When a First-Tier Bordeaux receives a score in
the 95–98 point range, this causes excitement among almost all of
its collectors. A First-Tier Bordeaux in this range is a big wine and
worthy of investment. Honestly, this is the target zone most investors should focus on, since most IGW score in this range. That
means many more opportunities for investment at far more reasonable prices.

Many end consumers don't want to pay for perfection, but they
do demand greatness. So they chase the 95- to 98-point First-Tier
Bordeaux. Currently, there are underpriced Bordeaux in this point
range available on the market. For example: 1995 Mouton Rothschild, rated 95 points by Parker, presently sells for $399 per bottle
while the 2005 Mouton future, rated (93–95) sells for $600 per bot-
tle. Even though 2005 is perceived to be a better vintage than 1995,
the points and price differential don't make sense. This is the type of
wine and price mismatch that you want to seek out as a wine investor. By the way, I expect that '95 Mouton will trade for $800–$1,000
per bottle by 2013—an annualized rate of return of between 15 and
20 percent, a meaningful return for a five-year holding period.

90–94 POINTS: The common wisdom used to be that First-Tier
Bordeaux rated in this range would rarely make for smart investments unless your cost of acquisition was far below the current market price. Recently, with the expansion of the global client base,
combined with the Asian market's lack of sensitivity to reviewer
scores relative to the overriding demand for wines with the biggest
names, these First-Tier Bordeaux have become good investments
and could continue to be. It all depends on how emerging markets
will come to value the reviewer point system.

For now, you could focus on wines like 1998 Latour, whose low rating of only 90 points by Robert Parker is offset by its low price of under $300 per bottle. With the 2006 Latour future scoring (93–96) and opening at more than $550 per bottle, the 1998 could have room to appreciate over the next few years. However, I'm not sure what price it might achieve given the uncertainty of just how the emerging markets will take to reviewer scores. My advice: If you're investing here, make sure you're buying wines that *you* like. Because if emerging-market consumers eventually gravitate toward reviewer scores, prices of the First-Tier Bordeaux in this range could stagnate, maybe even slip, as demand wanes. That would mean these are bottles you'll drink with dinner.

The Effect of Vintage on First-Tier Bordeaux Prices

Among First-Tier Bordeaux, vintage plays a variety of roles. Bordeaux collectors are hypersensitive to vintage and can sometimes overlook the score in favor of the year. Conversely, high-scoring wines from an unheralded vintage can be overlooked and not perform as great investments unless the entry price point is low.

BEST VINTAGES: When coupled with a high score, these vintages effectively have no price ceiling. Even wines with scores in the mid-90s will trade up during the best vintages. Perfect examples come from 1982, 1990, and 2000. Collectors want anything they can get from those years. The very best vintages—the so-called vintages of the century, like 1945—can basically become household names among wine's cognoscenti.

VERY GOOD VINTAGES: These vintages can trade to extremely high levels with the added support of higher scores. These wines tend to appreciate when the prices of the best vintages escalate, making these alternatives seem cheap by comparison.

Example: 1983 was a very good vintage in the appellation of Margaux but nowhere else in Bordeaux that year. Therefore, the market's overall perception of the 1983 Bordeaux vintage is that it's not so good, really. In 2007, the 1983 Château Margaux, although rated 99 points by Robert Parker, was selling for $800, approximately half the price of the 1982 vintage of that wine, even though the latter was rated at only 94 points. Vintage is the only differentiator.

Personally, I think that '83 Margaux is the equivalent of an underappreciated value stock. The price, from my vantage point, is likely to double over the next three to five years because there's a lack of drinkable back-vintage First-Tier Bordeaux with great scores, and that '83, as of this writing, trades at a $200 discount to the '05 Margaux futures—the still-in-the-barrel Margaux—which will not be drinkable until 2015, at the earliest.

AVERAGE/BAD VINTAGES: In the past, off vintages of First-Tier Bordeaux haven't fared well as investments, unless you were able to acquire them at prices significantly below market value. The recent spike in global demand suggests that the prices of these wines will increase in the same way that wines with lower scores are increasing. This goes back to the way emerging markets perceive those 90–94-rated First-Tier Bordeaux: The purchases at this point are based almost exclusively on brand appeal, so it's possible that this sector could reap more rewards than seasoned wine investors might anticipate. Be on the lookout for low-cost wines from off vintages by First-Tier producers.

But again, be warned: If emerging-market consumers begin to move past brand-name concentration, then the average/bad vintage wines you own might just become the bottles you pass around the table at your next meal.

The Downside of First-Tier Bordeaux

In this tier, we have those high—sometimes insanely high— entry-level prices. With wines in the multithousand-dollar-per-bottle range, the span of investors and consumers who can play in this sector of the Bordeaux market is relatively limited.

Dave Sokolin's First-Tier Bordeaux Predictions

OVERALL MARKET: Expect all First-Tier Bordeaux in every vintage to appreciate due to growing global demand, especially from emerging markets.

1982s: The current thirst for 1982 Lafite, Margaux, Latour, Mouton, and Cheval Blanc is unprecedented and will continue to grow, leading to ever-higher prices for these châteaux.

2005s: Even though this is the most expensive vintage ever released in Bordeaux, it is arguably one of the very best. To my taste, no other vintage has the fresh quality that is rampant in the '05s, although some can match the fruit. I think these wines are a great deal, especially compared to the 2006s, which aren't that much less expensive and aren't nearly as desirable. All '05 Bordeaux rated 95 and above from my lists of First through Third Tier will trade up in price, over time.

WINES TO WATCH: Expect Château Ausone to soon command the same prices as Pétrus, particularly in the 2000, 2003, and 2005 vintages, and going forward, in any future vintage that is stellar. This château certainly has no price ceiling.

Château Lafite Rothschild is a favorite in Asia, as is this producer's second wine, Carruades de Lafite. Expect every vintage of these two wines to move up.

Châteaux Latour and Margaux have taken serious, positive leaps in quality since the 2000 vintage, and that has made the efforts of these châteaux more valuable. Expect release prices and back-vintage prices to continue escalating.

Château Ausone Case Study

Even belles of the ball get bloodied from time to time, a fate that befell Château Ausone, a winery that dates to the eighteenth century and reputedly sits atop land owned back in the 300s by its namesake, the Bordeaux statesmen and poet Decimus Magnus Ausonius.

Though one of the great names of Bordeaux, Ausone throughout the 1970s, '80s, and into the '90s was producing wines that routinely earned rankings in the 80s and low 90s—some in the low 70s—making them middling at best and all but lost among Bordeaux's heavyweights.

But in 1995 a new proprietor, Alain Vauthier, took control of the château. Today, Ausone is a reinvigorated winery that has joined the ranks of the First Tier, an almost unprecedented event. After scoring 100 points from Robert Parker in the 2000 and 2003 vintages, plus a (98–100) range for the 2005 future, Ausone found itself swathed in an aura generally reserved for cult wines and the mighty names like Latour and Lafite.

Accordingly, the market reclassified Château Ausone, a fact witnessed by consumers paying as much as $2,000 per bottle for any one of these three immature, yet great vintages.

This sort of price appreciation isn't likely to have occurred with a wine from a lesser-pedigreed vineyard. Expect price increases on back vintages, starting with 1995, when Vauthier brought about a revolution in the quality of this estate's wines.

Second-Tier Bordeaux IGWs: "Super Second Growths"

Today's market has reorganized the 1855 Classification. Wine buyers are willing to pay up for a larger pool of Second-Tier Bordeaux, known in the trade as Super Second Growths. Although many of these wines were actually classified as Second Growth Bordeaux in 1855, some of the Super Seconds actually come way down in the ranks of the Fifth Growth châteaux, such as the world-renowned Château Lynch Bages. Moreover, some of the newer Right Bank estates, which did not exist in 1855, fall into the price tier of Super Seconds today.

This pool of Bordeaux's second-best wines offers profit potential for two key reasons: (1) There is a built-in customer base of former First Growth buyers now priced out of their traditional market, and they're buying the next best alternative; and (2) these wines have improved dramatically in recent decades and are currently priced at or below wines of lesser pedigree from California, Spain, and Italy.

Although Super Second quality and longevity can rival that of the hallowed First-Tier wines, even the absolute best example of the Super Seconds have price ceilings that keep them at roughly 25 to 50 percent of the prices of their similarly rated First-Tier peers. Nevertheless, Super Seconds can be profitable investments, with a $200 bottle of 2000 Lynch Bages doubling in a few years. Who's going to complain about that?

Second-Tier Bordeaux IGW

LEFT BANK	RIGHT BANK
Calon Ségur	Clinet
Cos d'Estournel	Figéac
Ducru Beaucaillou	La Clusière
Grand Puy Lacoste	La Conseillante
Haut Brion Blanc	L'Angélus
Laville Haut Brion	Larcis Ducasse
Léoville Barton	L'Église Clinet
Léoville Las Cases	L'Évangile
Léoville Poyferré	Pavie
Lynch Bages	Tertre Rôteboeuf
Montrose	Troplong Mondot
Palmer	Trotanoy
Pichon Longueville Baron	Valandraud
Pichon Lalande	Vieux Château Certan

PRICE RANGE OF SECOND-TIER BORDEAUX IGW

Current release prices: $90–$300 per bottle
Highest-priced back vintages: $300–$5,000 per bottle

Greatness in Second-Tier Bordeaux

There's no question that First-Tier Bordeaux are some of the most exquisite liquids ever bottled. But that doesn't mean a Super Second can't step up and uncork a huge, valuable wine itself. Consider this commentary.

2003 Cos d'Estournel   **99 Points**

The prodigious, fantastic 2003 Cos d'Estournel is a candidate for "wine of the vintage." A blend of 68% Cabernet Sauvignon (unusually high for this château), 30% Merlot, and 2% Cabernet Franc, 17,500 cases were produced from low yields. An inky/blue/purple color is accompanied by a compelling perfume of black fruits, subtle smoke, pain grille, incense, and flowers. With extraordinary richness, full body, and remarkable freshness, elegance, and persistence, this is one of the finest wines ever made by this estate. The good news is that it will be drinkable at a young age yet evolve for three decades or more. Kudos to winemaker Jean-Guillaume Prats and owner Michel Reybier.

Robert Parker, *The Hedonist's Gazette*

For the record, this '03 effort began life priced at about $75 a bottle and as of mid-2007 sells for nearly $200.

The best part for investors is that there is a growing market of consumers looking for premium Bordeaux wines priced between $100–$400 per bottle. These Second-Tier Bordeaux fill that role because, at least for the time being, many of these high-scoring wines fall into that price range.

Why Super Seconds Increase in Price

■ Historically, the correlation between the prices for Super Seconds and their First-Tier counterparts has been similar in that, as the top class rises, the rest float up as well. The difference is that the Super Seconds move along a curve that is less steep.

■ In recent years, the price gap separating First- and Second-Tier châteaux has grown abnormally large, due mainly to the huge re-valuation the '05 vintage had on the highest end of the market. The good news for investors is that this revaluation of the world's best wines will only serve to push prices of the Second-Tier Bordeaux higher.

■ With respect to other winemaking regions, Bordeaux's Super Seconds are currently underpriced. These wines consistently demonstrate greater demand, and both their pedigree and their trading histories are superior. If only they did not live under the shadow of the First-Tier Bordeaux, these Super Seconds would be considered the best wines in the world.

For my money, the Super Seconds represent a potentially wonderful arena for an investor, because there's room for significant price appreciation as this lower-priced category is pulled along in the wake of ascending prices for First-Tier wines.

Scores and Vintage: Numerical Impacts on the Super Seconds

SCORES: In short, scores have a far greater impact on the Super Seconds than on the First Tier, if only because the First Tier are gold-plated brand names that are almost always in demand, while names like Clinet and L'Angélus aren't immediately as recognizable among wine lovers. For that reason, the Super Seconds typically need a big score to stand out; otherwise they're largely lost among the crowd of wines that are released every year.

Investors, then, should stick to Super Seconds with scores of at least 95. Anything below that should not be considered investment-grade, though they'll be good, relatively affordable wines to impress friends when out at dinner one evening.

VINTAGE: The same trend holds here. Second-Tier Bordeaux pricing is always more sensitive to the wine's vintage than is that of First-Tier châteaux.

Big vintages, as I noted earlier, have the power to almost single-handedly drive the price for Bordeaux, and that's especially true of the Super Seconds. Amid a blockbuster vintage, First-Tier prices go nuts. So, too, do the Super Seconds, but again, not to the same level. When consumers get around to drinking a superb vintage, they will eagerly gobble up the Super Seconds because even though the prices are big, they're not nearly as big as the prices for the superstar First-Tier wines.

And just as lower scores should be avoided by investors, so too should vintages that are widely considered weak. What's the point of owning a less-than-stellar brand name in a vintage no one cares about? With a decent score, a Super Second in an off vintage might appreciate over time, but the degree of appreciation will be subpar to what you'd get with its counterpart from a great vintage. Therefore, avoid off vintages for investment purposes—though, once again, these can be phenomenal wines for you to consume.

The Downside of Being Number 2

No one ever remembers who came in second. It's the sad fate assigned to those who are "almost good enough to be the best."

Super Second wines, while almost good enough to be the best, nevertheless aren't the best. These wines cannot trade as high as First-Tier Bordeaux. You will undoubtedly see many a joyous gain over the long term by investing in wines from Second-Tier châteaux, but ultimately you should extinguish any dreams that these wines might just one day muster enough demand to tippytoe their way up into the stratospheric price levels attained by stars like Latour or Ausone or Pétrus. No Super Seconds are good enough to play in that rarified air.

Also, some of these châteaux produce wines in Texas-sized quantities, and all that Bordeaux flowing about—even if it does have a big score from a big vintage—can affect the wine's ability to appreciate to the highest levels.

Dave Sokolin's Second-Tier Bordeaux Predictions

OVERALL MARKET: The great vintages—again, 1982, 1990, 2000, and 2005—all have big potential, simply because these vintages are seen as the best in modern times. Consumers and collectors have these vintages etched into their collective consciousness, and they instinctively gravitate toward the best.

But beyond the great vintages, Super Seconds in the above-average vintages should fare well, too, given that they function in a price range that is more accessible for a larger group of discerning consumers.

1982s: Château Léoville Las Cases was trading at $750 per bottle in mid-2007. I'd expect it, along with its 100-point Robert Parker–rated sibling Château Pichon Lalande, to trade for over $1,000 per bottle in the near term. The 1982 Château Cos d'Estournel is trading at $500 per bottle, and it will sell for more than $750 per bottle by 2010.

WINES TO WATCH: Cos d'Estournel is one of most highly sought-after châteaux among clients of D. Sokolin Company. This château's best vintages once topped out at about $200 per bottle. Soon you'll have to ratchet that up by a factor of five. Already the '82 has hit $500 a bottle.

Pichon Lalande has a new owner and prices that have already started to nudge higher. That's likely to continue under the new regime—but, then again, the wine is worth it. Look for cheaper back vintages—1986, 1989, 1990, 1995, 1996—and expect the château's best vintages, such as 2000, to hit new price levels of more than $400 per bottle, up from its mid-2007 level of $225.

Château Palmer has a new winemaker who will push this wine's quality even closer to that of a First Growth than it already is. That push, along with Palmer increasing its release prices, has the potential to significantly recalibrate prices for this château's back-vintage wines.

Château Lynch Bages is a wine once famous for being a great value for the rating, long trading in the $60–$100 per bottle range. Those days are gone. The quality remains, but the wines are now quickly moving into the $200–$400 range, especially in legendary vintages like 1989 and 2000.

Like Palmer, Château Montrose has hit a new quality level, and the word is spilling out. High-scoring vintages like those from 2003 and 2005 will double in price, even though they are already priced higher than older vintages of Montrose.

Château Pavie is a potential First-Tier Bordeaux, with several of its best vintages approaching $500 per bottle. This wine is a Parker darling and has garnered high scores in every vintage since 1998. Expect to see the '00 Pavie trade up to near $1,000 per bottle—or possibly above—by 2013.

Third-Tier Bordeaux IGW: Rising Stars

Don't let Third-Tier status deter you. These are potentially the most interesting and profitable wines in Bordeaux. While the market might place lower values on these wines at lower prices, the possibility you have to consider as an investor is that some of these châteaux can easily jump up to Second-Tier pricing levels after a château notches a string of high-scoring vintages. The impact of such a run can be that all subsequent vintages of that wine will be priced higher going forward.

Bordeaux's list of rising stars is less about past performance than it is about present greatness and future potential. One of the defining characteristics of Third-Tier wine is the sense of newness, even though many of these wines come from very old châteaux. The common thread running through most of these châteaux is a recent cash infusion or change in ownership that has resulted in noticeably higher-quality wines. Although many of the châteaux in this sector are ancient names in Bordeaux, some are new boutique brands. The value of Third-Tier Bordeaux comes from their recent achievements and critical acclaim. Rising stars, therefore, are a bit like microcap stocks—an area where few investors have the real skills to pick the best and avoid the rest but that represents an opportunity for informed investors to buy into a nice brand before the rest of the world catches on.

Third-Tier Bordeaux IGW

LEFT BANK	RIGHT BANK
Bahans Haut Brion	Barde Haut
Beychevelle	Beau Séjour Bécot
Boyd Cantenac	Beauséjour Duffau
Branaire Ducru	Bellevue
Cantemerle	Bellisle Mondotte
Cantenac Brown	Bon Pasteur
Carruades de Lafite	Canon
Clerc Milon	Canon La Gaffelière
Clos du Marquis	Certan de May
Du Tertre	Chapelle d'Ausone
Duhart Milon	Clos de l'Oratoire
Ferrand Lartigue	Clos Dubreuil
Giscours	Clos Fourtet
Gloria	Croix de Labrie
Gracia	Destieux
Grand Puy Ducasse	d'Issan
Grand Puy Lacoste	Faugères
Gruaud Larose	Fombrauge
Haut Bages Libéral	Fonbel
Haut Bailly	Gazin
Haut Bergey	Grand Mayne
Haut Marbuzet	La Bienfaisance
Kirwan	La Confession
La Lagune	La Croix St. Georges
Lafon Rochet	La Fleur de Boüard

(*continued*)

Third-Tier Bordeaux IGW (*continued*)

LEFT BANK	RIGHT BANK
Lagrange	La Fleur de Gay
Langoa Barton	La Fleur Pétrus
Lascombes	La Mondotte
Les Carmes Haut Brion	L'Arrosée
Les Forts de Latour	Latour à Pomerol
Malartic Lagravière	Le Gay
Maléscot St. Exupéry	Lynsolence
Marojallia	Magrez Fombrauge
Pape Clément	Moulin St. Georges
Pavie Décesse	Pavie Macquin
Pavillon Rouge	Peby Faugères
Pontet Canet	Rol Valentin
Prieuré Lichine	
Rausan Ségla	
Sociando Mallet	
Talbot	

PRICE RANGE OF THIRD-TIER BORDEAUX

Current release prices: $30–$100 per bottle
Highest-priced back vintages: $200–$300 per bottle

Why Third-Tier Bordeaux Increase in Price

■ Third-Tier Bordeaux are underpriced in comparison to their counterparts from Italy and California. Many Brunello di Montalcinos sell for over $150 per bottle, and countless California Cabernets play in that price range as well. Some Third-Tier Bordeaux have been stuck in a tradition that has held their prices down. The market is quickly recalibrating, and the trick is to catch this trend as early as possible.

For example, the '05 La Lagune is an exceptional, delicious wine

A Rising Star Rises:
A Third-Tier Wine Jumps to the Second Tier

Just to prove that the Third Tier isn't comprised of a bunch of wannabes that will never amount to much beyond a fairly decent glass of Bordeaux with your steak and pommes frites, consider this Parker commentary on a 2005 Bordeaux that, as of this writing, remains in barrel.

2005 Château Larcis Ducasse   (96–100) Points

This offering has been controversial as its price increase ranged between 300–400%, but this is a great terroir, and since the remarkable winemaking team of Nicolas Thienpont and Stéphane Derenoncourt took over in 2002, Larcis Ducasse is finally showing its true colors. Located near Pavie, it possesses undeniable potential as demonstrated by the profound 2005. A 3,000-case blend of 78% Merlot, 20% Cabernet Franc, and 2% Cabernet Sauvignon fashioned from yields of 27 hectoliters per hectare, it underwent all of the standard *garagiste* winemaking techniques. It is not surprising that just about all the famous estates in this neighborhood on the Côte Pavie, including Pavie and Troplong Mondot, did unbelievably well in 2005. A dark, dense purple color is followed by an extraordinary perfume of roasted herbs, espresso, tapenade, crème de cassis, and sweet kirsch. It is a wine of sheer opulence, extravagant richness, sweet tannin, and an amazingly layered texture as well as length. A blockbuster with superb elegance, finesse, and precision, it represents an exceptional achievement. Kudos to everyone involved for turning out this modern day legend. Anticipated maturity: 2011–2030.

Robert Parker, *The Wine Advocate*

This Larcis Ducasse in the summer of 2007 was trading on Liv-ex for $1,800 a case, or $150 a bottle, the highest price for any wine available from this château. This also bolsters the point made a few pages back about Third-Tier wines with high scores in a big vintage. The Larcis owes a lot to the kind hand of Mother Nature in 2005, and because its score is so high, there's a fine chance this wine's price will increase as well.

Margaux's on a Roll

I believe that certain wines from a few renowned and revamped estates in the region of Margaux, such as Château Giscours, are primed to price-appreciate. The Margaux appellation is almost a brand in itself, and I believe that many of these wines are currently underpriced with respect to their level of quality.

2003 Giscours, which most recently scored 93 points in a Parker blog, will eventually trade in the $100 range in the next five years, though it was trading at around $50 at the time of this writing. There's good potential for a handsome profit to be made in wines from a number of high-achieving Margaux estates.

with serious longevity ahead of it. The qualitative equivalent of this wine in California would exceed $100 per bottle, while 2005 La Lagune sold for a remarkably low opening price of only $35 a bottle. By 2007, it had climbed to about $50, and I would expect this is a wine that can reach $120 by 2013. While those nominal numbers don't seem as astonishing as a $2,000 bottle of wine, you can't whine too much about an expected 19 percent annualized return on investment.

■ Many Third-Tier estates have incredible brand-name equity. Although some did fall on hard times between the Second World War and the 1990s, they've now recovered and there's a renaissance in many of these châteaux that has gone largely unnoticed, masked by their 92–94-point scores.

Scores and Vintage:
Numerical Impacts on the Third Tier

Don't expect these wines to get 100 points. None has—yet. A few of the '05 Third Tier Bordeaux have the potential for a 100-point score since several picked up ratings of (96–100) in the futures market. If one of them lands that coveted 100-point score once bottled, history will be made.

The sweet spot for investors in Third-Tier Bordeaux is 94–99 points.

Interestingly enough, Château Lascombes received 94 points from Robert Parker in the ordinary 2001 vintage, but it quickly became an IGW. (This might disprove my earlier statements about the importance of vintage, since '01 was not a knockout vintage, Overall, this is an exception rather than the rule.)

Lascombes aside, stick to the best vintages when investing in the Third Tier, such as 2000, 2003, and 2005. Research also the history of the estate, looking in particular for signs that the château has been consistently improving its quality and building a better, more reputable wine. Invest in the more recent vintages in this sector, and shy away from older wines that, despite having once received a high score, may have already hit their peak of drinkability.

The Downside of Third-Tier Bordeaux

Aside from the fact that few of these wines consistently register big scores, the biggest deficit Third-Tier investors face is that these

---

The Future of Bordeaux Pricing?

Bordeaux châteaux seek to keep prices from year to year within a price range in an attempt to make almost as much money in bad vintages as they do in great vintages and to keep a constant revenue stream.

As release prices keep rising, a new pricing strategy will have to emerge—one that heavily discounts less desirable vintages and charges an even heftier price for the best vintages, which some people will gladly pay. This will naturally allow lesser vintages that are best for early consumption to go to price-sensitive consumers and for the best vintages to veer off to the highest-bidding investors.

châteaux are not coveted by wealthy connoisseurs and collectors. This makes them potentially more susceptible to economic down-turns. Also, not every Third-Tier château has a track record that ensures that it will remain in this group in the future.

Dave Sokolin's Third-Tier Bordeaux Predictions

WINES TO WATCH: A few Third-Tier stars have begun to emerge since 2003 that resemble Second-Tier Bordeaux in terms of their quality and the reviewer scores and respect they receive. The fol-lowing wines are among those poised to start trading as Super Sec-onds: Pape Clément, Troplong Mondot, and Larcis Ducasse. The quality that began shining in 2003 was exceeded in 2005, and now these châteaux are on a tear. Many of the '05 vintage wines traded for more than $200 per bottle in the futures market in 2007, and they're on track to essentially double, in turn raising the ceiling on what the subsequent vintages can command.

A Note about Points for Wine Drinkers

The bulk of this book is aimed at investing in wine, not drinking it. But what would a wine book be if it didn't offer some advice on imbibing one of the world's greatest beverages?

If you're looking to find an amazing Bordeaux to drink today, look to those rated between 89 and 92 points. They'll definitely cost less—and substantially so—but they'll often be more approachable and drinkable young than higher-scoring counterparts from the same vintage.

A great example: the '90 Calon Ségur. It's a wine rated 93 by *Wine Spectator* and 90 by Robert Parker and admittedly hasn't been an easy sale because of the fairly mediocre score. Despite that, each time I've brought it to a 1990 Bordeaux tasting, people have preferred it to the 1990 Lafite and Margaux, which were still infants and, thus, not yet ready to drink. This is a wine I was selling to clients for $80 per bottle a few years ago, and today it sells for more than $150. It remains a wine I love to drink personally, and one I routinely turn my friends on to.

How Bordeaux Wines Accrue Value

When Bordeaux wines are released, consumers, investors, and collectors buy them and take them off the market, causing supplies to dwindle and prices to rise. These basic market forces are accelerated if a wine receives a high score, which will stimulate increased sales and fuel higher prices.

The initial release price sets the tone for its eventual valuation. In the past, a period of price stagnation during the five years immediately following a wine's release has been the norm. During this period, the wines are usually laid down in cellars, no one is drinking them, and, ergo, there is no demand.

Barring any review upgrades that jostle the price higher, the tipping point occurs when the wines are ready to drink, typically a decade after the vintage. The resultant consumption causes supply to begin shrinking and the prices to move up.

Another variable to keep in mind: the wines' drinkability. Vintages that drink early, such as Bordeaux's 1982, 1990, and other wines that never go "dumb," are wines whose prices appreciate quickly because people start drinking them very young. The '82s were being consumed in 1991, whereas late in 2005, the 1986s weren't being consumed in large numbers because they still weren't in peak drinking condition.

The '86 vintage is considered excellent because of its incredible longevity, but in the eighth year after the respective releases of the 1982s and the 1986s, their relative prices were appreciating in direct relationship to their evolution as drinkable wines. As a result, the '82 supplies were getting depleted on a daily basis and zooming up in price, while '86 prices stagnated.

The best advice across the board is to either buy wines young and cellar them, or buy them when they are close to maturity. We've seen wines that are completely ignored for years, such as the top wines of the 1995 Bordeaux vintage, which was a great year. This wine was released at historically high prices at the time. As is the norm, these prices did not move for many years, as the wines lay all but forgotten in their cellars. But right before they started drinking well, and as the new wines were being released at higher prices, the 1995s started to reappear on the market and their prices have shot up.

Beyond those châteaux, look for wines in vintages after 2000 from revamped Margaux châteaux, such as Giscours, Branaire Ducru, Lascombes, d'Issan, and Kirwan, to name a few. These were trading at $40–$60 per bottle in 2007, and they have the quality to climb toward $200 per bottle in the next decade.

The St. Émilion appellation is also loaded with high-scoring Third-Tier Bordeaux that are priced below $75 per bottle and that are prime candidates for upgrades, such as Clos Fourtet and Destieux.

Pontet Canet is a rising star from Pauillac, with neighbors the likes of Lafite, Latour, and Mouton. This wine is close to First Growth in quality, and the reviewers and the wine-buying public know it. The '05 Pontet Canet is of as high a quality as many California cult wines currently trading for ten times the price. Plus, Pontet Canet benefits from the special soil characteristics of its Bordeaux terroir. Trading at $99 per bottle in mid-2007, this will soon be a bottle of wine for which consumers will be paying $200 to $300.

9

BURGUNDY

Lifestyles of the Rich and Famous

Some of my most memorable experiences with wine have come while tasting red and white Burgundies. At their best, I must admit that these are my favorite wines. Due to the extremely limited production of Burgundy's finest wines, this sector represents no more than about 5 percent of the investment-grade wine market. Burgundy is as fascinating as it is complex, an area where expertise is almost mandatory and where beginners should be wary—assuming you can actually locate and purchase these rare wines.

Unlike Bordeaux, production of most investment-grade Burgundy is minuscule, ranging from one to ten barrels or 25 to 500 cases. Think about that: 25 cases; that's just 300 bottles, not enough to supply some restaurants for a single night's diners. Even 500 cases wouldn't be enough to sate the thirst of the crowd at a pro football game.

Such scarcity presents investors with both a challenge and an opportunity. On the challenge side of the ledger is the fact that it's hard to put together a sizable position of the extremely rare Burgundies that trade up in price. Too many collectors are already lined up, and there's simply not enough to go around. Investors are

Wine Psycho: Profiling the Burgundy Buyer

Hunters know their prey. Whether it's avid fisherman stalking large-mouth bass or FBI profilers chasing fugitives, those who track others know a little something about their quarry before the hunt ever begins. Burgundy investing is no different; you need to understand what's going on inside the buyer's mind. What is it lurking deep in the psyche of Burgundy buyers that compels them to pay as much as $15,000 for a bottle of wine?

Let me break it down for you:

Obsessed: Burgundy collectors are positively fixated on the way that Pinot Noir from a few specific plots of land tastes when it matures (I am, too). There's nothing else like mature Red Burgundy on planet Earth. When you develop a taste for it, you're done. It's an expensive habit, like gambling (I'll explain the element of chance in a moment). But just recognize that collectors of Burgundy essentially can't help themselves. They are so drawn to these wines that their passion for Burgundy borders on fanaticism.

Informed: Many obsessed Burgundy collectors have visited the region and have intimate knowledge about the producers and, more specifically, the individual plots that are each producer's best. They have deep relationships with the merchants who can procure these wines, and they know exactly what they want.

These physical ties to the region instill a sense of vicarious ownership, not unlike that of home buyers who walk through an open-house event and fall in love with the home. They're hooked, and they immediately envision themselves living there. The seller who recognizes this has the upper hand in striking the better bargain.

Rich: Most Burgundy collectors are extremely well off financially, if not

forced to pay a premium well above the release price to own these wines.

The upside of scarcity, however, is that if you do manage to score a case of the best Burgundy from the best years, it will usually trade up in price and continue to do so for a long period of time. The typical strategy in the Burgundy market is overpaying for the best and knowing that there will be someone down the line willing to do the same. Quite simply, Burgundy is a cult of oenology and collectors downright rich. Combine unlimited funds with a profound obsession, and you can see why a small pool of low-production wines can quickly become so expensive. I know plenty of men who have taken their obsession to the ultimate level: They buy vineyards in Burgundy with cartels of their buddies to ensure a supply of their favorite tipple.

Cliquey: The Chevaliers du Tastevin is the most prestigious Burgundy-tasting group in the world. Most serious collectors of Burgundy are members who show off their wine collections to one another at elaborate chapter dinners. Once every two years, the Burgundy harvest festival known as La Paulée comes to New York City, where collectors pay $1,000 a head to eat and drink, although the great wines supplied by the event are generally left untouched. The main event is what the guests bring to the table. Almost everyone, myself included, struts his stuff on these nights. While most show up with bottles in the $4,000 range, the whales lug in $50,000 double magnums of Burgundy—about six pounds of wine that serve nearly twenty people.

After nights like this, you'll often see a run on the Burgundy market as the next day attendees rush to buy the wines that showed the best. Securing the few remaining bottles on the market becomes the primary objective, price be damned.

And that pretty well sums up the collectible Burgundy market: obsessed, informed rich people form an exclusive clique because of price and scarcity. Having celebrated Burgundies in a collection and displaying them at these events doesn't just move a market, it can make it. *Hint:* If you have a truly great Burgundy that you want to sell for a fortune, bring it to La Paulée and pour it for as many well-heeled party attendees as you can.

are always hunting for the best. Unlike Bordeaux, there is such small supply from this region that there are almost no serious aftermarket sellers, making Burgundy a sweet spot for the individual investor with a supply of any back-vintage wines to offer in a market that is desperate to locate any Burgundy at almost any price.

Scarcity aside, the big problem for investors is that, unlike Bordeaux, Burgundy isn't terribly easy to understand. In Bordeaux, the name of the producer is synonymous with the estate on which the

wine was grown and bottled. In Burgundy, the wines' names are associated with the locations in which they are grown. One producer
will often make wines from a variety of vineyards, and the name of
the vineyard is often as important as—or even more important
than—the producer, a fact especially true of Second- and Third-
Tier Burgundy.

The estates of Burgundy have been divided up through the gen-
erations, according to Napoleonic inheritance laws, and today several different winemakers grow their own rows of vines on a single,
world-renowned, tiny plot of land.

As if all that weren't enough, producers' names have routinely
changed over the years, thanks to marriages and divorce, though,
thankfully, what remains constant are the names of the famous
vineyards and the distinct flavors imparted by the certain highly
prized plots of land—the terroirs.

That said, in terms of reputation some of the greatest brand
names in history hail from Burgundy, so much so that many times
the producer's name can far outweigh both the vintage rating and
the wine's score. Burgundy's investment-grade wines are determined chiefly by a combination of the producer's reputation and
the renown of the vineyard's designation. Collectors of Burgundy
buy in every vintage because the best producers are capable of making different shades of greatness every year.

Burgundy is known for both its red and white wines, and both
are investment caliber due to their remarkable longevity, a trait
that's unique given that whites are generally not known for their
longevity and, thus, are largely disregarded as an investment candidate in most other parts of the wine-producing world. The only
simple fact about Burgundies is that at least you don't have to think
about what blend of grapes goes into the wine. Burgundies are not
blends. The great red wines are made strictly from Pinot Noir grapes;
the collectible whites are made exclusively from Chardonnay.

Pinot Noir is a difficult grape to cultivate and to transform into
wine, and when first bottled it can be difficult to gauge, sometimes
tasting thin and acidic. Upon release, red Burgundy rarely elicits

the exuberant reviews that Bordeaux, California, and Italian wines get. Time is a mandatory factor for Burgundy to take on its secondary nuances and for its true greatness to emerge. Anywhere from five to twenty years are required for these nuances to develop. But when they do, few wines from any region can equal the magic of Burgundy.

Indeed, Pinot Noir grapes grown in the most esteemed Grand Cru plots and fashioned into red Burgundy by the best producers in the best vintages are the most expensive wines in the world, priced even higher than Bordeaux's most-sought-after legends. One example: in June 2007 a twelve-bottle original wooden case of the 1990 Domaine de la Romanée-Conti's flagship wine sold for $119,500—nearly $10,000 per bottle.

THE BURGUNDY MYSTIQUE

Whereas Bordeaux is a fairly simple game of high scores, respected reviews, well-known châteaux, and blockbuster vintages, there is a bit of mystery and mystique to the wines of this region:

- **Complex Nomenclature:** Burgundy has hundreds of producers sharing the same small vineyards, making wines with the same names. The only thing that distinguishes one product from another is the producer's name. For instance, there can be 100 wines released each year that list "Gevrey-Chambertin" somewhere on their labels.

- **Ultralimited Production:** Some wines are produced in one twenty-five-case barrel. That's it. No more. When that allotment of bottles is gone . . . well, there's always next year. The largest volume among Burgundy's investment-grade wines peters out at about 800 cases. Consider the 15,000 or so cases that some of the premier Bordeaux release each year and the prices awarded to those wines, and you begin to realize the difference of scale involved.

■ **Uncertain Longevity:** A common misconception about Burgundy is that it cannot age. In some cases, that's true, as the wines can be especially sensitive to storage conditions. But in the category of "every rule has its exceptions," the best Burgundies can age for 100 years. Indeed, some that are more than twenty years old are still considered too young to drink. The long and short of it is that investment-grade Burgundy can age well, giving the wines plenty of time to appreciate in value.

■ **Unpredictable Price Appreciation of Back Vintages:** Not every Burgundy makes it. Sometimes wine from the best producers in the best vintages won't live up to your expectations, while some of the lesser ones will unexpectedly excel. Burgundy is ruled by the fickleness of the thin-skinned Pinot Noir grape, the harvests of which are often subject to frost and hailstorms. Obsessed collectors generally don't lose heart, instead writing off bad vintages and using them as house wines—very expensive house wines. The unpredict-

---

A Burgundy Ghost Story

A friend of mine tells of a recent visit to one of Burgundy's finest First-Tier domaines, which I must keep nameless.

During recent renovations to the domaine's ancient subterranean storage cave, several skeletons were unearthed. Near to this now disturbed gravesite rested the domaine's different wines, maturing in casks.

Not long after the bones were discovered, the winemaker detected a mysterious off flavor in the entire production of this producer's vintage. The spooky irony is that this vintage had been highly rated overall by the critics, and neighboring domaines had all produced top-flight wines.

Sure, there could be any number of reasons for the faulty wines, but some *Bourguignons* began to speculate that the wines were actually haunted.

It was the "Ripley's Believe It or Not!" of wine—fitting for a region so steeped in mystery and amazing that such a rumor can gain any credence in the modern age.

ability of Burgundy is the antithesis of the predictability of Bordeaux, making this a region for the pros.

Appellation and Cru System of Burgundy

Burgundy's vineyard designations, which have existed for centuries, are used to distinguish among 400 different types of soil in this region. Today, the vineyards are regulated by the *Appellation d'origine contrôlée* (AOC).

In addition, the ancient cru system—the equivalent of growths in Bordeaux—indicates the wine-growing potential of a vineyard plot and is uniquely based on the average amount of sunlight the plot receives. This is, after all, northern France, straddling the same latitude as the United States/Canadian border. The crus are divided into Grand Cru, Premier Cru, and AC, or village wines. The main thing for the investor to know is that investment-grade Burgundy comes primarily from the Grand Cru vineyards, though there are exceptional Premier Cru plots.

Collectible Burgundy Vintages

Vintage is extremely important when investing in Burgundy. The great ones don't come around often. When mature, the classic vintages of the best red Burgundies trade up more than any other kind of wine. With global warming, it seems as if a great vintage of Bordeaux can occur several times a decade, but in Burgundy, this is not the case. A very good, investment-worthy vintage will come around once or twice in a decade. However, twenty or more years can sometimes elapse between legendary vintages of red Burgundy. Here are examples of great vintages:

• 2005	• 1993	• 1969
• 2003	• 1990	• 1964
• 2002	• 1985	• 1962
• 1999	• 1978	
• 1996	• 1971	

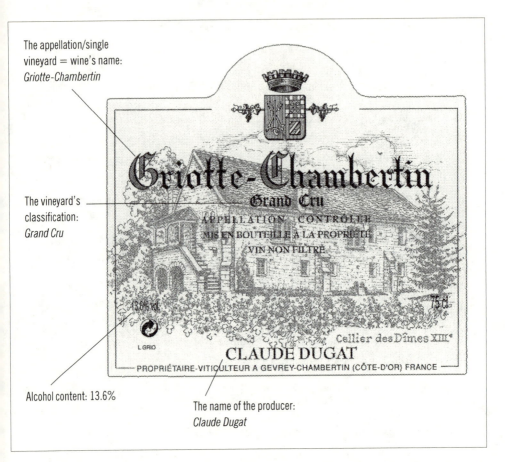

The appellation/single vineyard = wine's name: *Griotte-Chambertin*

The vineyard's classification: *Grand Cru*

Alcohol content: 13.6%

The name of the producer: *Claude Dugat*

How to Read a Burgundy Label

When you look at a Burgundy label, you can instantly see why Burgundy is for connoisseurs. More than in any other region, the hedonism of Burgundy is spiced by more than a little bit of intellectualism. The vineyard, in this case Griotte-Chambertin, is not as important as the producer, Claude Dugat. Adding to the confusion, there are multiple Dugats, making Bordeaux seem easy by comparison.

Burgundy's Grands Crus

REDS	WHITES
Bonnes-Mares	Bâtard-Montrachet
Chambertin	Bienvenues-Bâtard-Montrachet
Chambertin-Clos de Bèze	Chablis Grand Cru
Chapelle-Chambertin	Charlemagne
Charmes-Chambertin	Chevalier-Montrachet
Clos de la Roche	Corton-Charlemagne
Clos des Lambrays	Criots-Bâtard-Montrachet
Clos de Tart	Montrachet
Clos de Vougeot	
Clos Saint Denis	
Corton	
Échezeaux	
Grands Échezeaux	
Griotte-Chambertin	
La Grande Rue	
La Romanée	
La Tâche	
Latricières-Chambertin	
Mazis-Chambertin	
Mazoyères-Chambertin	
Musigny	
Richebourg	
Romanée-Conti	
Romanée-Saint-Vivant	
Ruchottes-Chambertin	

First-Tier Burgundy: High-End Sharecroppers

Burgundy's First Tier is comprised of thirty-nine wines, made by ten of the most respected producers from vines grown on twenty-six different terroirs. And you wonder why Burgundy can be so confounding. Bordeaux is a paint-by-numbers set in comparison. In the most rare instances, some properties are owned by only one producer and are known as *monopoles*. Although to confuse the matter, several of these top wines are made from the same handful of shared Grand Cru vineyards, such as in Musigny, responsible for the four First-Tier Burgundy producers listed below, all of which make world-renowned wines. Burgundy's greatest estate, Domaine de la Romanée-Conti, produces wine from grapes grown on six different plots—three of which are monopoles—and these vineyards produce the most expensive wines of Burgundy.

In my tasting experience, the best vintages of these wines are the best wines ever made. Prices in this sector have no ceiling, and as the proliferation of global wealth marches on, these wines will continue to skyrocket. In terms of the quantity produced and the artistic value, these are the closest things to collectible art that the wine market offers. The following passage from a *Financial Times* article perfectly illustrates the price trends that routinely roll through Burgundy:

> . . . At $400 or $500 a bottle, they say, a wine such as Christophe Roumier's Musigny, produced in minuscule quantities (little more than a barrel annually) from what some insist is Burgundy's finest *grand cru* vineyard, was absurdly inexpensive. For better or worse, the $1,500 or so per bottle that Roumier's 2005 Musigny is fetching more accurately reflects the wine's quality and scarcity. (John Gilman, who publishes a bimonthly review called *View from the Cellar* and who is currently writing a book about Musigny, expects the price of

the 2005 Roumier to rise to over $5,000 a bottle in the next two years or so.)

Some of the First-Tier Burgundies have traded up to such high prices that their owners cannot bear to drink them—yet these same collectors refuse to sell these five-figure bottles of wine, leery of giving up what they've become attached to and recognizing that the price is likely to track even higher.

For others, this is not the case. A high price is good reason to sell.

A good friend of mine owns six bottles of 1978 Domaine de la Romanée-Conti, Romanée-Conti (aka DRC, RC), which my father sold to him years ago for $200 each. Today, those bottles are worth $15,000—apiece. Many a wine collector would balk at drinking such a wine, but this collector doesn't flinch, arriving in the Hamptons each summer with a bottle for us to enjoy.

On the following page, in alphabetical order, are the top Burgundy producers and vineyards to look for.

Why First-Tier Burgundies Are Increasing in Price

- Production has remained static for 200 years and cannot increase.
- Microscopic production combined with a fanatical base of obsessed buyers, as well as a growing global market of new buyers, means inevitably higher prices.
- The reputations of many of these estates are unrivaled by almost any other consumer goods or luxury products.

The Effect of Scores on First-Tier Burgundy

In Burgundy, wine scores are less important than vintage perception and pedigree because collectors know that these producers make great wines every year. However, in the best vintages, Bur-

First-Tier Burgundy IGW

REDS	WHITES
Armand Rousseau Chambertin	Coche-Dury Corton-Charlemagne
Armand Rousseau Chambertin-"Clos de Bèze"	DRC Montrachet
Claude Dugat Charmes-Chambertin	Étienne Sauzet Chevalier-Montrachet
Claude Dugat Griotte-Chambertin	Étienne Sauzet Montrachet
Comte de Vogüé Chambolle-Musigny "Les Amoureuses"	Leflaive Bâtard-Montrachet
Comte de Vogüé Musigny "Vieilles Vignes"	Leflaive Montrachet
DRC Grands Échezeaux	Michel Niellon Bâtard-Montrachet
DRC La Tâche	Michel Niellon Chevalier-Montrachet
DRC Richebourg	Ramonet Bâtard-Montrachet
DRC Romanée-Conti	Ramonet Chevalier-Montrachet
DRC Romanée-Saint-Vivant	Ramonet Montrachet
Dujac Bonnes-Mares	
Dujac Clos de la Roche	
Georges Roumier Chambolle Musigny "Les Amoureuses"	
Georges Roumier Bonnes-Mares	
Georges Roumier Charmes-Chambertin	
Georges Roumier Musigny	
Georges Roumier Ruchottes-Chambertin	
Henri Jayer Échezeaux	
Henri Jayer Nuits-Saint-Georges	
Henri Jayer Nuits-Saint-Georges "Meurgers"	
Henri Jayer Richebourg	
Henri Jayer Vosne-Romanée	
Henri Jayer Vosne-Romanée "Beauxmonts"	
Henri Jayer Vosne-Romanée "Cros Parantoux"	
Henri Jayer Vosne-Romanée "Les Brûlées"	
Leroy Chambertin	
Leroy Clos de la Roche	
Leroy Latricières-Chambertin	
Leroy Grands Échezeaux	

First-Tier Burgundy IGW (continued)

REDS	WHITES
Leroy Musigny	
Leroy Richebourg	
Leroy Romanée-Saint-Vivant	
Ponsot Chambertin	
Ponsot Chapelle-Chambertin	
Ponsot Clos de la Roche "Vieilles Vignes"	
Ponsot Griotte-Chambertin	
Ponsot Latricières-Chambertin	

PRICE RANGE OF FIRST-TIER BURGUNDY IGW

Current release prices: $600–$6,000 per bottle
Highest-priced back vintages: $10,000+ per bottle

gundy producers create magic. With the rise of Allen Meadows (aka "Mr. 90 Points") as Burgundy's most influential critic, many of the best Burgundies in history can be rated at only 95 points. Therefore, Burgundies in this price tier are somewhat insulated from scores.

A great example of this is the 1985 DRC La Tâche, of which I sold a twelve-bottle case for $66,000 in June 2007. Both *Burghound* and Robert Parker rated this wine at 90 points, the latter commenting, "Performances such as this are further proof that Burgundy is indeed the wine for free-spending masochists."

99 AND 100 POINTS: Unlike Bordeaux, very few First-Tier Burgundies are ever rated this high. It's perplexing that some of history's greatest wines do not receive a perfect or near-perfect score when wines with substantially less pedigree and quality from other regions routinely rack up monster scores. Neither Allen Meadows nor Stephen Tanzer, the two critics whose judgments on Burgundy

High-scoring First-Tier Burgundy is the Holy Grail of wine. It's so rare, it's almost mythical. The reviews of these top-rated Burgundy read like effusive love letters to the wine. Reviewers refer to the impossibility of describing the wine or else employ mystifying terms, such as "sève" (which required a Google search to unearth its arcane meaning).

2002 Leroy Latricières-Chambertin   98 Points

. . . the most elegant nose . . . with kaleidoscopic complexity and a breadth of expression to which words cannot do adequate justice. The powerful, unctuous flavors are linear and incredibly detailed yet there is a serene quality to this wine. . . . The finish is painfully intense and builds and builds and then simply explodes and despite the youthful vigor, this is not severe or austere. . . . In sum, this is one of the greatest young Burgundies of my experience and a compelling wine.

Allen Meadows, *Burghound*

1993 Leflaive Montrachet   98 Points

An incredibly fresh nose of intense and extremely expressive white flower and citrus aromas combined with massive yet defined and well-focused, full-bodied flavors that possess solid ripeness and terrific underlying sève plus stunning length, balance and overall harmony. In sum, this is a great success for the vintage as well as the wine is very "Montrachet" in style and character. It can be approached now with much pleasure though to be sure, it will live for another decade plus.

Allen Meadows, *Burghound*

(By the way, "sève" is a French term applied to botany. It is essentially the sap that circulates through a plant to transport nutrients. So, basically, sève is vital liquids.)

are the most watched by the trade, has ever awarded a 100-point score to *any* wine. Of the twelve Burgundies to which *Burghound* has awarded 99 points, most are vintages before 1949. None came after 1992.

Tanzer has never handed out even a 99-point rating to a Burgundy.

In principal, this is fine. Critics are entitled to their opinions on where a wine falls along any given scoring scale. However, I find it humorous that there isn't even room for a third digit—i.e., 100—in the search engine of Meadows's database on *Burghound* .com. From a more serious perspective, though, why should Burgundies be held to a higher standard than Bordeaux? Or, conversely, why should Bordeaux be graded any easier? Both Robert Parker and *Wine Spectator* are more generous, having awarded approximately forty-four red and white Burgundies a rating of between 99 and 100 points.

One thing is certain when it comes to Burgundy: Given the prices these bottles already fetch, if you ever do find a First-Tier Burgundy with a 100-point score, your cost of acquisition will be exorbitant.

95–98 POINTS: Even this is an oxygen-deprived range for many of Burgundy's best efforts. Very rarely will you see Domaine de la Romanée-Conti's best vintages fall into this range, and DRC stands at the pinnacle of the Burgundy market. To put this in perspective, it would be like Latour, Lafite, and Mouton, the quintessential examples of Bordeaux's excellence, rarely earning scores above 95.

Again, pedigree and vintage trump points in Burgundy, but for investment purposes you should keep your eyes peeled for wines in this point range.

90–94 POINTS: More often than not, this is the range in which you will find many investment-grade Burgundies, especially many of the older legends whose reviews are not current.

I'm not saying you should feel comfortable investing in this point range in any other region. But if you're going to buy Burgundy, the reality is that most of the ones you'll want—the ones consumers covet—fall into this range, if only because so few ever get rated any higher.

The Downside of First-Tier Burgundy

First off, even though the merchant makes a market in them, you may never see merchants offer top-flight Burgundies. Most tend to sell them only to their best customers, which is another reason it's wise to buy your wines—both the investment-grade bottles and the stuff you want to drink—from a limited pool of suppliers. It's that you-scratch-my-back-I'll-scratch-yours approach to wine investing. If you routinely show loyalty to a particular merchant, that merchant at some point will feel compelled to give you first look at his new gems.

Second, the price of entry can be so prohibitively high that it makes you wonder if it can ever go higher—and it makes you question whether you can fit the price tag into your budget. Each time a new great vintage is released, the threshold of pain is tested, though ultimately always absorbed. First-Tier Burgundy is the Marquis de Sade. The producers know that because of the scarcity and fanaticism, their clients will take whatever price/pain they wish to inflict—and they wish to inflict a lot.

Dave Sokolin's First-Tier Burgundy Predictions

Again, because great Burgundies exist in such miniscule quantities, they have the potential to trade like one-of-a-kind paintings, especially when older. Don't be afraid to buy and hold at what seem like insane prices. If you have the money, the time, and the fortitude to resist the urge to pop the cork, you stand to make egregious profits.

Personally, I'll argue that every wine among the list of First-Tier Burgundy is headed higher. Although the entry price of the 2005 vintage is steep compared to previous vintages, I'm confident that all of the '05 First-Tier Burgundies will prove profitable. These '05s are the new standards of excellence, and they'll trade up to—and eventually exceed—the legendary 1978 vintage because they have a longer future ahead of them.

Since the prices for the '05s are so high compared to the great vintages of the past, there's an opportunity to purchase older vintages at somewhat friendlier price tags. Years such as 1993, 1995, 1996, 1999, and 2001 can be bought at a discount of typically 20 to 70 percent of the '05s. These older vintages will recalibrate to the new release price levels, possibly as early as 2009.

Second-Tier Burgundy

As with Second-Tier Bordeaux, the rapid and steep valuation of investment-grade Burgundy has priced some First-Tier collectors out of the market. This dislocation has many buyers looking for replacements from neighboring domaines in the Second Tier, a migration that has caused prices of those wines to soar.

Additionally, there are venerable players that fit into this category of high-level Burgundy that just miss the First Tier because their wines do have a price ceiling—though this ceiling is rising at a faster clip than many expected.

Some of these Second-Tier Burgundies can trade at more than $700 per bottle. Many eventually break the $2,000 mark when mature. As such, the Second Tier of Burgundy is higher priced than any other Second-Tier wine in the industry.

Burgundy's Second Tier can be broken down into two groups. The first is made up of wines made by First-Tier producers, but from vines grown on less-pedigreed properties. The remainder of Second-Tier Burgundies are made by less-pedigreed producers, but from vines grown on Grand Cru properties. Basically, the Premiers Crus made by First-Tier producers trade at prices similar to the Grands Crus made by Second-Tier producers. Again, we're back to why Burgundy can be such a confusing category.

In this Second Tier, the hierarchy of producer pedigree has remained unchanged for years, unlike in Bordeaux's Second Tier, where the landscape of producers has changed over the past few decades due to market forces.

Why Second-Tier Burgundies Are Increasing in Price

- Their prices share a historical correlation with the prices of the First-Tier wines, and as First-Tier prices escalate, Second-Tier prices rise along a similar trajectory, but at lower price points.
- The price gap between First- and Second-Tier Burgundies has grown abnormally large, indicating that the high prices of the First Tier will continue to drag this sector upward.

The Effect of Scores on Second-Tier Burgundy

As I've said, in Burgundy pedigree is everything.

But among the Second-Tier wines, points and vintage play a greater role in their pricing. Extremely high scores—again, extremely rare—can help these wines appreciate with greater speed. Collectors focus on vintage reputation and will pay up for back-vintage Second-Tier wines from the great years when these wines are mature.

A relative newcomer, superstar producer Perrot-Minot made some of the finest wines in the '05 vintage. Now they're priced through the roof. Minot's '05 Chambertin "Clos de Bèze Vieilles Vignes" (or VV, which means "old vines") scored a whopping 99–100 points from David Schildknecht, who tracks Burgundy for Robert Parker's *The Wine Advocate*. I can see future vintages achieving similar critical acclaim, which in the Second Tier would flow through directly to pricing.

The Downside of Second-Tier Burgundy

These wines never appreciate as much as First-Tier Burgundy, and the need for an encyclopedic knowledge of the region's esoterica keeps them from becoming household names.

As a result, Second-Tier Burgundies don't achieve the bragging rights and the prices associated with the best. And unlike Burgundy from the First Tier, there's an ego deflator for collectors: You can't

Second-Tier Burgundy IGW

RED	WHITE
Anne & François Gros Clos Vougeot "Le Grand Maupertuis"	Bonneau du Martray Corton-Charlemagne
Anne & François Gros Richebourg	Comte Lafon Meursault "Charmes"
Armand Rousseau Chambertin "Clos des Ruchottes"	Comte Lafon Meursault "Genevrières"
Armand Rousseau Charmes-Chambertin	Comte Lafon Meursault "Les Perrières"
Armand Rousseau Clos de la Roche	Étienne Sauzet Bâtard-Montrachet
Armand Rousseau Gevrey-Chambertin "Aux Combottes"	Étienne Sauzet Bienvenues-Bâtard-Montrachet
Armand Rousseau Gevrey-Chambertin "Cazetières"	Étienne Sauzet Chevalier-Montrachet
Armand Rousseau Gevery-Chambertin "Clos St.-Jacques"	Henri Boillot Bâtard-Montrachet
Armand Rousseau Mazis-Chambertin	Henri Boillot Chevalier-Montrachet
Armand Rousseau Ruchottes-Chambertin	Henri Boillot Corton-Charlemagne
Bernard Dugat Charmes-Chambertin	Louis Latour Montrachet
Bouchard Beaune Grèves "Vigne de L'Enfant Jésus"	Leflaive Bienvenue Bâtard-Montrachet
Bouchard Chambertin "Clos de Bèze"	Leflaive Puligny Montrachet-Combottes
Claude Dugat Gevrey-Chambertin	Leflaive Puligny Montrachet-Pucelles
Claude Dugat Gevrey-Chambertin "Lavaux St.-Jacques"	Château de la Maltroye Bâtard-Montrachet
Clair-Daü Bonnes Mares	Raveneau Chablis Les Clos
Clos de Lambrays	Raveneau Chablis Valmur
Drouhin Musigny	Raveneau Chablis Blanchot
Dujac Chambolle-Musigny	William Fèvre Chablis Bougros
Dujac Charmes-Chambertin	William Fèvre Chablis Bougros "Cote Bouguerots"
Dujac Échezeaux	William Fèvre Chablis Les Clos
Emmanuel Rouget Échezeaux	William Fèvre Chablis Valmur
Emmanuel Rouget Vosne-Romanée "Cros Parantoux"	William Fèvre Chablis Vaudésir
Faiveley Chambertin-Clos de Bèze	
Faiveley Clos de Vougeot	
Faiveley Corton Clos des Cortons	
Faiveley Latricières-Chambertin	
Faiveley Mazis-Chambertin	
Faiveley Musigny	

(continued)

Second-Tier Burgundy IGW (*continued*)

RED

Faiveley Nuits-Saint-Georges "Les St.-Georges"

Georges Lignier Bonnes Mares

Georges Lignier Clos de la Roche

Groffier Bonnes Mares

Groffier Chambertin-Clos de Bèze

Groffier Chambolle-Musigny "Les Amoureuses"

Gros Frère et Soeur Clos de Vougeot "Musigni"

Gros Frère et Soeur Grands Échezeaux

Gros Frère et Soeur Richebourg

Henri Lignier Charmes-Chambertin

Henri Lignier Clos de la Roche

Jean Grivot Clos du Vougeot

Jean Grivot Richebourg

Jacques-Frédéric Mugnier Bonnes Mares

Joseph Roty Charmes-Chambertin

Joseph Roty Charmes-Chambertin "Très Vieilles Vignes"

Joseph Roty Gevrey-Chambertin "Les Fontenys"

Joseph Roty Griottes-Chambertin

Joseph Roty Mazis-Chambertin

Marquis d'Angerville Volnay "Clos des Ducs"

Méo-Camuzet Richebourg

Méo-Camuzet Vosne Romanée Au "Cros Parantoux"

Michel Lafarge Volnay "Clos du Château des Ducs"

Mongeard-Mugneret Bonnes Mares

Mongeard-Mugneret Grands Échezeaux

Mongeard-Mugneret Vosne-Romanée "Les Suchots"

Mommessin Clos de Tart

Ponsot Chambolle-Musigny "Les Charmes"

Ponsot Charmes-Chambertin

Robert Arnoux Clos de Vougeot

Second-Tier Burgundy IGW (*continued*)

RED

Robert Arnoux Romanée-Saint-Vivant

Robert Arnoux Vosne-Romanée "Les Suchots"

Vicomte Liger-Belair "La Romanée"

Vougeraie Bonnes Mares

Vougeraie Musigny

PRICE RANGE OF SECOND-TIER BURGUNDY IGW

Current release prices: $90–$300 per bottle

Highest-priced back vintages: $300–$2,000 per bottle

show these wines off to someone who isn't a total wine geek, because most people have never heard of them. That helps limit price appreciation, because for the collector, showing off your collection is part of the fun.

Dave Sokolin's Second-Tier Burgundy Predictions

Short and sweet:

1. Look for wines by Ponsot, Rousseau, and Arnoux. These are big names associated with quality in Burgundy.
2. Focus on vintage vintage vintage. You will succeed if you confine your purchases to the '05 vintage or pay lower prices for the 1993, 1999, or 2001 vintages of these three producers' wines.

Third-Tier Burgundy

Third-Tier Burgundy consists of both famous-name Second-Tier producers growing in Premier Cru vineyards of ancient pedigree, as well as a group of newer, progressive producers that have used their cutting-edge techniques to elevate their status.

1996 Faiveley Corton Clos des Cortons   **94 Points**

Deep ruby color. Multidimensional aromas of violet, coffee, dried rose, clove, rare steak and seductive oak. Huge and tactile; really implodes in the mouth today. Extremely deep and lush, with the sheer sweetness to buffer its considerable acids and tannins. Oaky. Finishes extremely long, with very fine, tooth-coating tannins. With aeration, some of the baby fat melted away, and the wine's powerful structure was manifest. Headspinning, old-style Burgundy, and very impressive.

Stephen Tanzer, *IWC*

2000 Henri Boillot Chevalier-Montrachet   **96 Points**

Reticent, deep aromas of pineapple, powdered stone and minerals, with a roasted, oily aspect. Like liquid silk in the mouth, with extraordinary thickness of texture for Chevalier-Montrachet. Superripe flavor of pineapple framed by stone. An incredible wine, suppler and larger-scaled than the young 2001. Almost too large for the mouth. One of the greats of the vintage.

Stephen Tanzer, *IWC*

But beware: the Third Tier can be tricky.

Many of these wines are expensive, but they don't have a history of trading up very much. That could change, since some Third-Tier estate reputations are starting to improve, as are collector perceptions, thanks largely to the influential critics. Because pedigree is so crucial in Burgundy, it wasn't until recently that the critics had any impact on this market. Today, Burghound and Tanzer can have a profound impact on buyer perceptions, causing a run on prices overnight.

This new trend may be profitable, but homework here is mandatory. If you're serious about Burgundy as an investment, you might even consider visiting the region and the estates to get a feel for what these wines are all about, and to meet the producers and get an understanding of truly rare and investment-worthy wines. The wines below have already been discovered, so they've already priced up, though that doesn't mean you can't find some value here to hold on to for the longer term. But there are producers that haven't hit the collectors' radar yet; they haven't even hit my radar. Spending time in the region may result in uncovering potential stars on your own.

Overall, Burgundy's Third Tier is a field for the true aficionado.

Third-Tier Red Burgundy IGW

Alain Hudelot-Noellat Richebourg

Alain Hudelot-Noellat Romanée Saint-Vivant

Alex Gambal Chambolle-Musigny "Les Charmes"

Alex Gambal Clos Vougeot

Alex Gambal Vosne-Romanée "Vieilles Vignes"

Amiot Clos de la Roche

Amiot Clos St.-Denis

Bertagna Clos de Vougeot

Bertrand Ambroise Corton "Le Rognet"

Bruno Clair Chambertin-Clos de Bèze

Camille Giroud Clos de Vougeot

Camille Giroud Latricières-Chambertin

Camille Giroud Romanée-Saint-Vivant

Comte Armand Pommard "Clos des Epeneaux"

Denis Mugneret Romanée-Saint-Vivant

Drouhin-Laroze Chambertin-Clos de Bèze

Drouhin-Laroze Chapelle-Chambertin

Drouhin-Laroze Clos de Vougeot

Drouhin-Laroze Latricières-Chambertin

Dominique Laurent Chambertin

Dominique Laurent Charmes-Chambertin

Dominique Laurent Grands Échezeaux

Dominique Laurent Mazis-Chambertin

(*continued*)

Third-Tier Red Burgundy IGW (continued)

Dominique Laurent Musigny

Dugat-Py Chambertin

Dugat-Py Charmes-Chambertin

Dugat-Py Mazis-Chambertin

Dupont Tisserandot Corton "Rognet"

Frédéric Magnien Chambertin-Clos de Bèze

Frédéric Magnien Chambolle-Musigny "Charmes Vieilles Vignes"

Frédéric Magnien Charmes-Chambertin

Frédéric Magnien Nuits-Saint-Georges "Les St.-Georges Vieilles Vignes"

Fourrier Griotte-Chambertin "Vieilles Vignes"

Geantet-Pansiot Charmes-Chambertin

Henri Gouges Nuits-Saint-Georges

Henri Gouges Nuits-Saint-Georges "Les St. Georges"

Henri Gouges Nuits-Saint-Georges "Les Vaucrains"

Henri Gouges Nuits-Saint-Georges "Pruliers"

Henri Perrot-Minot Chambolle-Musigny "d'Orveaux"

Henri Perrot-Minot Charmes-Chambertin

Henri Perrot-Minot Clos de Bèze "Vieilles Vignes"

Henri Perrot-Minot Mazoyères-Chambertin

Henri Perrot-Minot Morey-Saint-Denis "Riotte Vieilles Vignes"

Henri Perrot-Minot Nuits-Saint-Georges "La Richemone Vieilles Vignes"

Henri Perrot-Minot Vosne-Romanée "Champs Perdrix Vieilles Vignes"

Hubert de Montille Volnay "Champans"

Jayer-Gilles Échezeaux

Jacques Prieur Clos de Vougeot

Jacques Prieur Musigny

Jean Grivot Vosne-Romanée "Beauxmonts"

Jean-Louis Trapet Chambertin

Jean-Louis Trapet Latricières-Chambertin

Lignier-Michelot Clos de la Roche

Louis Jadot Bonnes-Mares

Louis Jadot Chambertin-Clos de Bèze

Third-Tier Red Burgundy IGW (*continued*)

Louis Jadot Chambolle-Musigny "Les Amoureuses"

Louis Jadot Chapelle-Chambertin

Louis Jadot Latricières-Chambertin

Louis Jadot Musigny

Lucien le Moine Bonnes-Mares

Lucien le Moine Chambolle-Musigny "Les Amoureuses"

Lucien le Moine Clos de la Roche

Lucien le Moine Clos de Vougeot

Lucien le Moine Mazis-Chambertin

Lamarche Vosne-Romanée "La Grande Rue"

L'Arlot Romanée-Saint-Vivant

Michel Magnien Charmes-Chambertin

Nicolas Potel Bonnes-Mares

Nicolas Potel Chambertin

Nicolas Potel Charmes-Chambertin

Nicolas Potel Clos de la Roche

Nicolas Potel Clos-Saint-Denis

Nicolas Potel Échezeaux

Nicolas Potel Vosne-Romanée "Les Gaudichots"

Pierre Damoy Chambertin-Clos de Bèze

Perdrix Échezeaux

Pousse d'Or Corton "Bressandes"

Pousse d'Or Volnay "Clos de la Bousse d'Or"

Pousse d'Or Volnay "Clos de Soixante Ouvrées"

Raphet Charmes-Chambertin "Cuvée Unique"

Raphet Clos de la Roche "Cuvée Unique"

Vincent Girardin Bonnes-Mares

Vincent Girardin Chambertin-Clos de Bèze

Vincent Girardin Charmes-Chambertin

PRICE RANGE OF THIRD-TIER BURGUNDY IGWS

Current release prices: $50-$400 per bottle

Highest-priced back vintages: $200-$600 per bottle

Why Third-Tier Burgundy IGW Are Increasing in Price

■ These wines are underpriced compared to First- and Second-Tier Burgundies. And many are growing vines on some of the exact same plots. In other words, the wine name or vineyard designation is the same as more expensive wines but the producer doesn't have as much cachet . . . yet.

■ These wines are capable of critical acclaim, and many times they achieve the same scores as wines that sell for thousands of dollars more per bottle.

The Effect of Scores & Vintage on Third-Tier Burgundy IGW

Don't expect newcomers to fight above their weight class.

In other words: the Third Tier struggles to outdo its pedigree, and it usually fails unless a wine picks up a score of 95 points or more—and we know how rare those ratings are. A Third-Tier 2002 Henri Boillot Chevalier-Montrachet rated 95 points by *Burghound* sells for $300 per bottle, whereas the Second-Tier 2002 Domaine Leflaive Chevalier-Montrachet, which Meadows rated at 93 to 95, can trade for $700 per bottle. You get the picture; pedigree still means a lot more than points do in Burgundy.

Vintage also carries more weight in the Third Tier than it does in the Second Tier since the producer names are less well known.

The Downside of Third-Tier Burgundy

Some of these wines could be trendy, and their ability to age may be questionable. And as you now know, longevity pays huge dividends with investment-grade wine, particularly in Burgundy, where questions about longevity abound.

Also, while the wines are less expensive for an investor to buy into, the chances that the price will never move dramatically higher—that your money is effectively dead—are far greater.

The message: In a region that is already a challenge to understand, playing around in the Third Tier should be reserved for investors who have spent time in Burgundy and know that they're getting in on the ground floor of an up-and-coming producer. Otherwise, the risks are great.

Dave Sokolin's Third-Tier Burgundy Predictions

The pedigreed Domaine Camille Giroud has been recently revamped, and its wines are positioned to appreciate in the 2005 vintage and good vintages going forward. Keep a look out for Vougeraie, Perrot-Minot, and Faiveley. With the high scores their wines have received in recent years, they are among the producers staking their claim to a more visible spot in Burgundy's hierarchy.

But I can't emphasize enough: Investment in the Third Tier is for experts only.

10

RHÔNE AND THE
"BORDEAUX EFFECT"

Pressed hard against the Swiss and Italian borders, the vineyards of France's Cotes du Rhône region shadow the Rhône River's run from Vienne to Avignon. Much wine comes from the Rhône—a greater diversity than found in either Burgundy or Bordeaux. But mass quantity does not equate to a larger number of investment opportunities. Much of the wine here is made for drinking, not investing.

By my estimates, less than 2 percent of investment-grade wines currently comes from the Rhône Valley. The wines, though, are uniquely positioned to become the beneficiary of what I've come to call the "Bordeaux Effect," my theory that rising prices in one sector must eventually drive frustrated end consumers to discover the high-quality wines from other regions. The resounding critical acclaim awarded to many Rhône wines by the likes of Robert Parker and others, and the exceptional value available throughout the region, are driving increased interest in these wines and investment opportunities in the area.

The most notable characteristic shared by many investment-worthy Rhônes is the remarkable consistency of high scores they earn, year in and year out. It's not uncommon for a top-flight Rhône to receive 98, 99, or even 100 points from all of the most influential reviewers in the region. Parker loves Rhônes. On his website alone, there are 99 Rhône wines to which he has awarded 100 points, as well as the single highest-scoring wine in history, the 2003 Pégaü "Cuvée da Capo," with 100+ points. At times, it seems as if Parker's unstated pet project is to bring the Rhônes into the forefront among wine lovers who have become fixated on Bordeaux, Burgundy, Super Tuscans, and California's cult Cabs.

For investors, the Rhône represents the last sector where you'll find pedigreed, long-lived wines with huge scores, trading at affordable prices. This, to my way of thinking as a wine investor, is why so much possibility exists in the Rhône.

Until 2000, Rhône wines were the arcane preserve of hard-core wine aficionados. Despite the legendary trilogy of vintages—1989, 1990, 1991—Rhône wines couldn't gain the attention afforded to those made in Bordeaux, California, and Italy. A string of bad vintages in the Rhône in the mid-1990s plunged the region into obscurity at a time when other regions were blessed with an abundance of blockbuster vintages that consumed wine connoisseurs. During Rhône's Dark Ages, the wines were perceived to be "peppery" and "vegetal"—never a good combination—and my clients were not at all receptive to my suggestion that they try some of the region's better wines.

All of that changed in 2000, when Robert Parker reviewed the 1998 vintage and proclaimed:

> I have been visiting France professionally as a wine critic for twenty-two years, and have never seen such a quality transformation in a viticultural region as I have witnessed in the Rhône Valley over the last four or five years.

Thus 1998 marked a new era for the Rhône. The work of a new generation of winemakers had finally begun to emerge after years of decline. Almost every wine made in the Rhône Valley that year was great, and the best producers made history by putting this once-sleepy region back on wine collectors' radar. Many wines were awarded high scores, and the rave reviews were so persuasive that they resembled sales pitches. Domaine du Pégaü's 1998 Châteauneuf-du-Pape "Cuvée da Capo" received 100 points from Parker, and within seven years, it had traded up to nearly $700 per bottle from its $200 release price.

After the '98 vintage, there was a slew of great years, and by mid-2007 there were exactly one hundred different wines with Parker scores of between 98 and 100 points. The cellars of many wine collectors are now full of post-'98 Rhônes, though these wines are only now, in 2007, being tasted for the first time. And collectors are realizing that they love what's inside. The Rhônes are aging well—very well. The '98s are now trading up in price, and don't be surprised to see the full effects of this upgrade in the next few years as demand for top-flight Rhônes increases.

In the meantime, the market is flooded with 95- to 97-point Rhône wines priced well under $100 per bottle, some even under $40. For now, Guigal's rarest single-vineyard Côte Rôties are furiously trading at Burgundian prices, many at more than $1,000 per bottle. Is this a harbinger of what could someday happen with other boutique cuvées with larger productions? I'm guessing it is, although it may take some time.

What's the Deal with Rhône?

Rhônes have every condition in place for success as investment-grade wines: high scores and rave reviews; a proven ability to age well for several decades; price appreciation of great back vintages; pedigree and famous producer names; and production that's large enough for investors to find the wine and build a position.

With the exception of the slightly more complex wine names, the only stumbling block to the price appreciation of Rhônes seems to be that the demand for them is not yet commensurate with supply, meaning that at this point supply exceeds demand. That should begin to change. As the post-'98 wines begin to drink better and better, and as Parker continues his one-man marketing campaign to raise the profile of the region, demand will begin to soak up the supply. Rhônes, therefore, could be quite the profitable trading opportunity for investors willing to take their position ahead of the curve and hold on for the ride.

Rhône Appellations

Rhônes do not have simple or catchy names, like Bordeaux's Le Pin or California's Screaming Eagle. Similar to Burgundies', Rhône wine names are associated with the locations where they are grown.

Several different producers make wines bearing the same name, such as in Châteauneuf-du-Pape, a medieval town and an appellation for several hundred producers. Adding to the confusion, all Châteauneufs come in the same crest-embossed bottle.

What distinguish Rhônes from one another are their producer names or, in some cases, the names of their special cuvées, which always come after the appellation's name—such as Domaine du Pégaü Châteauneuf-du-Pape Cuvée Laurence. Some producers make five different Châteauneuf-du-Pape cuvées, each name often long and cryptic, like "Cuvée de la Reine des Bois" or "Cuvée de Mon Aïeul." These longer-named wines are generally low-production boutique cuvées, and in a few instances they have performed marvelously as investments, trading up several hundred percent from their release prices.

Rhône's vineyard designations are regulated by the same AOC system that's at play in Burgundy. The main distinction for Rhône collectors is whether a wine comes from the northern or southern end of the Rhône Valley. The two areas have different microclimates, and different varietals of grape are planted there.

The Importance of Vintage in Rhône Wines

With so many good wines produced, a Rhône's vintage is at least as important to its potential price appreciation as a Bordeaux's. Collectors are looking for *the best* of the best. Outstanding older vin-

The Rhône: A Geography Lesson in Grapes

The Rhone is packed with different types of wines made from different types of grapes. Only a few, though, hit the charts as investment-worthy wine.

Northern Rhône

The two investment-grade appellations in the northern Rhône are Côte Rôtie and Hermitage, where all wines made from 100 percent Syrah grapes. Côte Rôtie and Hermitage are towns where several producers make wines that carry these local names. As such, the name of the producer is the critical factor in distinguishing between the collectible wines and those that are not collectible.

There are about ten important producers in the region, and some are considered to be in the top echelon of global winemaking.

Southern Rhône

This area is home to one of the best-known names in wine, Châteauneuf-du-Pape, which is made from a blend of up to fourteen grape varietals, usually dominated by Grenache. Many Châteauneufs have high production and are sold for low prices. But fifteen distinguished producers take their best barrels and make cuvées in all but microscopic amounts, which can trade for between $100 and $700 per bottle. These ain't your daddy's Châteauneufs.

tages of the highest-level Rhônes, such as 1961 Jaboulet Hermitage "La Chapelle," are capable of commanding over $50,000 per case.

Here are the recent Rhône vintages that stand out among collectors and, as such, should be high on an investor's list as well.

NORTHERN RHÔNE

- 2003 (exceptional)
- 1999 (exceptional)
- 1998
- 1991
- 1990
- 1989
- 1988
- 1985
- 1978

How to Read a Rhône Wine Label

The appellation + single vineyard (or special cuvée)
= Wine name: *Ermitage "Le Pavillon"*

"Ermitage": The northern Rhône appellation, is more commonly spelled: "Hermitage"

The name of the producer: *M. Chapoutier*

"Biodynamique" = Organic

Alcohol content: 13.5%

SOUTHERN RHÔNE

- 2005 (exceptional)
- 2003 (good)
- 2001 (exceptional)
- 2000 (exceptional)
- 1999 (good)
- 1998 (exceptional)
- 1990 (exceptional)
- 1989 (exceptional)

First-Tier Rhônes

The cream of the crop in the Rhône, both north and south, is names that are well known and respected by almost any serious wine collector: Hermitages, Côte Rôties, and Châteauneuf-du-Papes. These wines share the common elements of low production and, generally speaking, huge scores in just about every major and not-so-major vintage. Therefore, it is essential to focus on the best of the best wines in years with the absolute highest scores. A 99- or 100-point wine combined with a famous vintage is always a safe bet and the only investment I would recommend at present.

First-Tier Rhône IGW

NORTHERN

Chapoutier Hermitage "Le Pavillon"

Chapoutier Hermitage "L'Ermite"

Chave Hermitage

Chave Hermitage "Cuvée Cathelin"

Guigal Côte-Rôtie "La Landonne"

Guigal Côte-Rôtie "La Mouline"

Guigal Côte-Rôtie "La Turque"

Paul Jaboulet Aîné Hermitage "La Chapelle"

SOUTHERN

André Brunel Châteauneuf-du-Pape "Cuvée Centenaire"

Beaucastel Châteauneuf-du-Pape "Hommage à Jacques Perrin"

Henri Bonneau Châteauneuf du Pape "Réserve des Céléstins"

Pégaü Châteauneuf-du-Pape "Cuvée da Capo"

Rayas Châteauneuf-du-Pape

PRICE RANGE OF FIRST-TIER RHÔNE IGW

Current release prices: $300–$1,000 per bottle

Highest-priced back vintages: $1,000–$6,000 per bottle

Why First-Tier Rhônes Are Increasing in Price

- Limited-production cuvées are akin to the finest red Burgundies and are in the elite circle of retailers' and auction houses'

If you like wine as a drink and not just an investment, make the effort to taste one of the Guigal Côte-Rôtie "La La" cuvées. It's worth the time and the money—about $1,100 a bottle.

2003 Guigal Côte-Rôtie "La Mouline"   100 Points

. . . by far the most delicate and elegant wine (11% Viognier is co-fermented with 89% Syrah) but the enormous aromatics of spring flowers intermixed with creme de cassis, black raspberry, mocha, caramel, and cola, and enormous full-bodied opulence and striking velvety, seamless texture make for one of the most memorable wines anyone could ever drink. This wine should age effortlessly for 25–30 or more years.

Robert Parker, *The Wine Advocate*

---

offerings, widely recognized as being among the world's best wines.

- Rhônes are adored by critics, and they routinely garner big, big scores.
- Their ability to age well is proven.
- Price increases for top-flight Bordeaux are pushing wine buyers into the Rhône region on a hunt for great wines at equally great prices.

The Effect of Scores on First-Tier Rhônes

100 POINTS: Since so many Rhônes earn a 100-point rating, a perfect score is almost a must to help your cases of wine stand apart from the flood of Rhônes on the market.

Rhône is probably the highest-scoring region on the planet among investment-grade wines. Guigal's single-vineyard Côte Rôties, for instance, achieves 100-point scores year in and year out. So many 100s abound in Rhônes—about forty-three among the First Tier—that the wines trade for surprisingly low prices, though I'd expect that to change in the future.

99 POINTS: There are nineteen wines with 99 points in the First Tier, and all are worthy of investment, despite the fact that there is a significant price difference between what collectors will pay for a 100-pointer versus a 99-pointer

95–98 POINTS: Because so many of the Rhône Valley's best wines get high scores, a 95- to 98-point rating barely makes a dent in the consciousness of points-oriented collectors and consumers. Exercise caution here. Don't invest.

90–94 POINTS: Stay away. This point range is investment poison, not just for a First-Tier Rhône but for any Rhône. Again, with so many high-scoring Rhônes floating around, what's the point of owning a relatively low-rated wine that isn't likely to have tremendous demand in the future?

The Downside of First-Tier Rhône IGW

Despite their collector cachet and critical acclaim, it is doubtful that these wines will ever catch up to the popularity of Bordeaux. Emerging markets are not as enamored with Rhônes as they are with Bordeaux, so until this changes there will be less of a market for these wines, no matter how great they are.

And because there's such a plethora of highly rated Rhônes, the price appreciation will likely be somewhat constrained for all but the absolute best the region has to offer.

Dave Sokolin's First-Tier Rhône Predictions

Back vintages of Guigal's single-vineyard Côte-Rôtie "La Mouline," "La Landonne," and "La Turque" will trade up to even higher levels, based on the market's acceptance of the exorbitant release prices of the 100-point '03 vintage. Expect the best back vintages—1989, 1990, 1991—to double in price, since they're currently priced at levels similar to the '03s and have the same scores. Expect the lower-scoring back vintages to rise with the tide as well, though not to the same degree.

The 2003 Pégaü "Cuvée da Capo" received the highest Parker score ever—100+ points, the "plus" designation being the first time Parker has employed that descriptor. Parker called the 1998, 2000, and 2003 vintages of this cuvée "Some of the greatest wines I have ever tasted in my life." In mid-2007, D. Sokolin & Co. was selling the '03 for $800 per bottle at a brisk clip. What do you think this "100+" wine will trade for in ten years, considering that it is expected to be in peak drinking condition through 2035? My guess is that in 2035, when Parker is retired and his reviews will be relied upon by people who may not have even been alive in 2003, this "da Capo" may be trading for as high as $8,000 per bottle. In the near term, I would expect this wine to trade at $1,200–$1,500 per bottle by 2013.

Rayas Châteauneuf-du-Pape has earned worldwide attention for decades, and it will continue to trade up in future vintages. Even the 1998 Rayas, rated 94 by Parker (low for a Rhône, let alone a Rayas) is trading at over $400 per bottle on the momentum of the vintage alone. That '98 opened at $100 a bottle and could trade up toward $1,800 in five years. The 1990 Rayas, rated 100 points, has already hit $1,500, thanks to its amazing score.

Second-Tier Rhônes

Second-Tier Rhônes are an enticing area for the casual collector, though potentially more risky for the investor. These Rhônes often pick up tremendous scores, accumulate mouthwatering reviews, and possess all the criteria present in other successful wine investments—except for the kind of price appreciation that you might otherwise expect. The reason is fairly simple: So many highly rated First Tiers are available at such affordable prices that the superb Second Tiers are generally overlooked. On the upside: You can purchase highly rated wines at low prices and in serious quantity.

For instance, 2003 Pégaü Châteauneuf-du-Pape "Cuvée

Réservée" is a wine that opened for $47 per bottle, but after receiving an upgraded 99-point score from Parker, it now trades at about $140. The wine is made by Domaine du Pégaü, the same producer behind the First-Tier "Cuvée da Capo." As such, you'd expect a much higher price, based on pedigree and points. Yet that high price isn't forthcoming in this corner of the Rhône market. I expect "Cuvée Réservée" to trade for over $300 per bottle by 2013, and I think that it has potential to become a $500 wine in the longer term, since its anticipated maturity is 2026. But that's a long wait and, depending upon the time necessary to reach loftier price levels, a potentially tepid return on investment.

Second-Tier Rhône IGW

NORTHERN

Chapoutier Côte-Rôtie "Mordorée"

Chapoutier Ermitage "de l'Orée"

Délas Côte-Rôtie "Landonne"

Délas Hermitage "Les Bessards"

Guigal Côte-Rôtie "Château d'Ampuis"

Guigal Hermitage "Ex Voto"

Marc Sorrel Hermitage "Le Gréal"

Michel Ogier Côte-Rôtie Cuvée "Belle Hélène"

Remizières Hermitage "Cuvée l'Éssentiel"

Réné Rostaing Côte-Rôtie "Côte Blonde"

SOUTHERN

Beaucastel Châteauneuf-du-Pape

Beaurenard Châteauneuf-du-Pape "Boisrenard"

Chapoutier Châteauneuf-du-Pape "Barbe Rac"

Clos des Papes Châteauneuf-du-Pape

Domaine du Caillou Châteauneuf-du-Pape "Réserve Clos du Caillou"

Henri Bonneau Châteauneuf-du-Pape "Cuvée Marie Beurier"

Second-Tier Rhône IGW (continued)

SOUTHERN

Henri Bonneau Châteauneuf-du-Pape "Cuvée Spéciale"

Marcoux Châteauneuf-du-Pape "Vieilles Vignes"

Mordorée Châteauneuf-du-Pape "Cuvée de la Reine des Bois"

Mordorée Châteauneuf-du-Pape "La Plume du Peintre"

Paul Avril Châteauneuf-du-Pape "Clos des Papes"

Pégaü Châteauneuf-du-Pape "Cuvée Laurence"

Pégaü Châteauneuf-du-Pape "Cuvée Réservée"

Pierre Usseglio Châteauneuf-du-Pape "Mon Aïeul"

Pierre Usseglio Châteauneuf-du-Pape "Réserve des Deux Frères"

Roger Sabon Châteauneuf-du-Pape "Le Secret de Sabon"

Vieille Julienne Châteauneuf-du-Pape "Réserve"

Vieille Julienne Châteauneuf-du-Pape "Vieilles Vignes"

PRICE RANGE OF SECOND-TIER RHÔNE IGW

Current release prices: $90–$300 per bottle

Highest-priced back vintages: $300–$5,000 per bottle

Why Second-Tier Rhônes Are Increasing in Price

The highest-scoring wines in this price tier are currently under-priced. Second-Tier Rhônes are made by esteemed producers, they have huge scores, and they will improve for years, so there is plenty of time for these wines to appreciate. The question is: How long will it take? If demand for Rhônes escalates to the point that the First Tier become increasingly difficult to find at reasonable prices, then the natural inclination of investors and consumers will be to step down to the Second Tier, which will ultimately push those prices higher as well. But it's a matter of both "if" and "when."

So, if you're looking to invest in the Second Tier, concentrate almost exclusively on wines from the best vintages with the highest scores.

The Downside of Second-Tier Rhône IGW

As I mentioned above, these wines might require many years before they generate a meaningful return on investment. Pain awaits as well if demand never picks up or picks up exceedingly slowly. Finally, if the Rhône Valley racks up even more great vintages in succession, then the number of standout, highly rated wines is bound to increase, thereby jacking up the supply and keeping a lid on prices.

Dave Sokolin's Second-Tier Rhône Predictions

Beaucastel Châteauneuf-du-Pape is an amazing investment-grade wine. It drinks young and improves for years. Its First-Tier special-cuvée sibling, "Hommage à Jacques Perrin," can trade in the $1,000-per-bottle range, yet as of this writing, the regular Beaucastel has not hit the $200 mark. That day is coming.

Second-Tier Rhônes from great vintages such as 1989 and 1990 are currently selling for less than $200 per bottle, and they're poised to double in price. Newer vintages such as 1998, 2000, and 2005 were released on the cheap, at around $100 per bottle. By 2013, they will likely have doubled as well.

Third-Tier Rhônes

A bevy of high-scoring Rhônes is currently available at price points below $50 a bottle, and these are wines that, in my opinion, have the potential to trade up. That said, I'm not recommending these as investment-worthy wines, though they are potentially collectibles. You could fill an entire cellar full of these wines for the price of a few cases of First-Growth Bordeaux, and some of them might just pay dividends in the future.

But investing is about the risk-reward balance, and in Third-Tier Rhône wines, the risk outweighs the reward these days. There are just too many excellent First-Tier wines for investors to play around down here. But I will say this: Investors who are price-conscious consumers should, when buying investment-caliber Rhônes, spend a few dollars on Third-Tier Rhônes just for the pleasure of drinking them.

Third-Tier Rhônes

NORTHERN

Délas Hermitage "Marquise de la Tourette"

Guigal Hermitage

Joseph Jamet Côte-Rôtie

Michel Ogier Côte-Rôtie

Remizières Hermitage "Cuvée Emilie"

Réné Rostaing Côte-Rôtie "Cuvée Classique"

Tardieu-Laurent Côte-Rôtie

SOUTHERN

Beaurenard Châteauneuf-du-Pape "Cuvée Boisrenard"

Bois de Boursan Châteauneuf-du-Pape "Cuvée des Félix"

Clos Saint Jean Châteauneuf-du-Pape "Deus ex Machina"

Cuvée du Vatican Châteauneuf-du-Pape

Cuvée du Vatican Châteauneuf-du-Pape "Réserve Sixtine"

Domaine Charvin Châteauneuf-du-Pape

Domaine du Caillou Châteauneuf-du-Pape "Les Quartz"

Domaine Grand Veneur Châteauneuf-du-Pape "Cuvée Les Origines"

Domaine Grand Veneur Châteauneuf-du-Pape "La Fontaine Vieilles Vignes"

Eddie Féraud Châteauneuf-du-Pape

Font de Michelle Châteauneuf-du-Pape "Cuvée Étienne Gonnet"

Le Vieux Donjon Châteauneuf-du-Pape

Marcoux Châteauneuf-du-Pape

Monpertuis Châteauneuf-du-Pape "Cuvée Tradition"

Paul Autard Châteauneuf-du-Pape "Côte Ronde"

Pierre Usseglio Châteauneuf-du-Pape

(continued)

Third-Tier Rhônes (*continued*)

SOUTHERN

Roger Sabon Châteauneuf-du-Pape "Cuvée Préstige"

Tardieu-Laurent Châteauneuf-du-Pape "Cuvée Spécial Vieilles Vignes"

Vieux Télégraphe Châteauneuf-du-Pape

PRICE RANGE OF THIRD-TIER RHÔNES

Current release prices: $30–$100 per bottle
Highest-priced back vintages: $200–$300 per bottle

Dave Sokolin's Third-Tier Rhône Predictions

In the world of emerging-market investments, there has long been a saying that "Brazil is the next great investment opportunity . . . and always will be." The point is that for all of its positive attributes, investors just haven't latched onto the South American giant as anything other than a side bet that might or might not pay off one day.

The Rhône is similar—a region bursting with potential, but potential that has not yet arrived in the mind of the consumer.

For now you should focus on the highest-end, ultra-limited-production cuvées that have a track record of price appreciation in the highest-scoring vintages. Steer clear of high-production wines unless the score is 99 or, preferably, 100 points. I'm sure that at some point, wine buyers will look back and remember these as being the good ol' days of Rhône prices, but we're not there yet. Investing based on your palate may never generate the kind of returns you seek.

The high-scoring producers will inevitably raise their release prices on a significant but more gradual basis than producers of wines with similar price points from other regions, such as Bordeaux.

I'm not saying this is my best investment pick, so don't gamble the kids' college fund, but there is a play on the highest-scoring best vintages of certain wines priced under $50 per bottle. The upcoming release prices for many of these wines should exceed the $50 mark in the next five years, and that will make the more desirable back vintages look cheap by comparison. Names to be on the lookout for in the '03 vintage from both the Northern and Southern Rhône include: Délas Côte-Rôtie "La Landonne," Janasse Châteauneuf-du-Pape "Cuvée Vieilles Vignes," Pierre Usseglio Châteauneuf-du-Pape "Réserve des Deux Frères" and "Cuvée de Mon Aïeul," Beaurenard Châteauneuf-du-Pape "Cuvée Boisrenard," and Bois de Boursan's Châteauneuf-du-Pape "Cuvée des Félix."

11

CHAMPAGNE

Bubble?

People love Champagne. It has such a luxury air about it with its froth and bubble, a drink to toast New Year's and weddings, births and business deals, and winners of the Formula One race. It's a common thread in modern urban music with singers and rappers routinely referring to the loads of cash laid down for bottles of Cristal and Dom Pérignon. Read any men's or women's magazine for the just-out-of-college-and-looking-for-fun set, and you will almost assuredly find a recommendation to keep a bottle of bubbly in the refrigerator for those impromptu moments when a potential mate is hanging around and you want something classy to lubricate the evening.

For investors, though, Champagne isn't so effervescent.

Due to a general lack of awareness about Champagne's longevity and just how well the best ones improve with age, this is a tricky market. For most people, Champagne is an "event" drink, something that gloved servers ferry around on platters in banquet halls. It's not the stuff of daily imbibing.

It is a little-known fact that some Champagnes age as well as the finest wines. Most people, though, tend to drink the finest Champagnes too young, largely because they don't know any better, which means that very few price-appreciate to a significant degree and the back-vintage market is small in relation to the quantities produced. I see it all the time in my business: end users of the best Champagnes—Dom Pérignon, Cristal, Krug, and other special reserves, known as *têtes de cuvées*—have turned these wines into brute commodities by focusing solely on the lowest prices rather than the best vintages.

To most consumers of high-end Champagne, the vintage is not as important as the label, which has the cachet—the "bling," as urban America refers to it—to get the job done. In the world of hip-hop music, the best Champagnes are omnipresent in music videos and at Hollywood clubs, cuffed in the hands of moneyed urban moguls. When Jay-Z raps about "Six model chicks, six bottles of Cris," he's referring to Louis Roederer Cristal, that brand's tête de cuvée.

Who would've ever predicted that rap stars would make this formerly obscure luxury item a fixture of global pop culture and synonymous with success? Imagine what might happen to the investment-grade wine market if rappers were to extol the delights of Lafite Rothschild or Latour? It would be an IGW collector's dream to see a double magnum of Lynch Bages in a rap video. Don't count out the effect that pop culture can have on the wine business.

Too bad for IGW collectors, though, that Jay-Z never mentioned the vintage of the Champagnes he was drinking. It might have helped investors' efforts—including my own—to score big profits on a 1990 Dom Pérignon play that ultimately fizzled.

My company and many of our clients/investors thought we'd cornered the market for this classic Champagne, buying over 10,000 cases of the high-scoring '90 vintage year before the millennium arrived, betting the price would spike as the '90s became ten years old and scads of drinkers rushed to buy this particular vintage for their new-millennium celebrations. As it turned out, many people purchased the less expensive and much lower scoring 1992 and 1993 vintages and partied just the same. It was a sobering lesson in the way the Champagne market works—namely, that it's all about brand name at the cheapest prices. Fortunately, the 1990 retained its value and we didn't book a loss.

Investment-Grade Champagne Vintages

Be careful paying up for older vintages, since most buyers of these wines look for the lowest-priced brand with a label that still impresses. They don't—and generally won't—pay a premium for an excellent vintage. A tiny handful of cognoscenti will pay a huge premium for extremely rare, well-stored back vintages of the best, such as 1972 Dom Pérignon. It's a tricky region, for connoisseurs only. And similar to Burgundy, where premiums are paid for reputation over scores, it's a region driven by the rabid demand of just a few well-heeled experts.

CHAMPAGNE'S BEST VINTAGES

- 1999
- 1996
- 1995
- 1990
- 1989
- 1988
- 1986
- 1985
- 1982
- 1976
- 1975
- 1971

Investment-Grade Champagnes

Bollinger R.D.

Krug Clos de Mesnil

Krug Vintage

Louis Roederer Cristal

Louis Roederer Cristal Rosé

Moët & Chandon Dom Pérignon

Investment-Grade Champagnes (*continued*)

Moët & Chandon Dom Pérignon Rosé

Pol Roger Cuvée Sir Winston Churchill

Salon Blanc de Blancs Le Mesnil

Salon Vintage

Taittinger Comtes de Champagne

Veuve Clicquot La Grande Dame

Veuve Clicquot La Grande Dame Rosé

Dave Sokolin's Champagne Predictions

The best older vintages of Dom Pérignon are sublime and can age for forty years. I have a few Champagne-o-phile friends who might scoff at my remarks because they will pay stratospheric prices for well-stored older vintages, but they are in the minority.

Each Champagne that I've listed above can age for decades and, as a result, is investment worthy in the best vintages. But at the end of the day, Champagne is best as an investment in your own pleasure. I strongly suggest cellaring Champagne in your wine collection for that purpose only, rather than on the expectation that the bottle prices will soar to new heights.

Champagne Dreams

1999 Roederer Cristal **98 Points**

One of the finest Champagnes I have ever brought to my lips, the 1999 Cristal bursts from the glass with fresh hazelnut and apple scents. Elegant, deep, and silky-textured, this medium to full-bodied beauty is immensely concentrated, pure, packed with apple flavors, and astoundingly long in the finish.

Robert Parker, *The Wine Advocate*

12

ITALY

Why So Few Investment-Grade Wines?

taly has always been one of the most popular and critically acclaimed winemaking countries of the world, home to some of the most celebrated names in the business and some of the most beloved, highest-scoring wines. So why is it, then, that so few investment-worthy bottles of vino come from this boot-shaped slice of the wine world?

Simply put: Most don't age very well.

The common trait shared by all of the most profitable investment-grade wines is their ability to age and, for their back vintages, to dependably increase in price over time. Some Italian wines are capable of aging, but most just don't age very well. Thus, it's rare for older-vintage Italian wines to command a significant premium among wine buyers. For that reason, Italian wines account for only a sliver, maybe 3 percent or so, of the investment-wine market.

Make no mistake: Italian wines are extremely popular upon release. Clients line up to prebuy the best. Restaurant demand is massive, and the retail trade is huge because Italian wines require no cellaring. Some of the most discriminating collectors of rare Bordeaux and Burgundy routinely buy Italian wines to serve at home because they're so good.

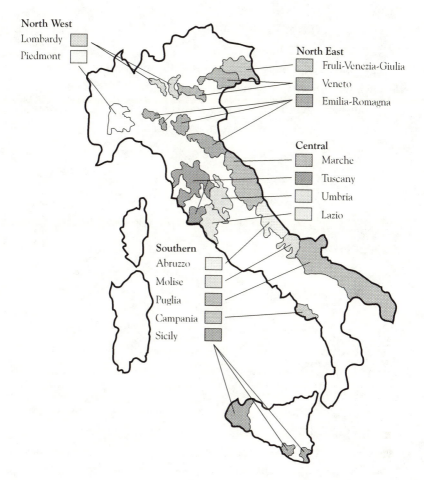

North West
Lombardy
Piedmont

North East
Fruli-Venezia-Giulia
Veneto
Emilia-Romagna

Central
Marche
Tuscany
Umbria
Lazio

Southern
Abruzzo
Molise
Puglia
Campania
Sicily

But overall the market for top-flight Italian wines resembles what we'll see in California in chapter 15: The greatest price appreciation happens in the first five years after release; then it goes flat. Where the Italian market diverges is in quantity. While the cult California Cabernets regularly produce tiny quantities, the greatest Italian wines tend to be produced in large quantities, which, in that whole supply-demand equilibrium, pushes the scales markedly toward the supply end, keeping prices tame.

The two most important investment-grade wine regions of Italy are Piedmont, with its Barolos and Barbarescos, and the more famous Tuscany, where Brunello di Montalcino and a host of Super Tuscans are made. Similar to California wines', their release prices are high. The independent buyer's primary edge is the ability to buy these wines before they're reviewed, before their prices go higher. Buying on the hope that the reviews will be good is also a risk. If the reviews are not so good, well, then, so much for that rapid price escalation you were hoping for, in which case, *mangia, bevi e sii felice!*

The Italian Appellation of Tuscany

Tuscany is the wine region where the traditional systems of classification are the least important in determining a wine's price. The kingpins of Tuscany are the new guard, the so-called Super Tuscans. These wines are produced in a style that breaks from ancient local tradition, and they are designated *vini da tavola* or table wines by the Italian government's version of the French AOC.

However, these superboutique wines are a far cry from standard table wines in terms of their extremely high quality and their prices. Super Tuscans—often fashioned from a blend of Bordeaux varietals, such as Merlot and Cabernet Sauvignon, as well as the region's traditional Sangiovese grape—have been anointed by leading reviewers and the consuming public as Italy's best. And the best Super Tuscans are worthier investments than are their classified counterparts, the Brunello di Montalcino, none of which is in the First Tier of Tuscan investment-grade wines.

The Great Tuscan Vintages

- 2004
- 2001
- 1999
- 1997
- 1990
- 1985

How to Read a Tuscan Wine Label

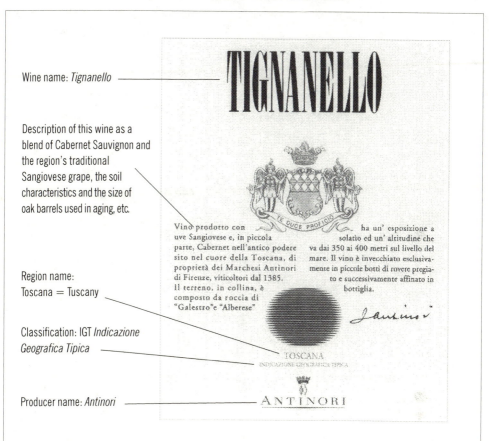

Wine name: *Tignanello*

Description of this wine as a blend of Cabernet Sauvignon and the region's traditional Sangiovese grape, the soil characteristics and the size of oak barrels used in aging, etc.

Region name:
Toscana = Tuscany

Classification: IGT *Indicazione Geografica Tipica*

Producer name: *Antinori*

First-Tier Tuscans

Although some Super Tuscans can command higher prices when older, I've found through the years that simply having any of these wines in stock, regardless of age or vintage, is enough to satiate client demand. Vintage is usually less important than brand name, which is part of why Tuscans rarely make for good investments.

Sometimes it's easier to sell the less expensive, latest vintages than the older, rarer, and slightly more expensive vintages with similar reviews. It has become clear that people like these wines young and don't want to pay more than the lowest price at which they can be had. In other words, this is a consumer market, not a collector's market, and consumers buy the most affordable version of the best brands. (Similar to Champagne, where customers generally care more about simply serving Dom Pérignon than any particular vintage of it.)

All that said, there are a few rare instances where Italian wines can trade into the stratosphere on the power of a review. The best example of this is 1985 Sassicaia, rated 100 points by Parker and 99 points by *Wine Spectator*. This wine was released at $600 per case and now sells for $36,000—assuming you can find a dozen pristine bottles still packed in their original wood case.

Examining why that '85 Sassicaia appreciated so much, a few things become clear.

- Sassicaia is made not from traditional Tuscan grape varietals but rather Cabernet Sauvignon, the star of Bordeaux.
- Parker calls the '85 Sassicaia "a monumental Cabernet Sauvignon, it is one of the greatest wines made this century," and he mentions that he misidentified it in a blind tasting as a 1986 Mouton Rothschild, a wine that he also rated at 100 points. Parker's anticipated maturity date of 2025 gives this Italian wine the distinctly un-Italian trait of a four-decade life span.

In essence, this Sassicaia, though dressed fashionably in Italian, is a Bordeaux on the inside. And that has given it a very Bordeaux-like price trajectory.

First-Tier Tuscan IGW

Antinori Masseto

Antinori Solaia

Tenuta San Guido Sassicaia

Tua Rita Redigaffi

The Italian Appellation of Piedmont

The collectible wines from Piedmont (*Piemontese* in Italian) are confined exclusively to the villages of Barolo and Barbaresco and are made from the Nebbiolo grape.

Most Piedmont IGW follow the traditional guidelines of the Italian wine regulatory body, the highest classification of which is DOCG (*Denominazione di Origine Controllata e Garantita*). Piedmont wine names are similar to those of Burgundy and the Rhône, where you'll see numerous producers making Barolo and Barbaresco and where just one producer makes several wines in one village, all under several different single-vineyard designations. Piedmont

How to Read a Piedmont Wine Label

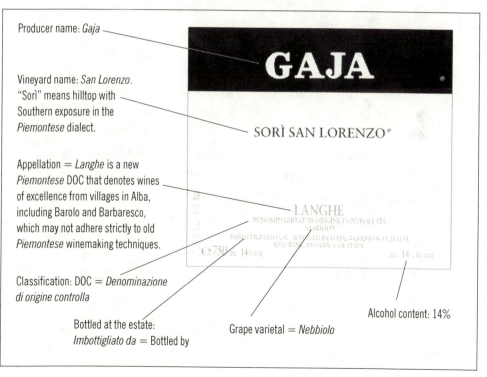

Producer name: *Gaja*

Vineyard name: *San Lorenzo.* "Sorì" means hilltop with Southern exposure in the *Piemontese* dialect.

Appellation = *Langhe* is a new *Piemontese* DOC that denotes wines of excellence from villages in Alba, including Barolo and Barbaresco, which may not adhere strictly to old *Piemontese* winemaking techniques.

Classification: DOC = *Denominazione di origine controlla*

Bottled at the estate: *Imbottigliato da* = Bottled by

Grape varietal = *Nebbiolo*

Alcohol content: 14%

GAJA

SORÌ SAN LORENZO®

wines are gaining in popularity because they are now being made in an increasingly fruit-forward style, which gives them the ability to be drunk earlier without sacrificing their longevity.

The Great Piedmont Vintages

- 2004
- 2001
- 2000
- 1999
- 1998
- 1997

- 1996
- 1990
- 1989
- 1988
- 1985
- 1982

First-Tier Piedmonts

The new releases of Piedmont rarely garner the attention heaped upon the wines of Tuscany. However, because Piedmont's Barolos and Barbarescos take more time to mature and have a greater longevity than their sexier Tuscan counterparts, they may have better investment potential should the Bordeaux Effect begin to make itself felt in this region, as disaffected Bordeaux customers decide to explore Piedmont more deeply.

Some of the most sought-after, older wines from Italy are Barolos from the 1971 vintage. The best examples of these can trade for more than $2,000 a bottle. Barolos from as far back as the 1940s are still actively traded, and I find that a handful of cognoscenti are happy to pay a premium to get these mature wines, as much as $2,000 per bottle for some wines that may have been released for as little as $2 per bottle decades ago. Following are the First-Tier Piedmonts. You'll notice that there are few producers growing on a number of plots:

First-Tier Piedmont IGW

Aldo Conterno Barolo "Bussia Soprana"

Aldo Conterno Barolo "Gran Bussia" Riserva

Bruno Giacosa Barbaresco "Santo Stefano" Riserva

Bruno Giacosa Barolo "Rocche del Falletto" Red Label Riserva

Gaja Barbaresco "Sorì San Lorenzo"

Gaja Barbaresco "Sorì Tilden"

Gaja Barberesco "Costa Russi"

Giacomo Conterno Barolo "Monfortino" Riserva

Luciano Sandrone Barolo "Cannubi Boschis"

Luciano Sandrone Barolo "Le Vigne"

PRICE RANGE OF FIRST-TIER TUSCAN AND PIEDMONT IGW

Current release prices: $200–$300 per bottle

Highest-priced back vintages: $1,300–$2,000 per bottle

Why First-Tier Tuscan and Piedmonts Are Increasing in Price

■ Quality levels are improving with new technology that marries the traditional trait of longevity with the ability to drink young, a combination that didn't previously exist. Years ago, great vintages of the best Italian wines needed to be cellared for twenty years. But today, consumers can drink these wines younger, causing them to become scarcer sooner—a fantastic characteristic for investors who own the premier examples of Tuscans and Piedmonts.

■ The reputations of some of these estates are unrivaled among their fans, giving investors a built-in base of buyers.

The Effect of Scores on First-Tier Tuscan and Piedmont IGW

There's no two ways about it: You absolutely must stick with 97- to 100-point Super Tuscans and Piedmonts to be a successful investor.

The Burgundy and Bordeaux of Italy

You may have picked this up from previous pages, but Piedmonts and Tuscans are effectively Italy's version of Burgundies and Bordeaux, and not just because of the confusing etymology at play.

The Tuscans tend to reflect the Bordeaux style of wine, while the Piedmonts are Burgundian at heart.

Here's how Parker and Suckling reviewed a Tuscan and a Piedmont, both of which earned the coveted 100-point score. Their analysis sheds some light on the differences in each region's style.

2000 Tua Rita Redigaffi   100 Points

The prodigious . . . 2000 Redigaffi (a 400-case 100% Merlot cuvée) is a wine of extraordinary distinction and intensity. It boasts a fabulous perfume of melted licorice mixed with high quality espresso roast, black cherry and currant liqueur, white flowers, and toast. Boasting great intensity, glorious ripeness, formidable purity, and a finish that lasts nearly a minute, this is the stuff of dreams! Its dry extract number is about as high as one will find in a dry red wine. Additionally, its 14.8% alcohol is incredibly well-concealed beneath the wealth of glycerin and fruit. A brilliant achievement! Kudos to winemaker Stefano Chioccioli and proprietors Rita Tua and Vegilio Bisti. Anticipated maturity: 2007–2018.

Robert Parker, *The Wine Advocate*

2000 Giacosa Barolo Le Rocche del Falletto Riserva   100 Points

Fabulous purity of crushed fruit—strawberries and raspberries, with hints of fresh roses. Full-bodied, with an amazing concentration and a palate that goes on and on and on. Ultraripe tannins. This is the Romanée-Conti of Barolo. Terrific balance and richness. Best after 2012. 1,200 cases made.

James Suckling, *Wine Spectator*

Even at these high levels, consumers will often choose the lowest-priced example of a particular brand instead of worrying about vintage. So if you want a wine that's likely to appreciate in value—and isn't that why you're an investor?—your only option is to go with the highest-rated Tuscans and Piedmonts. And be sure to read the reviews and anticipated maturity dates; you want a wine that the critics expect will age well for a long time.

The Downside of First-Tier Tuscans and Piedmonts

Only a small handful of the highest-scoring wines from the very best vintages trade up significantly over time. Even though I've included a list of First-Tier wines that command high prices, I'm not convinced personally that they're great investments, despite their pedigree and the longevity that some can muster. At this time, the vast bulk of wines of Tuscany and Piedmont are not capable of investment-worthy returns.

Dave Sokolin's First-Tier Tuscan and Piedmont Predictions

TUSCANY: Sassicaia has proven that it can trade to extremely high levels in the best vintages.

Priced at $180 per bottle as I write this, the 2001 and 2004 vintages seem underpriced relative to other wines of similar stature. I expect these vintages to trade to $300 per bottle over the next five years, despite their 93- and 94-point scores, if only because of the brand name and the wine's demonstrated and unique ability among Super Tuscans to improve with age.

PIEDMONT: In short, I'm concerned about the high release prices of these wines, relative to the prices for back vintages. Bruno Giacosa's Barolo "Rocche del Falletto" Red Label Riserva is one of the most desired wines from the region, and I expect the best back vintages of this wine, such as the 2000, to trade up. I find price resistance on the legendary wines of Gaja as they plow up toward $300 per bottle. The wines are masterful, no doubt, but I'm not sure the investment potential is there.

Elsewhere in Piedmont I see few glaring opportunities to lay in cases of wine with the expectation that you'll rack up respectable gains. For my money, Piedmont is not the place to invest.

Second-Tier Tuscan and Piedmont IGW

The Second Tier of Italian wines reads like a Who's Who of famous producers—Tignanello, Ornellaia, and Altesino. But most of these wines do not currently make for great investments.

Although these are some of the greatest wines in the world, collectors rarely step up and pay a premium for the older vintages. Except in the rarest cases, back vintages of Brunello di Montalcino, which make up a large part of this price tier, are not big price gainers, despite their fame and wide fan base. The upside in this market is realized early after the release of these wines, when trading in the highest-scoring wines can be quite frenetic.

The opportunity with Second-Tier Piedmont wines is that, unlike Bordeaux, they are released into the market before they're ever reviewed. So basically we're talking about a lottery, not an investment. If scores of a particular wine come in very high, then the buyers who are lucky enough to have bought that wine upon release have a chance to turn the big score into, well, a big dollar score.

Of course, if the scores are low, don't expect to earn much of a profit. You can just drink the wines since they go so wonderfully with food.

The scores you'll be waiting for will come from *Wine Spectator*, the most influential force in Italian wine. The magazine drives prices across the market, with much of the action and profit potential coming immediately following the publication of *Wine Spectator*'s yearly "Top 100" issue, published each December. You can be sure to find many of these wines on this list. If your early purchase happens to become "Wine of the Year," you may instantly have made a fortune, since virtually everyone will be chasing it.

But again, we're talking lottery, not investing.

Second-Tier Tuscan IGW

Altesino Brunello Montalcino "Montosoli"

Antinori Tignanello

Argiano Solengo

Banfi Brunello "Poggio all'Oro"

Brancaia Il Blu

Caparzo Brunello di Montalcino Riserva

Casanova di Neri Brunello di Montalcino "Cerretalto"

Casanova di Neri Brunello di Montalcino "Tenuta Nuova"

Castello Rampolla Vigna d'Alceo

Ciacci Piccolomini Brunello di Montalcino "Santa Caterina d'Oro"

Fanti Brunello di Montalcino

Fontodi Flaccianello

Fuligni Brunello di Montalcino

Guado Al Tasso

La Poderina Brunello Montalcino "Poggio Banale"

Le Macchiole Merlot Messorio

Ornellaia

Petrolo Galatrona

Salvioni Brunello di Montalcino

San Giusto a Rentennano Percarlo

Siro Pacenti Brunello di Montalcino

Soldera Brunello di Montalcino Riserva

Tua Rita Giusto dei Notri

Valdicava Brunello di Montalcino

Second-Tier Piedmont IGW

Bruno Giacosa Barbaresco "Rabajà"

Bruno Giacosa Barolo "Falletto"

Bruno Giacosa Barolo "Le Rocche"

Ceretto Barolo "Bricco Rocche"

Conterno-Fantino Barolo "Sorì Ginestra"

(continued)

Second-Tier Piedmont IGW (*continued*)

Domenico Clerico Barolo "Ciabot Mentin"

Fratelli Revello Barolo "Vigna Rocche Annunziata"

Gaja Barolo "Conteisa"

Gaja Barolo "Sperss"

Giuseppe Mascarello Barolo "Monprivato"

La Spinetta Barolo "Vigneto Campe"

La Spinetta Barbaresco "Vigneto Gallina"

Massolino Barolo "Vigna Rionda Riserva"

Paolo Scavino Barolo "Bric del Fiasc"

Paolo Scavino Barolo "Rocche dell'Annunziata Riserva"

Pio Cesare Barolo "Ornato"

Pira Barolo "Cannubi"

Roberto Voerzio Barbera Riserva "Pozzo dell'Annunciata"

Roberto Voerzio Barolo "Brunate"

Roberto Voerzio Barolo "La Serra"

Roberto Voerzio Barolo "Rocche"

Roberto Voerzio Barolo "Rocche dell'Annunciata Torriglione"

Vietti Barolo "Villero Riserva"

PRICE RANGE OF SECOND-TIER TUSCAN AND PIEDMONT IGW

Current release prices: $90–$300 per bottle

Highest-priced back vintages: $200–$300 per bottle

The Effects of Vintage and Score on Second-Tier Tuscan and Piedmont Prices

Certain vintages, like 1997, become so popular that they transcend the brand name on the bottle and effectively become brands in their own right. Although this rarely happens, I continued to see demand for the 1997 Brunellos long after they were released. People were willing to pay up just to have that vintage in their cellar. They couldn't care less about the producer.

Still, Second-Tier Piedmont and Tuscan wines must be rated

between 97 and 100 points to be considered for investment, and even then you're stretching the definition of investment.

The Downside of Second-Tier Tuscan and Piedmont IGW

Sometimes even the best Tuscan vintages don't age well. I have recently read unflattering reviews about the best Brunellos of the legendary 1990 vintage. Some of them are falling apart, and they're not even twenty yet. These are not long-lasting wines.

Conversely, while the 1990 Piedmont Barolos are finally drinking well, you don't see much interest in or huge premiums for the Second Tiers, unless their scores are sky high.

Dave Sokolin's Second-Tier Tuscan and Piedmont Predictions

TUSCANY: The 2001 Casanova di Neri Cerretalto received an earth-shattering 100-point *Wine Spectator* score. This was an anomaly in this region.

Still, at the mid-2007 price of $350 per bottle, having already ascended from its $160 release price, I don't have much confidence that there's room for dramatically more appreciation. First movers won the lottery on this wine.

I do think there's some potential for profits in this sector, but it's tricky. I see more demand for the back-vintage Barolos than those of Tuscany. The key producers to invest in are those who produce a more modern style of Barolo and Barbaresco, with high scores, that both drink young and have the ability to age for a long time. There will be great vintages in the future, where the quality of the vintage is known before the wines' scores are published. This is where you will have the best opportunity to buy ahead of the curve.

In the final analysis, Second-Tier Italian wines are the same as Third-Tier Rhônes: for experts only.

13

THE SPANISH
INQUISITION

S pain has never been known for producing investment-grade
wines, but this could be changing. Until recently, there was
little interest in Spanish wines, with the notable exception
of Vega Sicilia's "Unico," a rare and highly collectible investment-
grade wine. The '68 Unico was rated 98 points by Parker and exploded onto the marketplace in 1991, when it was finally released
by its producers with twenty-two years of bottle age, a most unusual
tactic. Opening at $130 per bottle, the '68 Unico traded up to
$1,500 in a span of fifteen years.

The trading history of Vega Sicilia wines sheds light on how
Spain's relatively immature investment market is taking shape.
Despite its stature as a great producer, Vega Sicilia's brand iden-
tity among the mass market of consumers is less of a factor in its
investment-worthiness than the reviewer scores and praise that its
individual wines receive. No other vintage of Unico has inspired
the same degree of critical adulation, nor has any other traded at
anywhere near the prices attained by that 1968 vintage.

Fast forward to February 2007, as Dr. Jay Miller takes over the
Spain beat for Robert Parker's *The Wine Advocate*. In his first report, Miller makes history by awarding 100 points to five wines from

the 2004 vintage. This may be the most exciting thing ever to happen to Spanish wines. Neither Parker nor the *Wine Spectator* had ever previously rated any Spanish wine at 100 points, much less five from one vintage and in one issue of a publication. In essence, Spain became a player overnight.

There were those in the trade who questioned Miller's credibility, given the totally unprecedented, extreme enthusiasm he expressed for Spanish wines. However, Miller had been Parker's tasting partner for more than fifteen years, and Parker had hand picked him for the job. As *The Wine Advocate*'s publisher, Parker would probably have let these groundbreaking reviews make it into print if he didn't agree with them.

Whatever the case, the market bought into Miller's enthusiasm and consumers were quickly laying out more than $1,000 a bottle for the limited-production, 100-point '04 Pingus, a wine that just a few months previously had been released at $400 per bottle. This could be a harbinger for the future of Spain's top-flight wines, at least in the best vintages. Expect more 99- and 100-point scores, which will serve to fuel the status of Spain's microcuvées, with productions of less than 500 cases, as collectibles. And as we all know, whether it's Beanie Babies, baseball cards, or microcuvée Spanish wines, where collectors emerge, the profit opportunity is not far behind.

In the same issue of *The Wine Advocate*, a larger-production cuvée, the '04 Numanthia Toro, received a whopping 98 points from Miller, with an anticipated maturity date of 2042 and an opening price of $57 per bottle, suggesting that there will be more opportunities to invest in reasonably priced and readily available Spanish wines that possess all of the criteria to make them profitable investments over the long term. Numanthia's superdeluxe microcuvée, the '04 Termanthia, received a perfect score, with an open-ended, unforeseeable anticipated maturity date, something that is rarely seen and that sheds light on the investment appeal of the wines from Spain. These wines can mature for a long—long—time.

Spanish wines are growing in popularity at a grassroots level.

Every day, more consumers are impressed by the new, low-priced, high-quality Spanish wines that are popping up on the market. These wines play as if they're from the New World, with an obvious, fruit-driven style. Yet they also appeal to collectors of European wines. After the publication of Miller's initial reviews, his highest-scoring wines all but flew out of stock, prompting my team to reconsider Spain as a potentially significant revenue stream in the near future, whereas previously it had been a nonfactor.

I believe we're seeing the emergence of a new investment-grade wine sector in Spain, and the early movers will be able to capitalize on the relatively low price-to-points ratio of these wines on release. As people drink these wines over the next few years, and if they age as well as expected for several decades, you can anticipate that connoisseurs will be requesting these Spanish wines down the line.

Until then, there's no way to bet on Spanish wines that isn't speculative. Back-vintage trading histories are very thin, meaning there's no discernable trend to help guide your investment efforts. The best you can do is pay attention to the wines emerging today and follow them as they age. If you see a trend emerging in which the new vintages earn big scores and the older vintages are still drinking well on later reviews, you'll know that Spain really is emerging as a producer of investment-grade wines.

The four appellations where most of the critically acclaimed Spanish wines are grown are Rioja, Ribera del Duero, Priorat, and Toro. However, the overall market is not yet sensitive to the specific region a Spanish wine comes from, and aside from Rioja, many people have probably never heard of these places. The proliferation of boutique collectible wines in Spain is very new, so it could take some years for these regional appellations to acquire significance in the marketplace. The wines' producer names are far more relevant, having just recently caught the attention of reviewers. High reviewer scores are the most overwhelmingly important element in the investment-worthiness of Spanish wines right now, so pay attention to them.

The Best Spanish Vintages

In looking at Spain, a reason for the country's relative obscurity and absence from the collections of wine aficionados could be the dearth of great vintages in its main wine-growing regions throughout much of the 1980s and 1990s, especially in its best-known region, Rioja. Interestingly, during this same period, we saw the rise of many new producers from other regions, primarily Ribera del Duero, where, starting with 1999, there were a string of six good vintages in a row.

RIOJA VINTAGES
- 2004
- 2001
- 1996

PRIORAT VINTAGES
- 2004
- 2003
- 2001

RIBERA DEL DUERO VINTAGES
- 2005
- 2004
- 2003
- 2001
- 2000
- 1999
- 1996
- 1995

TORO VINTAGES
- 2004
- 2003
- 2002
- 2001
- 1999
- 1998

Spanish IGW

Alion

Álvaro Palacios Priorat "L'Ermita"

Artadi Rioja "El Pisón"

Artadi Rioja "Grandes Añadas"

Artadi Rioja "Pagos Viejos"

Benjamin Romeo "Contador"

(continued)

Spanish IGW (*continued*)

Benjamin Romeo "La Viña de Andrés Romeo"

Clos Erasmus Priorat

El Nido "Clio"

El Nido El Nido

Finca Villacreces Nebro

Mas d'en Compte Planots

Mas Doix Doix Costers de Vinyes Velles

Mas Romani (Mas Alta) La Creu Alta

Muga Rioja Aro

"Ester" Nin Nit de Nin

Numanthia Toro "Termanthia"

Numanthia Toro

Pesquera Ribera del Duero "Janus"

Pingus

Pingus "Flor de Pingus"

René Barbier Priorat "Clos Mogador"

Roda Rioja Cirsion

Rotllan Torra Tirant

Sierra Cantabria "El Bosque"

Vall Llach

Vega Sicilia "Unico"

Spanish Rock Star

2004 Numanthia Toro   **98 Points**

Any aspiring collectors should add a case of this to their stash. . . . The vines for this cuvée range from 70–100 years of age with tiny yields of 1 ton of fruit per acre. The wine undergoes malolactic fermentation in barrel followed by 19 months in new French oak before being bottled unfined and unfiltered. The wine is a glass-coating opaque purple with a killer nose of mineral, pencil lead, wild blueberry, and blackberry liqueur that roars from the glass. On the palate the wine is full-bodied, dense, and already beginning to show complexity within its layers of spicy black fruits. There is immense power, well-concealed ripe tannin, and the well-delineated finish lasts for over one minute. This is a sensational effort which in a perfect world should be cellared for a decade and enjoyed over the following 25+ years. However, the elderly among us should not feel guilty about opening a bottle now.

Dr. Jay Miller, *The Wine Advocate*

14

PORT

A Safe Harbor?

Vintage Port is similar to Sauternes, which we'll get to in chapter 17, in that it pairs with very few foods and is consumed primarily as a dessert wine. Port's big problem is that it suffers from the slackening demand for sweet and fortified wines by modern wine consumers. Similarly to Sauternes, vintage Ports mature at a glacial pace, as do their price appreciations. There are rare instances where these wines trade up quickly, and, again, it's always the latest-release, 99- and 100-pointers that seem to achieve this.

Although I understand this effect, I'm always perplexed by how a new, high-scoring Port release can trade at higher price levels than an older, ready-to-drink Port that may be rated a few points lower. Vintage Port takes a minimum of fifteen to twenty years to become drinkable, and my professional taste buds would prefer to pay a premium for an aged Port. But I'm not the market, and the market today seems to overlook the drinkability factor and to focus almost exclusively on high scores.

It is for this reason that a 95-rated 1963 Taylor, one of Port's top four producers, trades in the same $300-a-bottle range as the 100-point 1992 Taylor.

Whereas other IGW regions benefit to varying degrees from the price escalation that drives consumers to lower-priced, high-quality, back-vintage wines, Port seems to be the anomaly. It's just not happening in this market. Maybe this is due to the fact that Port can seem especially inaccessible to wine novices; maybe it's because Port largely sits on merchants' shelves because, let's face it, there are not many Port drinkers. This is a low-demand wine that's seasonal to boot. Who wants to drink a heavy Port in the summertime?

However, I should mention that my father paid for my sister's expensive Tufts University education with an investment in Port. So why am I so hesitant to recommend investment in this sector? Because my father bought Ports back in the late '70s, when the 1963 vintage could be purchased for $100 per case during a lackluster market. Today the market has matured and prices have risen commensurately, but I don't see them moving much higher in the near term. There's little broad interest in Port from the same emerging-market consumers who are driving prices higher in Bordeaux and other profitable IGW sectors.

The irony is that you'd think the newer markets would prefer sweeter wines. In Asia, many of the new, wealthy wine drinkers seek to impress their guests and business relationships with high-price Bordeaux like Pétrus and Latour—but then spike their own glass of wine with Coca-Cola to sweeten the taste.

Investment-Grade Port Vintages

Great Port vintages are few and far between:

- 2000
- 1992
- 1985
- 1977
- 1966
- 1963
- 1955

Investment-Grade Port Producers

Unlike just about every other wine market, Port is dominated by only a few key players. Spend more than thirty seconds looking at this and you're a Ph.D. candidate in Port-ology:

First-Tier Port IGW

Quinta do Noval "Nacional"

Qunita do Noval

Fonseca

Taylor Fladgate

Second-Tier Port IGW

Dow

Graham's

Warres

There you have it—the seven wines that constitute the entire investment-grade Port market and the tiers into which they fall.

Dave Sokolin's Port Predictions

I don't get it: Why isn't this market more expensive?

It's amazing, but as I write this, you can still grab a bottle of 1955 Dow Port in the $300 range and buy the legendary 1963 Fonseca—rated 96 by Parker and 98 by *Wine Spectator*—for under $500 per bottle.

I'm not suggesting Port is my number-one investment pick, but if you are so inclined, buying the back vintages probably makes the most sense. As you can see, there is a lack of good vintages between 1977 and 1992, and that could lead to a dearth of mature, drinkable Port in near future. Moreover, those old Ports are drinkable now, and there's still not a huge price premium. So what's to make anyone think that young Ports still in need of decades before they're ready to drink will appreciate in value any quicker? Because their prices move at glacial paces, the oldest Ports you can find are the ones riding the leading edge of that glacier.

Could the highest-rated Ports of the seemingly underpriced 1977 and 1985 vintages trade up? Sure. And I will continue to stock

---

Any Port in a Storm

This review is interesting, not only for what it says about this wine but also for what it says about the other great vintages of this and other Ports of the late twentieth century.

1963 Quinta do Noval "Nacional"   99 Points

Amazingly, the importer still has tiny stocks of such legendary ports as the 1970, 1963, and 1962 Nacionals. In most vintages the production of Quinta do Noval Nacional is no more than 250–275 cases. The 1970, 1963, 1962, and 1994 are candidates to achieve perfect scores. The 1963 Nacional's opaque purple color is remarkable, looking more like a 1992 than a 33-year old port. The wine possessed a fabulously smoky, cassis, black-cherry, peppery nose. After thirty minutes in the glass, fruitcake notes and more evolved aromas emerged. This port is so concentrated it defies belief, with extraordinary balance, and, like its two siblings, well-integrated alcohol and tannin. The impression is one of a silky, succulent, voluptuously-textured mouthful of exceptionally extracted port. This is a legend in the making. In 30–40 years it may well be considered, along with the 1931, as one of the greatest ports ever produced. Those lucky few with a bottle or two should plan to hold onto them for another decade before pulling the cork. It, too, is a hundred-year port.

—The Wine Advocate

them for clients whose tastes lead them to these older wines. But I'm not saying these Ports will lead to huge gains anytime soon.

My best bets:

- 1985 Graham's, rated 96 points by both Robert Parker and *Wine Spectator*
- 1977 Fonseca, rated 100 by *Wine Spectator*
- 1977 Taylor, rated 96 by Robert Parker

15

CALIFORNIA DREAMIN'

The "Members Only" Wine Market

S
ome of the most talked-about, sought-after, limited-production wines on Earth come from California, so it may be a bit surprising that these wines make up less than 1 percent of the overall investment-grade wine market. And because the production volume of the most influential wines is so tiny, professional wine investors—the wine funds—rarely, if ever, put their money to work in America's premier wine market.

California's IGW market differs greatly from Bordeaux's in that it's not yet twenty years old. Global demand for these wines does not even begin to compare to that for even Third-Tier Bordeaux. Nevertheless, Napa and Sonoma Valley are all the rage among collectors of these boutique wines. Some of the most highly collectible California wines are made in such small quantities that their production is consumed by a handful of restaurants and private collectors who are lucky enough to make it onto these wineries' mailing lists.

Boutique wine was born in California in the early 1990s. The science of winemaking was perfected there, as were the vineyard management and marketing tactics that made wineries into successful businesses, a prospect that was never particularly easy for winegrowers to accomplish. In fact, the winemaking technologies developed in California are today used across France, Italy, Spain, and everywhere else fine wine is produced.

California cult wines broke away from the volume-based business model of their regional predecessors, leading the way for other producers around the world to charge higher release prices for higher-quality wines produced in smaller batches. Even Bordeaux's best First Growth wines were trading at a significant discount to California cult wines in the early 1990s, since California producers were first to recognize and ultimately command a market value of their wines from a base of hard-core fans. Today, most of the collectible California wines are Cabernet Sauvignons from the Napa Valley, though the idea of appellation in California wines is less significant than is a producer's reputation and reviewer score.

Screaming Eagle is perhaps at the pinnacle of the cult-wine movement. With a total production of 600 cases, releases priced at $300 per bottle easily and quickly trade up beyond $2,000. Harlan Estate, another cult wine, might be released to list members at $300 as well and hit $1,000 after only a few months on the market. While the price appreciation attained by these wines is often immediate, it's a bit like a flashover fire, quick to ignite but then just smoldering, meaning the price surges on release but the premium for the older vintages generally creeps along.

When people ask me how to make money on these wines, my answer to them is that it's almost impossible unless you're able to get on those precious mailing lists, most of which are closed to new buyers for three or more years. The most sought-after wines of California, including Screaming Eagle and Harlan Estate, are sold directly to long-standing clients who purchase every year, in good vintages or bad. They get the best allocations of these wines at prices that are a fraction of what they are worth on the street. However, even the best clients get only a few bottles annually, often not more than a case, maybe only half a case.

California's most expensive cult wines, therefore, do not fit the criteria for investment-grade wines—namely because there's no real way to purchase them except at already inflated prices, which, by definition, pretty well limits your return on investment.

In addition, the most expensive cult wines have no track record of longevity. After all, their earliest vintages are from the 1990s, and there is a perception that these cult Cabernets—it's almost always Cabs that emerge as cult wines—are made to drink only when young. Indeed, more than one reviewer who has tasted older vintages has called into question most of these wines' ability to age.

When investors hold back great vintages of Bordeaux, they can expect to make money over time. But in California, the opposite might be true. As you know by now, longevity is crucial to the investment-worthiness of wine. But when you examine the California market, you see a steep price curve early on, because people start drinking these wines upon release. You don't see, as of yet, a proven ability to live beyond the first few years. That means investors are taking a huge risk in paying up for cult wines and *hoping* they survive the years and improve with age. If your hope turns out

How to Read a California Wine Label

The producer name (Screaming Eagle) is pretty much all you need to know.

to have been hype, then you're doubly in trouble: not only is your investment under water, but also if the wines are breaking down, they won't even be that good to drink.

In sum, low production, exclusive mailing lists, little vintage variation, high release prices, a minimal premium for back vintages, and no proven longevity make for a relatively bearish market for investors eyeing California's cult wines.

The good news: There are other highly rated California wines that you can actually buy because their production is much higher. These Second-Tier wines are chased by collectors and adored by restaurateurs, who especially appreciate these wines' ability to drink young.

The Best California Vintages

Below is a list of California's most highly collectible vintages.

- 2004
- 2002
- 2001
- 1997
- 1995
- 1994
- 1991
- 1990

The 1996, 1993, 1992, 1987, and 1985 vintages are also considered to be good years, when many exceptional wines were produced; however, they are not considered to be "the greatest of the great years," like the vintages listed above. Also, the earlier years precede the existence of the top California producers of today.

First-Tier California IGWs

The following are the seven top cult wines whose winery mailing lists you must be on in order to buy them at release prices. Some will accept your name but alert you that it may take three or more years before you're on the official list that makes you eligible to buy wine. Others won't even have an option for joining the list because the current waiting list to get on the main list is already so long that your grandchildren might not even have a shot.

But try if you must. All of these vineyards have websites that will generally point you toward instructions on how to get your name into the system.

First-Tier California IGW

Bryant Family

Colgin Herb Lamb Vineyard

Dalla Valle Maya

Groth Napa Cabernet Sauvignon Reserve

Harlan Estate

Heitz Cabernet Sauvignon Martha's Vineyard

Shafer Cabernet Sauvignon Hillside Select

Screaming Eagle

PRICE RANGE OF FIRST-TIER CALIFORNIA IGW

Current release prices: $300–$1,000 per bottle
Highest-priced back vintages: $1,000–$3,000 per bottle

Where Eagles Scream

1997 Screaming Eagle   **100 Points**

It doesn't get any better than 1997 Cabernet Sauvignon, a perfect wine. Representing the essence of cassis liqueur intermixed with blackberries, minerals, licorice, and toast, this full-bodied, multi-dimensional classic is fabulous, with extraordinary purity, symmetry, and a finish that lasts for nearly a minute. It has the overall equilibrium to evolve for nearly two decades, but it will be hard to resist upon release. Anticipated maturity: now–2020.

Robert Parker, *The Wine Advocate*

Why First-Tier California IGW Are Increasing in Price

■ There are so few wines in this sector, and they're produced in such micro quantities that the competition among buyers pushes prices to sometimes obscene levels within months of release.

■ The wineries release wines with higher and higher prices in each vintage, helping back vintages to price-appreciate as well, albeit much more modestly.

The Effect of Scores on First-Tier California IGW

Cult wines routinely score in the upper 90s, so the real differentiation comes at the 98-, 99-, and 100-point marks. Still, anything less than that will still be snapped up by the fanatical followers who absolutely must have a complete collection of whatever winery they've fallen in love with.

The Effect of Vintage on First-Tier California IGW

Although somewhat important, these wines' vintages matter less than their reviewer scores. A prime example is the 1992 Screaming Eagle. The vintage is not considered to be the most outstanding, but the wine received 100 points, making it a cult classic. Originally released for $50, it was selling for $3,000 per bottle in mid-2007.

The Downside of First-Tier California Wines

Some of these producers are increasing their productions and diluting their brands. For instance, since they can't actually increase the output of their flagship brand, Harlan Estate is introducing other product lines.

In the past, owning a wine from Harlan meant more than it does now because more people can own the different cuvées such as Harlan's "IX" or "The Maiden," its two newer offerings.

And, I'll say it again, there are those infernal mailing lists. It's seems easier to book a meeting with the Pope than it is to get your name on the mailing list for California's trendiest wines. Good luck trying.

Second-Tier California Wines

California's Second Tier of wines is comprised of a pool of roughly ten wines, many with names that even a casual consumer would recognize. These are produced in large enough quantity that many people have seen them on retailers' shelves or tasted them in restaurants outside the immediate bounds of the Bay Area and Los Angeles.

Joseph Phelps Insignia, a blend of Bordeaux varietals made in Napa, is amazing for its incredibly high quality. The wine regularly receives high scores in spite of its huge 13,000-case production, a Bordeaux-like number. One interesting distinction between Insignia and others in this tier is that these wines have a distinct ability to age and command higher prices for back vintages—a very un-Californian characteristic. Another example of Second-Tier excellence: the 1991 Dominus, made in California by Bordeaux star Christian Moueix of Château Pétrus. It was rated 98 points by Robert Parker and was trading in the $300 per bottle range in mid-2007. It is safe to assume that it will go higher, given Parker's estimated 2027 maturity date. And I wouldn't be surprised if the 1991 Opus One hits $1,000 a bottle during its life span.

Current release prices of both Dominus and Phelps Insignia are quite reasonable, in the $100–$140 per bottle range. The fun part is that these wines are actually available for sale at your local merchant. This price tier is about mass-appeal-meets-longevity in vintages with high scores, making the Second Tier of California IGW similar to that of Bordeaux.

Second-Tier California IGW

Abreu

Araujo Eisele Cabernet Sauvignon

Bond Vineyards Melbury

Bond Vineyards St Eden

Bond Vineyards Vecina

Caymus Special Selection

Dalla Valle Cabernet Sauvignon

Dominus

Dunn Cabernet Sauvignon Howell Mountain

Etude Cabernet Sauvignon

Grace Family Cabernet Sauvignon

Harlan The Maiden

Joseph Phelps Insignia

Kistler Pinot Noir Camp Meeting Ridge

Kistler Pinot Noir Cuvée Catherine

Kistler Pinot Noir Kistler Vineyard

Kistler Pinot Noir Occidental Cuvée Elizabeth

Lokoya Mount Veeder Cabernet Sauvignon

Martinelli Jackass Hill Vineyard Zinfandel

Merryvale Profile

Merus Cabernet Sauvignon

Mondavi Reserve Cabernet Sauvignon

Montelena Cabernet Sauvignon

Opus One

Paul Hobbs Cabernet Sauvignon Beckstoffer To Kalon Vineyard

Pahlmeyer Merlot

Pax Cellars Syrah Cuvée Keltie

Pax Cellars Syrah Obsidian

Peter Michael Les Pavots

Philip Togni Cabernet Sauvignon

Pride Mountain Vineyards Cabernet Sauvignon Reserve

Pride Mountain Vineyards Reserve Claret

Second-Tier California IGW (*continued*)

Robert Foley Vineyards Claret

Ridge Montebello Cabernet Sauvignon

Seavey Cabernet Sauvignon

Silver Oak Napa Valley Cabernet Sauvignon

Sine Qua Non E Raised

Sine Qua Non Imposter McCoy

Sine Qua Non Heart Chorea (Syrah)

Sine Qua Non Hollerin' M

Sine Qua Non Just for the Love of It

Sine Qua Non In Flagrante

Sine Qua Non Incognito

Sine Qua Non Midnight Oil

Sine Qua Non SQN (Grenache/Syrah)

Sine Qua Non Papa (Syrah)

Staglin Family Cabernet Sauvignon

Stag's Leap Cabernet Sauvignon Cask 23

Turley 101 Vineyard Zinfandel

Turley Hayne Vineyard Petite Sirah

Turley Library Vineyard Petite Sirah

Turley Rattlesnake Ridge Petite Sirah

Verite La Joie Proprietary Blend

PRICE RANGE OF SECOND-TIER CALIFORNIA IGW

Current release prices: $90–$200 per bottle
Highest-priced back vintages: $300–$400 per bottle

Why Second-Tier California IGW Are Increasing in Price

■ Increased release prices are pulling up the prices of back vintages.

■ With an extremely high level of quality in their best vintages, they're just a notch behind the cult wines. The only difference:

Their high production keeps their prices, and their cachet, lower than the cults'.

■ They can actually command a premium for rare back vintages because the end-consuming collectors of these wines like drinking them older.

The Effect of Scores on Second-Tier California Wines

With so much attention paid to the First-Tier cults, the Second-Tier wines must—*must!*—pick up a rating of at least 96. Anything less, and you have a wonderful wine for drinking but not for investing.

The Effect of Vintage on Second-Tier California Wines

Honestly, we're talking about California here, where everyone wants cachet. So in this market the vintage must have a "buzz" around it because these names alone can't produce major price appreciation. Stay away from bad vintages, such as 2000, 1998, 1988, and 1983.

Dave Sokolin's Second-Tier California Predictions

Look for Dominus to begin releasing wines at a higher price level. It is simply one of the region's best wines, and it is marketed by the masters of high prices, Château Pétrus.

Phelps Insignia has potential as well, because the prices of its best vintages have shown the ability to double their release prices in relatively short order, making Insignia a candidate for a price hike that will push the best, older vintages even higher.

The '91 Caymus Special Selection and the '97 Peter Michael Les Pavots are Second-Tier wines that command high prices in the highest-scoring vintages. These rare vintages could command

$500+ per bottle by 2013, whereas today they trade at roughly half that level.

Third-Tier California IGW

There is an upside to distribution of California wines via mailing lists in that it is an interesting, fun, and experimental way to potentially make a profit. Many of the people on the top of Screaming Eagle's list were wine-collecting pioneers who traveled around California and became the first clients of this fledgling boutique vineyard.

These kinds of opportunities still exist, but they take time, luck, and lots of tasting. I'm constantly getting feedback from clients who travel to northern California, telling me what they think is going to be the "next big thing." Generally, their predictions don't become cult wines, but some do go up in price, becoming the new top boutique wines of California. An example of a new breakout wine that has exploded onto the scene is David Arthur's Elevation 1147, which is quickly becoming a cult wine. It's possible to be ahead of the curve in this area and to have fun in the process. It helps to spend lots of time in northern California.

Third-Tier California IGW

Groth Napa Reserve

Kistler

Martinelli Jackass Hill

Montelena

Pahlmeyer

Paul Hobbs

Pride Mountain Vineyard

PRICE RANGE OF THIRD-TIER CALIFORNIA IGW

Current release prices: $30–$100 per bottle
Highest-priced back vintages: $200–$300 per bottle

The Effect of Scores on Third-Tier California IGW

High scores are what have put these wines on the map, so make sure that your investment in this sector is based on wines with the highest scores you can find. Pride Reserve Claret can sell for over $400 per bottle with a great score, but less than $100 without one.

The other option is to essentially do what some options investors do on Wall Street and that is to "take a flyer," betting on Third-Tier, small-production wine before it's reviewed and before it finds a broader audience. If the wine scores well and does find that audience, then you're golden because you'll be buying wines at the release prices in the future and you can turn around and sell them with a huge markup in the secondary market.

The Downside of California Wines

Across the board, few California wines have been able to establish themselves as investment worthy, and when they do, their release prices are jacked up to levels that make them bad investments. Additionally, there is no huge premium paid for back vintages of many of these wines.

The stark reality is that for all the great wines California has to offer, I've never made much money in this sector. I guess that's because I'm not on many mailing lists. I'd like to be a bigger holder of stock from the next great vintages of Dominus and Phelps Insignia, where I can actually put together a nice position of wine. But for the vast lot of us who endeavor to invest in wine, the cult Cabs are basically off limits. It's as simple as that. There is no secret handshake or special code word that will help you snag an allotment of Screaming Eagle or Harlan or any of the others that sell out every year by way of their mailing lists.

The best advice is to get a jump on the next cult Cabs to emerge before the crowd catches on. You can find out about these wines by trolling the wine blogs online and reading what the relatively unknown critics are saying. Their reviews are not going to carry any substantial weight, but occasionally they catch wind of a new dar-ling earlier than Robert Parker or James Laube at the *Wine Specta-tor*. If these two critics ultimately rate the wine highly, it may suddenly become a cult Cab on everyone's to-buy list. But you may go through a hundred wines before you find a big winner.

You should also pay attention to vintners in California who cre-ate wines for multiple wineries. Those who score big successes in one place will sometimes re-create the magic at another winery not far away, though that's certainly not a given. Also, it's still possible to get your name on some boutique winery mailing lists, but they will almost all be new wineries that the mass of consumers don't yet know about and that haven't yet released a wine with a blockbuster score. As I noted back in the chapter on the futures market, your best bet here is to spend some time in Napa and Sonoma County on vacation, touring the new wineries or talking to vintners about which new wineries are releasing high-quality boutique wines, since not all of these will be open to tourists stopping by. With some luck, you might just stumble onto the next Screaming Eagle before the rest of the world does.

Maybe.

16

AUSTRALIA

High Ratings Down Under

T he fruit bomb exploded sometime in 2000.
Both the *Wine Spectator* and Robert Parker fell in love with the 1998 vintage coming out of Australia, awarding ratings of 95 and higher to many of the wines coming up from Down Under. In turn, consumers were sucking down these fruit-forward wines—known as fruit bombs—because of their high scores and modest prices. Suddenly, Australia was the hottest wine story since California's cult Cabs.

A decade later, demand for Aussie wines appears to have tempered markedly. My clients who adore massive fruit are repeat customers, but many of them have not maintained their initial fascination. Today, a few select superstars in Australian wine have held their ground and could one day emerge as profitable investment-grade wines. For the most part, though, investors circling around Australia will find little to sate their wants.

The Effect of Vintage on Australian Wines

As with every rule, there is one notable exception. In Australia, that exception is Penfolds Grange Hermitage, whose global notori-

ety long preceded the Aussie craze. "Grange," as most call it, dates
to the 1952 vintage, and the wines have proven capable of aging for
at least half a century. The '76 vintage picked up 100 points from
Parker, making it the most respected of all Grange wines. It is definitely one of the greatest wines that I have ever tasted, and it has
certainly generated respectable profits for those savvy enough to
tuck a few cases away as an investment all those years ago. Released
at $20 per bottle, original cases of Grange as of mid-2007 traded
hands at $24,000, a 10 percent annualized return, only slightly less
than that of the Dow Jones Industrial Average—and without nearly
the volatility.

The '76 Grange set the bar for where a 100-point Aussie could
trade. Inside that vintage are two familiar, critical hallmarks of an
IGW: (1) a 100-point Parker score and (2) a long window of drinkability. Add to this the fact that this wine has been at peak drinkability for over a decade, thrilling collectors and showing no signs of
decline. During this period, a significant buzz has developed among
those who have tried this Grange, and I'm convinced the 1976 will
be a $50,000 case of wine before 2020.

But Australia is more than Grange. Indeed, supermarket and
wine-shop shelves are chockablock with Aussie labels, many
decorated with animals in electric colors, as if a neon sign had exploded in a zoo. And there are certainly other 100-point Aussie
wines on the market. The question, though, is whether any of
these high-scoring critters have the stamina to last as long as
Grange.

Overall, this is a region notorious for wines that taste great out
of the gate but whose big fruit isn't enough to help them age gracefully or to achieve price premiums years down the line. As a result,
my focus in this region is strictly on wines with the highest scores
that have the ability to age. That means the 99- and 100-point
wines with reviewer-estimated maturities well into the future.
Wines like Grange, Clarendon Hills "Astralis," and Henschke "Hill
of Grace" all have track records of proven longevity and price appreciation.

The Effect of Scores on Australian Wines

All of the wines on the list below share a common trait: somewhere amid their list of vintages one of their wines has earned a 99- or 100-point score from the *Wine Spectator* or Robert Parker. But let's be clear: High scores alone are not enough.

Australian IGW

DRY

Amon-Ra Shiraz

Amon-Ra Shiraz McLaren Vale

Burge Family Draycott Shiraz Reserve

Chris Ringland (aka Three River) Shiraz

Clarendon Hills Astralis

Clarendon Hills Shiraz Astralis

Fox Creek Shiraz Reserve

Greenock Creek Alice Block Shiraz

Greenock Creek Apricot Block Shiraz

Greenock Creek Creek Block Shiraz

Greenock Creek Roennfeldt Shiraz

Greenock Creek Seven Acres Shiraz

Henschke "Hill of Grace"

Jim Barry "The Armagh" Shiraz

Kalleske Old Vine Grenache

Kay Brothers Shiraz Block 6

Kilikanoon Shiraz Attunga 1865

Kilikanoon Shiraz M Reserve

Kilikanoon Shiraz Reserve

Kilikanoon Shiraz Reserve Greens

Marquis Philips Shiraz Integrity

Mitolo Shiraz G.A.M.

Mitolo Shiraz Savitar

Mollydooker Carnival of Love Shiraz

Australian IGW (*continued*)

DRY

Noon Winery Reserve Cabernet Sauvignon

Noon Winery Reserve Shiraz

Penfolds Grange Hermitage

Shirvington Shiraz

Standish Shiraz/Viognier The Relic

Torbreck Descendant

Torbreck Factor

Torbreck Les Amis

Torbreck Run Rig

Two Hands Ares Barossa Valley Shiraz

Veritas Shiraz Hanische Vineyard

Veritas Shiraz Heysen Vineyard

Wild Duck Creek "Duck Mush" Shiraz

SWEET

Chambers Rosewood Vineyards Rare Muscat

Ralph Fowler Old and Rare Muscat

RL Buller & Son Calliope Rare Tokay

Trevor Jones Shiraz Liqueur

You'll notice sweet wines on the list. There is a sector of sweet dessert wines from Australia that always seems to garner very high 99- and 100-point scores. I haven't seen enough of them trade on the aftermarket to get a good sense of their investment potential, but the reviews are so enticing that they must be of value, and they do trade much higher than their release prices. Again, longevity will be the key for these wines. But dessert wines are generally long-lived to begin with, and they do tend to improve for longer periods of time than do dry wines, making for a potentially interesting investment area.

Entering the Australian Market

Price of entry is critical to investment success in Australian wines. Many have low release prices relative to where they end up trading. Most of these wines are produced in miniscule amounts, so don't get your hopes up about building large positions on these wines at opening prices. You'll likely have to pay up to obtain these wines. For that reason, I'm cautious about this sector. As a wine merchant, even I don't have great access to large quantities of these wines, so I doubt many others do either. Leveraging a relationship with a retailer who sells large quantities of these producers' lower-tier wines could potentially afford you access to a low-priced allocation. So if you really want to play Down Under, find a retailer in your area who sells the lower-priced brands, get to know the wine buyer, and routinely spend your money there to build that relationship.

Dave Sokolin's Australian Predictions

While some of my clients call me, bragging about how much high-scoring wine they just bought at low-opening prices, inevitably it turns out they got one case or less. This doesn't constitute a real wine-investment position; it's more of an IPO-like cherry that you can hope for as a gift for your extensive trading with some brokerage firm.

I'm extremely bullish on the ability of Penfolds Grange to trade higher, and there is the potential to buy this wine in seemingly greater quantity than you'll find for many other boutique Aussie wines. Other interesting prospects include Chris Ringland (formerly known as Three Rivers) Shiraz, Clarendon Hills "Astralis," and Henschke "Hill of Grace." All are capable of aging for at least two decades or longer. Mollydooker's 2005 "Carnival of Love" generated huge press, critical acclaim, and enthusiasm when this inaugural vintage grabbed a Parker score of 99 points. Created by Sparky Philips, formerly of Marquis Philips fame, the '05 Mollydooker was released at $60 a bottle and was trading at up to $180 less than a

---

OK, So Maybe My Comments
Were a Bit "Euro-centric"!

2002 Clarendon Hills Astralis Shiraz   **99 Points**

This compelling, black/blue-hued offering from 75-year-old Syrah vines tastes like blood of the vine. An extraordinary perfume of flowers, *creme de cassis,* blackberries, roasted meat, new saddle leather, and earth is followed by a wine with sweet tannin, sensational concentration, full body, an unctuous texture, and a full-throttle, tannic finish. Yet it reveals unbelievable elegance and finesse. Too many Euro-centric elitists argue that Australian wines are too rich and over the top, but all of these offerings have been made by someone with great talent and vision who takes the extraordinary ripeness and purity of fruit available from these old vine vineyards and crafts them into wines that are quite European in style . . . just richer and denser. The 2002 Astralis is a *tour de force.* Anticipated maturity: 2012–2025 + . Roman Bratasiuk is one of Planet Earth's greatest winemakers, and obviously a top-notch viticulturist given his obsession with sourcing extraordinary fruit from ancient McLaren Vale vineyards.

Robert Parker, *The Wine Advocate*

---

year later. It was a great short-term trade, no doubt. But because the wine's anticipated maturity is only 2016, investors shouldn't expect an ever-escalating price.

The Downside of Australian IGW

Overall, my take on Australia is that high entry prices and the inability to age for decades are the primary downsides investors face here, despite these wines' high scores. If you're an investor, it makes much more sense to own a Second-Tier Bordeaux, such as Léoville Las Cases, which is in the same price range as the First-Tier Australians, but which can age for over seventy-five years.

Moreover, I have seen a noticeable dearth of attention paid to back-vintage Australian wines. Maybe this is a function of the minuscule production; maybe it's the inability of Aussie wines to mature beyond a few years; maybe it's consumers who focus on Australia as mainly a source of high-quality wines for immediate consumption and thus who don't care about vintage so much as a good name for the weekend's dinner party.

Whatever the case, Australia is a land papered with high-scoring, delicious wines, but one where the investment-grade pickings are leaner than an anorexic kangaroo.

17

SAUTERNES

Sweet Investments?

We began this journey around the world of wine many pages ago in Bordeaux. Here, at the conclusion, we return to the same region for a sweet ending.

No, really. I literally mean *sweet*—as in sugary.

Along with the famous clarets that come from this corner of France, Bordeaux is known the world around for its sweet white wines—the Sauternes.

Despite the fact that Sauternes are a fantastic finish to a wonderful meal, they generally are not smart additions to the wine investor's portfolio, with a few outstanding exceptions. The underlying problem is the same one that afflicts Port: the intrinsic demand for dessert wines just isn't that strong, regardless of the high scores and fairly limited production. Many health-conscious wine drinkers prefer to allocate their caloric intakes to dry wines with food, often skipping dessert altogether. I don't see sugar-laden dessert wines as a growing trend, even though they are a hedonist's dream.

The Effect of Vintage and Series on Sauternes

Sauternes take many years—decades, really—to mature, and they last for many years longer. But over the course of my career, I've seen only rare instances where extreme premiums are paid for holding on to these wines over the long term. These notable exceptions occur when legendary vintages come along that produce Sauternes with 99- and 100-point scores. As in every other sector, wines with 100-point scores come about so rarely that they capture the attention of the entire wine-buying public. Collectors who don't focus on dessert wines tend to cross over and collect these rare exceptions simply because of the score.

Château d'Yquem

But unlike in every other region, only one Sauternes is king. And while there are certainly other producers, there are no real peers. Even back in 1855, when that famous classification was created, Château d'Yquem had its own designation as a "Superior First Growth" of Bordeaux whites, the *only* wine in the category.

Château d'Yquem is still today the only First Growth of Bordeaux sweet wines, and it's capable of aging for 100 years or longer. Demand for this wine exists the world over, and some of the most expensive investment-grade wines in the world are 100-point Yquems from famous back vintages, such as the legendary 1921, which was trading for up to $150,000 per case in mid-2007.

Produced in extremely small quantities in the far southern reaches of Bordeaux, Yquem has all the vitals necessary for profitable investing: high scores, tremendous longevity, huge brand awareness, untainted pedigree, and global demand.

The challenge for investors is building a position; Yquem isn't cheap, particularly in great vintages. In the futures market for '05, a standout vintage, a case of Yquem carrying a (95–100) rating exceeds $9,000—the third-most-expensive futures price behind

2001 YQUEM: Yes, It's *That* Good!

In rare moments, all the factors necessary to produce greatness align and something so magical comes about that world is in agreement: *This is good.* The 2001 Château d'Yquem is the by-product of one of those rare moments.

To get an idea of what constitutes greatness in a Sauternes, consider what Messrs. Suckling and Parker had to say about this particular wine:

2001 Château d'Yquem   100 points

The greatest young Yquem I have ever tasted from bottle. Yellow, with a golden hue and an almost green tint. Intense aromas of botrytis, spices and blanched almonds follow through to honey, maple syrup, dried apricot and pineapple. Full-bodied, sweet, thick and powerful, with layers of fruit and a bright, lively finish. Coats the palate yet remains exciting. So balanced and refined, showing the pedigree that only this Sauternes estate can deliver. Best after 2012. 10,000 cases made.

James Suckling, *Wine Spectator*

2001 Château d'Yquem   100 points

There are 10,000 cases of this perfect sweet white Bordeaux. The 2001 Yquem reveals a hint of green in its light gold color. While somewhat reticent aromatically, with airing it offers up honeyed tropical fruit, orange marmalade, pineapple, sweet crème brûlée, and buttered nut-like scents. In the mouth, it is full-bodied with gorgeously refreshing acidity as well as massive concentration and unctuousity. Everything is uplifted and given laser-like focus by refreshing acidity. This large-scaled, youthful Yquem appears set to take its place among the most legendary vintages of the past, and will age effortlessly for 75+ years. Anticipated maturity: 2010–2100+. (Release date, Sept. 1, 2005.)

Robert Parker, *The Wine Advocate*

Châteaux Margaux and Haut Brion, two of Bordeaux's five First Growth superstars.

A slightly cheaper alternative to the '05 is the '01, a vintage I particularly recommend. It's also rated 100 points by both Parker and the *Wine Spectator*. Though this particular wine was slow to ascend the price charts, it shot up to roughly $7,000 a case, and given its stupendous reviews and ratings, investors can expect a steeper price curve as the wine hits that point where it starts to drink well in the next few years. Better yet, this vintage is predicted to have another eighty-five years left to mature. That's longevity.

The new proprietors of Yquem, the European luxury conglomerate LVMH (Moët Hennessy-Louis Vuitton), have steadily increased its release price ever since their takeover in 1999. This has been a boon to those holding Yquem's back vintages, since they've effectively been revalued higher. On the day the '01 Yquem was released, the 99-rated '90 Yquem was trading at only $360 per bottle. But that no longer made much sense, given that the '01 came out at $400. The older vintage was soon trading at $600, on par with the younger sibling. The '90 vintage could ultimately increase in value at a more accelerated pace, if only because consumers will be drinking it sooner. Over time, though, it won't have the legs to reach the values the '01 is likely to see, and for one reason only . . . one little, but very significant, ratings point.

While Yquem is the king of Sauternes, a few other notable sweet wines exist in the region and in the neighboring area of Barsac. Their best vintages are also investment worthy, but they will never be Yquem.

Sauternes and Barsac IGW Producers

Château d'Yquem Sauternes

Climens Barsac

De Fargues Sauternes

Raymond-Lafon Sauternes

Rieussec Sauternes

Suduiraut Sauternes

Great Sauternes/Barsac Vintages

- 2001
- 1990
- 1989
- 1988
- 1986
- 1983
- 1976
- 1975
- 1971
- 1967

Dave Sokolin's Sauternes/Barsac Predictions

If you're going to invest in Sauternes, you might as well stick to the best. Consumption is so limited that the collectors who jump into the market tend to concentrate their efforts on Yquem. You will occasionally find investment-worthy names in the great vintages of La Tour Blanche and Château Rieussec, but they simply do not—and will never—command the kind of immediate attention that Château d'Yquem does.

If I'm building a portfolio of long-lasting Yquems, wines that I'm confident will double in value over the next five or so years and then keep marching higher from there, I'm going after these vintages: 1983, '86, '88, '89, and '90. All are in the $400 to $600 range as I write this. All are going much higher.

CONCLUSION

It is interesting to me that when people buy the most extravagant luxury items—rare cars, jewelry, yachts—most of the time those assets do not increase in price. Think about your own life, and you might see how common that is. Buy any typical mass-market car, and the price tumbles before you get to the first stop sign after leaving the dealership. Buy an diamond engagement ring from any old jeweler and then try to resell that ring for the same price or more, and you'll find that, at most, you can unload it for about a 50 percent discount. Or go buy the average boat you see plying the local lakes and rivers near your hometown, and then, when you get tired of it a few years later, try to sell it for a profit. You won't even get close to your original purchase price.

The fact is, the bulk of consumer items are unlimited, prosaic, mass-produced duplicates absent any inherent structural traits that allow them to increase in value over time. Rare assets, though . . . well, regardless of price they tend to trend higher over time simply because they are uncommon. They are unique, limited-edition originals that can't be replaced by another just like them or close enough that no one will notice or care. The man who bought the apartment in Manhattan for the record price of $10 million ten years ago—well, in 2007 he was selling it for $50 million. Recently, a friend of mine made a profit on a Gulfstream 4 jet when he traded up to a larger plane. In only two years, world demand for the limited supply of Gulfstream 4s had ascended to such a level that the price of his eight-year-old plane had risen by $2 million. Economies wax and wane, but a rare asset is, by definition, a rare asset. The cream, as the old saw goes, always rises to the top.

Wine is a rare asset as well. The same fundamental economic principles of supply and demand are at play. Just as they're not making any more Manhattan real estate, they're not making any more '61 Pétrus either—or '05 Pétrus, for that matter. Thus, even when investors pay up for a classic wine—that is, even when they pay what others see as insane prices—the market still generally goes higher over time because, again, these wines are diminishing assets, constantly being consumed, constantly shrinking in supply, and contantly in demand.

I'd be foolish to predict that the wine market will sustain in the future the same kind of ridiculous returns posted in recent years. Who knows if a string of lackluster vintages won't arrive to put a chill on wine prices for a while. But without question such potential exists. The main difference today is that the environment has become more complex, more competitive, and more dynamic, due to the increased number of buyers and the response by wine producers of charging much higher prices. In addition, there is newly accessible, real-time reviewer information, creating profound market impacts, often in real time as well. That can make it more challenging for wine investors, at times drowning the uninitiated in data. But that same trend gives informed buyers an edge they can use to effectively trade the wine market to their advantage.

But if you believe in the continued growth of the world economy over time and the continued emergence of markets such as Brazil, China, Russia, India, and others, and if you can see that investment-grade wine has a demonstrated history over several decades of increasing in value, then you have to be a believer in the future prospects of wine as an investment class. I said it in the introduction, and I will repeat it here: Individual investors who buy and properly store investment-grade wines are uniquely positioned to participate in the global expansion of wealth now under way. Because in the end, it is that rapidly expanding base of consumers and collectors with discretionary dollars who are increasingly willing to pay up to either enjoy or collect the world's rarest wines.

Wine is, first and foremost, a beverage. But there is an asset hidden in plain view inside this liquid. Investors increasingly recognize that asset and are moving money into fine wine, confident in their knowledge that when they find a market characterized by continually increasing demand and continually decreasing supply, they have found an investment opportunity.

And that is something to toast!

APPENDIX

The Bordeaux Classification of 1855

In chapter 6, I categorized investment-grade Bordeaux into three tiers to denote how they rank among the world's connoisseurs, collectors, and investors. But Bordeaux has its own official segregation that I've mentioned on several occasions, the Classification of 1855, which separates the various châteaux into five growths.

Below are the sixty-one wines that fall into the various growths, what the French know as *Les Grands Crus classés*:

FIRST GROWTH (PREMIERS CRUS)
- Haut Brion
- Lafite Rothschild
- Latour
- Margaux
- Mouton Rothschild

SECOND GROWTH (DEUXIÈMES CRUS)
- Brane Cantenac
- Cos d'Estournel
- Ducru Beaucaillou
- Dufort Vivens
- Gruaud Larose
- Lascombes
- Léoville Barton

- Léoville Las Cases
- Léoville Poyferré
- Montrose
- Pichon Longueville Baron
- Pichon Longueville Comtesse de Lalande
- Rauzan Gassies
- Rauzan Ségla

THIRD GROWTH (TROISIÈMES CRUS)

- Boyd Cantenac
- Calon Ségur
- Cantenac Brown
- Desmirail
- Ferrière
- Giscours
- d'Issan
- Kirwan
- La Lagune
- Lagrange
- Langoa Barton
- Malescot St. Exupéry
- Marquis d'Alesme Becker
- Palmer

FOURTH GROWTH (QUATRIÈMES CRUS)

- Beychevelle
- Branaire Ducru
- Duhart Milon Rothschild
- La Tour Carnet
- Lafon Rochet
- Marquis de Terme
- Pouget
- Prieuré Lichine
- Saint Pierre
- Talbot

FIFTH GROWTH (CINQUIÈMES CRUS)

- d'Armailhac
- Batailley
- Belgrave
- de Camensac
- Cantemerle
- Clerc Milon
- Cos Labory
- Croizet Bages
- Dauzac
- Du Tertre
- Grand Puy Ducasse
- Grand Puy Lacoste
- Haut Bages Libéral
- Haut Batailley
- Lynch Bages
- Lynch Moussas
- Pédesclaux
- Pontet Canet

INDEX

Printed in the United States
By Bookmasters